Soc

FAILURE TO RETURN THIS BOOK ON TIME
COULD INCUR A RECOVERY CHARGE.

Culture and Society

Calderdale College Library
Tel: 01422 399 350

13 JUN 1997		
27 JUN 1997	- 5 APR 2006	
- 5 NOV 1998	- 2 JUL 2007	
19 JAN 1999	31 MAR	
27 SEP 200		
20 MA		
5 JAN		
12 JUN 2013		

This book is issued subject to Library regulations, and is due
on or before the date marked above.

You may renew books in person or by telephone, quoting
the number on the book's Library barcode label.

Calderdale College

1080392

SOCIOLOGY FOR A CHANGING WORLD
Series Editors: Roger King and Janet Finch

Editorial Advisory Board:
Frank Bechhofer, Sheila Cunnison, Sara Delamont,
Geoff Payne and Liz Stanley

This new series, published in conjunction with the British Sociological Association, evaluates and reflects major developments in contemporary sociology. The books will focus on key changes in social and economic life in recent years and on the ways in which the discipline of sociology has analysed those changes. The books will reflect the state of the art in contemporary British sociology, while at the same time drawing upon comparative material to set debates in an international perspective.

Published
Rosamund Billington, Annette Fitzsimons, Leonore Greensides
   and Sheelagh Strawbridge, *Culture and Society*
Lois Bryson, *Welfare and the State: Who Benefits?*
Frances Heidensohn, *Crime and Society*
Glenn Morgan, *Organisations in Society*
Andrew Webster, *Science and Society*

Forthcoming
Angela Glasner, *Life and Labour in Contemporary Society*
Marilyn Porter, *Gender Relations*
Mike Savage and Alan Warde, *The New Urban Sociology*
Claire Wallace, *Youth and Society*

CULTURE AND SOCIETY

A Sociology of Culture

Rosamund Billington
Sheelagh Strawbridge
Lenore Greensides
Annette Fitzsimons

THE LIBRARIAN,
CALDERDALE COLLEGE,
FRANCIS STREET,
HALIFAX, WEST YORKS. HX1 3UZ.

M
MACMILLAN

© Rosamund Billington, Sheelagh Strawbridge, Leore Greensides and
Annette Fitzsimons 1991

All rights reserved. No reproduction, copy or transmission of
this publication may be made without written permission.

No paragraph of this publication may be reproduced, copied or
transmitted save with written permission or in accordance with
the provisions of the Copyright, Designs and Patents Act 1988,
or under the terms of any licence permitting limited copying
issued by the Copyright Licensing Agency, 90 Tottenham Court
Road, London W1P 9HE.

Any person who does any unauthorised act in relation to this
publication may be liable to criminal prosecution and civil
claims for damages.

First published 1991 by
THE MACMILLAN PRESS LTD
Houndmills, Basingstoke, Hampshire RG21 2XS
and London
Companies and representatives
throughout the world

ISBN 0–333–46038–3 (hardcover)
ISBN 0–333–46039–1 (paperback)

A catalogue record for this book is available
from the British Library

Printed in Hong Kong

Reprinted 1992

CALDERDALE
COLLEGE LIBRARY
HALIFAX

DATE 30|1|97
SOURCE GREENHEAD
CLASS 306
A/No. 53255
£11·99
COPY No.

Series Standing Order (Sociology for a Changing World)
If you would like to receive future titles in this series as they are published,
you can make use of our standing order facility. To place a standing order
please contact your bookseller or, in case of difficulty, write to us at the
address below with your name and address and the name of the series.
Please state with which title you wish to begin your standing order. (If you
live outside the United Kingdom we may not have the rights for your area,
in which case we will forward your order to the publisher
concerned.)

Customer Services Department, Macmillan Distribution Ltd
Houndmills, Basingstoke, Hampshire RG21 2XS, England

Contents

1080392

Introduction

As we drew up the plan for this book and even more, as we wrote it, we realised that no clearly defined 'sociology of culture' exists. Boundaries between sociological studies of culture and other areas of sociology are often difficult to draw and some of the most important contributions to the study of culture have been made by writers from outside the malestream of sociology. This means that any text in this area must be selective and will reflect the authors' interests and specialisms. Our text is no exception.

We have structured the book around what we see as important theoretical debates which inform empirical studies and we have included material not easily available in similar texts. Of necessity, we have been selective in the traditions we highlight, but it is our belief that the theoretical tensions on which we have focused, are encountered in all traditions, albeit in differing disguises. Our selectivity has been guided by the intention to deal with theorists who have explicitly used and developed 'culture' as a theoretical concept and a tool for analysing social processes. Consequently, we have been concerned not with these theorists and theories in themselves, but only as they contribute to the sociological study of culture.

An organising theme of the book is the way in which conceptual distinctions are made and theoretical perspectives defined, which then break down as they are refined and debated. For example, as the concept of culture was developed as a theoretical tool researchers sought to distinguish specifically cultural from other aspects of society and to understand the pattern of causal forces between them. The distinction made has often been between culture and social structure. As work has developed, the limitations of this distinction

CALDERDALE
COLLEGE LIBRARY
HALIFAX

have become apparent and further theoretical debate has ensued. Similarly, cultural beliefs, attitudes and values have been distinguished from knowledge, particularly scientific (and social scientific) knowledge. However, as the impact of culture on what is held to be knowledge in a society has been increasingly appreciated, this distinction has blurred, with consequences which are problematic for the very idea of knowledge.

As writers in differing theoretical traditions and perspectives have sought to develop and refine their ways of understanding the complexity of culture, they have borrowed concepts and insights from each other and boundaries between Marxists, Durkheimians, Weberians and others have become clouded. Indeed, the sociology of culture itself is increasingly difficult to distinguish from other disciplinary contributions to the study of culture. In this book, we have held on to a view of sociology as a discipline which seeks to go beyond description and provide explanatory frameworks for social processes. However, we are aware that as sociology has sought to define itself and its subject matter and to develop its research methods, it has engaged in a reflexive dialogue with other disciplines and again boundaries have been blurred. Moreover, the goal of some sociological traditions – that of developing a single over-arching explanatory framework encompassing all social processes – is increasingly being abandoned as overambitious and even inherently oppressive. Not only Weber's substantive concerns but also his overall view of sociology as essentially incomplete, its questions shifting with shifting value orientations in society, has gained influence as sociologists have focused on issues of modernity and post-modernity.

Our theme of the formation, clarification and subsequent breakdown of conceptual boundaries is a simplification, as all themes are likely to be. However, we believe that it is a useful organising principle which has helped us and will help our readers to make sense of an enormously complex field.

Among the range of writers, schools of thought and topics which might legitimately be seen as contributing to the sociology of culture but are not covered in this book, are the work of Peter Berger and 'social constructionist' theorists, Schutz and a whole range of symbolic interactionists and ethnomethodologists, including Erving Goffman. Norbert Elias's complex work on the 'civilising process' and the transformation of European society and culture is missing from our text, as is the work of Anthony Giddens, which appears to be moving to a synthesis of many previous theories of society and culture. A major area we have excluded is that of religion, which reflects, in part, the concentration of contemporary work in Britain on more secular aspects of culture, but ignores the continuing concern with religion in the work of American writers. Similarly, although we have recognised the importance of the anthropological and comparative study of culture, we have placed our greatest emphasis on Britain and America, including the imperialistic nature of British culture and the emphasis on pluralism versus integration in American culture. Other areas which might have been given greater prominence in this text − youth and youth cultures and mass media − are to be covered in separate volumes in this series.

The particular character of *our* 'sociology of culture' has been shaped both by our separate competencies and interests and by our debates concerning their interrelationships. Two of us are sociologists, one of us a literature, culture and communication specialist and one of us a psychologist-cum-social theorist. The form and content of this volume have also been shaped by our considerable collective experience of teaching students. We have attempted to bring together and make accessible both to sociology and other students a range of arguments and theories which are not always seen as interconnected, but which seem to us important aspects of a sociology of culture. The bibliography reflects the eclectic and wide-ranging approach we have taken. We have been mindful of recent developments in the field of 'cultural studies' and sociology and have introduced some exciting contemporary debates.

Each of us has been responsible for parts and sections of chapters and for specific tasks for this volume, reflecting our various competencies. Our involvement has been as follows: Rosamund Billington, Chapters 1, 2, 5, 6 and 7; Sheelagh Strawbridge, Chapters 2, 8 and 10; Lenore Greensides, Chapters 3, 4 and 5; Annette Fitzsimons Chapters 5, 6 and 9. Rosamund Billington has carried out the overall editing and coordination of the work and Sheelagh Strawbridge much of the clarifying and drawing together of our theoretical and conceptual focus. We take collective responsibility for both the merits and faults of our work.

We would like to thank Eric Sigsworth for reading the completed draft typescript and his helpful comments on this. Louis Billington

1 What is Culture?

Definitions

There are at least two everyday, commonsense meanings of culture. The first is the 'best' achievements and products in art, literature and music. The second is the artificial growth or development of microscopic organisms or species of plants, a meaning deriving from a much older usage of the verb 'to cultivate': meaning to husband, and originally referring to agricultural techniques. Both these meanings are relevant to what is discussed in this book. More immediately we need to remember that although sociology is concerned with commonsense meanings, it must also look beyond them for theories, explanations and interpretations. Durkheim saw the study of 'collective representations' and their symbolic meaning as central to a sociological understanding of the social. In a very different tradition, Max Weber saw sociology as one of the 'cultural sciences', concerned with values and meaning, developing concepts and interpretations relevant to the society in which they take shape (Weber, 1949). A basic proposition of modern sociology is that concepts, ideas, words and other symbolic systems arise out of the society or group in which they operate. In this chapter we shall see that the development and use of the concept 'culture' relates to the beliefs and values people have about societies, social change and the ideal society they seek. We shall also see that much work on the concept has come from writers outside academic sociology, including literature, philosophy, politics, history and anthropology. Indeed, it is difficult to argue that there is a distinctive sociology of culture at all.

The complex of social and economic changes we call industrialisation in Britain, Western Europe and North America brought with

1

CALDERDALE
COLLEGE LIBRARY
HALIFAX

them a range of theories and concepts through which people tried to explain the structural changes which were occurring, based on the belief that it was possible to study society 'scientifically'. From these theories the related disciplines of sociology and anthropology developed, both utilising the concept of culture in a variety of ways. By looking at some of these in detail we hope to clarify some of the issues, assumptions and problems involved in the definition and study of culture.

Anthropologists and culture

An important change in Western ideas in the nineteenth century was the notion of the 'evolution' of species in the natural world. Among other things, this theory established human beings as part of the animal world (see Burrow, 1970; and Jones, 1980). The pseudo-science of physical anthropology attempted to investigate some of the differences between the 'races' of humankind at the same time that 'armchair' anthropologists were studying their cultures. Since then, studies by ethologists of primates and other 'higher' animal groups have emphasised the complex group activities of animals. Scientists, including psychologists, have utilised animal studies as a basis for research on some aspects of human behaviour. In popular thought people commonly explain human behaviour and arrangements as an aspect of their 'animal nature' but sociologists and modern anthropologists reject such reductionist explanations. They begin from the premise that only humankind possesses culture, in the sense of the classical definition by the nineteenth-century anthropologist Tylor: 'that complex whole which includes knowledge, belief, art, morals, law, custom and any other capabilities and habits acquired by man [*sic*] as a member of society' (Tylor, 1891, p. 18).

Like sociologists today, anthropologists (who owe a considerable intellectual debt to Durkheim) have attempted to explain societies in their own terms, that is, not simply as the sum total of the activities of individuals or deriving from the biological properties of human beings, but as unique social entities. To distinguish society from the biological or organic, the American anthropologist Kroeber, for example, talked about culture as the superorganic, stressing that there was nothing about the varied cultures of the world which was biologically inherited. He made the important point that culture is learned and transmitted through groups and individuals in societies (Kroeber, 1952; also see Beattie, 1964). Other writers and anthropologists have stressed the importance of humankind's ability to symbolise and to communicate through symbols, in the development of culture. Culture is 'species specific': although other species can communicate, only humans can communicate through symbols, language being the most important symbol system (see Chapter 2). These ideas are part of the nature/nurture debate, in which sociologists and anthropologists agree on the importance of the social and cultural as determinants of human action. Through the use of symbols humans bestow value and meaning on objects, relationships and ideas, and studies by modern anthropologists have shown us the tremendous range of these.

Many early anthropologists and ethnologists were concerned to list cultural 'traits', that is to analyse abstracted items of culture, such as religious beliefs or kinship arrangements, or items of 'material' culture, often finding similarities in these items in different societies (Frazer's *The Golden Bough*, on primitive religions, is a good example). Their findings were used as evidence for constructing evolutionary typologies and theories of societies or institutions such as kinship and religion (see also Chapter 3). Partly in reaction against such theories and their wrenching of cultural items out of context (and their assumption that social evolution occurred in a similar way to biological evolution) later anthropologists stressed the importance of studying 'primitive' cultures as systematic wholes, to understand the significance, function and meaning for the cultures themselves of particular beliefs, customs and practices. Such a holistic approach to the study of other cultures usually adopted the structural–functionalist assumptions of Durkheim which have important implications for the study of culture, a point to which we shall return.

We have used the concept of 'culture' almost interchangeably with society, but in sociology and anthropology important distinctions between the two have been made. Beattie points out that because of the all-embracing nature of culture as defined by Tylor above, British social anthropologists have tended to concentrate on social structure – social institutions. Study of aspects of culture, for example, belief systems – has been in terms of the functioning of these for the institutional system. American anthropologists have concentrated more on culture *per se*. Beattie stresses that this is a matter of emphasis and all anthropologists are concerned with social relationships (Beattie, 1964, p. 20). More recently, Douglas has argued that attempts by cultural anthropologists to split off culture from the rest of human behaviour have been relatively unsuccessful (Douglas, 1980, p. 117).

What becomes clear, when we look at classical works of British and American anthropology, is that given humans' innate capacity to develop culture as well as the biological limitations on such development, we cannot fully understand social activities unless we understand the place of beliefs, values and customs – culture – in these activities (see, for example, Hirst and Woolley, 1982; Geertz, 1973; and discussion of Levi-Strauss in Chapter 2 below). This is shown in the discussion of culture by the American anthropologist Clyde Kluckhohn. He adds to previous definitions of culture, saying that it consists of different components, it is dynamic, structured and the means by which individuals adjust to social life and learn 'creative expression'. Kluckhohn argues that cultures do not merely have content but also structure. They are cultural systems in that they are not random but have organised patterns, independent of particular individuals. Cultures are 'designs for living', formed through historical processes. Social scientists need to study both the explicit culture, which can be directly observed and is largely consciously understood by participants, and the implicit culture, which Kluckhohn calls 'an abstraction of the second order' (Kluckhohn, 1951, p. 43). By this he appears to mean something similar to what the phenomenologist Schutz meant by the difference between 'commonsense' concepts – the shared meaning which culture has – and the more abstract concepts developed by social scientists to understand the symbolic and other meanings of culture.

Kluckhohn writes in the Durkheimian tradition, stressing the shared and normative nature of culture and its functions for integrating the individual into the group. He emphasises that although some aspects of culture are relevant only to particular groups – generational, sex, work, class – all aspects are interrelated and form a whole, although culture is not necessarily perfectly integrated. In particular, he points out that individuals in Western societies, because of the cultural stress on individualism and freewill, are not always willing to conform to cultural patterns. Two points are implied in this argument. One is that in general culture serves an overall integrative function in society and the second is that there is a functional if complex relationship between culture and social structure, an analysis similar to that of the sociologist, Talcott Parsons.

More recently Clifford Geertz has stressed the creativity of culture and the agency of human action in negotiating and manipulating culture, using an 'action frame of reference' derived from the sociology of Max Weber and Talcott Parsons (Austin-Broos, 1987). Geertz has also emphasised the particularity of cultures and the necessity for 'thick description', that is, an interpretative approach:

> the concept of culture . . . is essentially a semiotic one. Believing, with Max Weber, that man is an animal suspended in webs of significance he himself has spun, I take culture to be those webs, and the analysis of it . . . not an experimental science in search of law but an interpretative one in search of meaning (Geertz, 1973).

We will look again at culture as a semiotic system, but for the moment we need to look at a major theme in the sociology of culture, one which goes back to the great sociologist Durkheim – the notion that culture is functional for the continuation of society.

Functions of culture

Parsons' structural-functionalism has been one of the most influential theoretical approaches in sociology until quite recently. Despite his attempt to synthesise ideas from a variety of nineteenth- and twentieth-century social theorists most of his work is in a direct line from Durkheim in his stress on the nature and necessity of social integration (Parsons, 1937 and 1951). Parsons's theory (or theories) is complex and changed over time, but what is relevant here is the priority given in his most influential work to what he called the cultural system in the overall integration of society and the integration and socialisation of individuals into society. For Parsons, 'social action' by individuals, which results in what anthropologists call social institutions, involves choices based on values and norms which are specified within the cultural system. Put simply, people behave as they are expected to in a given situation because they have internalised the norms and values – the culture – of society (Durkheim termed this 'morality'). This ensures the stability both of the individual and society: the social action of individuals is functional for the maintenance of the social system.

Parsons conceptualises 'the social' in a highly abstract way – as a 'system of action', consisting of four components, which are also 'systems': the cultural system, the social system, and the psychological and biological systems of individuals. It is easier to understand this abstract schema if we think of it as a series of levels – both of analysis and of functioning for the total system of action. The cultural system represents the highest or most general level of analysis and is the most important in terms of its function for integration of the whole, because it ensures normative consensus, a common value-system. All parts of the social system are functional to the whole and this includes the system for allocating 'rewards and facilities', including power: the stratification system (Parsons, 1954). Here individuals are ranked and evaluated in terms of the 'value standards' prevailing in the cultural system and in Western societies achievement on the basis of merit and performance is most important.

This structural-functionalist theory of stratification appears to have logical and fundamental implications for the content and maintenance of the value/cultural system which are not spelt out by the theory. Individuals and groups who have power presumably have power over the content and continuing production of values/ culture. If this is so, then the 'value-consensus' central to Parsons's schema could be seen to be the 'property' of those at the top of the stratification system, not some overarching, reified and autonomous cultural system. The considerable criticisms of this theoretical approach to the role of culture, are dealt with in various parts of this book but we need to note here the similarities which exist between structural-functionalism and some nineteenth-century writers and theorists of culture. We need to note also that there is a continuing concern by Americans with the search for an integrated modern American culture (e.g. see Berger, 1977; Sennett, 1974; Bell, 1979; Bellah *et al.*,1985; Clecak, 1983).

Culture and industrial society

Sociologists and anthropologists are not alone in developing theories and ideas about culture. Raymond Williams has attempted to show

how modern notions of culture in Britain arose out of the
nineteenth-century changes and processes indicated by the 'keywords', industry, democracy, class, and art (Williams, 1958, 1963).
Williams is pointing essentially to what sociologists have called
social differentiation, the increasing specialisation of functions in
society. In the nineteenth century he argues, the concept of culture
'as an abstraction and an absolute' emerged 'as a recognition of the
practical separation of certain moral and intellectual activities' from
the rest of society, and as an attempt to create ultimate values at
which to aim and by which to judge other social and economic
activities' (Williams, 1963, p. 17). Williams stresses that this new
concept of culture was not simply a response to industrialisation but
a search for 'new kinds of personal and social relationship' – just the
concern of social theorists like Saint-Simon, Comte, Durkheim,
Spencer and Marx. Similar 'cultural consequences of modernization'
were felt in America too (Levine, 1988, pp. 223–6; Buhle, 1987, pp.
xii–xiii). If we accept that an essential part of the 'spirit of the age'
was the idea of human progress, then the various theories of culture
are part of the attempt to regulate and channel progress (e.g. see
Kumar, 1978). In the United States this attempt was couched in
terms of the need to develop a national culture commensurate with
democracy and freedom of the individual and one which was the
equal of European culture (Bellah *et al*, 1985; Levine, 1988;
Riesman, 1964).

The idea that humankind should seek perfection was not new, but
European, British and American writers in the late eighteenth and
early nineteenth centuries connected this search with the new
possibilities and problems of industrialism. In this context, the
concept of culture was equated with the idea of civilisation.
Underlying this equation, as we have seen, was some notion that
societies evolved from less civilised forms and Western industrialised
societies were closer to the top of this evolutionary scale – a notion
stated quite explicitly by early writers on primitive societies. But
writers like Coleridge, Mill and Arnold also began to distinguish
culture (with particular emphasis on the arts and philosophy) from
the more general terms civilisation and progress. Doubting (like
Durkheim and other sociologists) that the prevailing philosophy and
practice of Utilitarianism was adequate to deal with morals and
standards, they specified conditions necessary for a culture to
develop which would provide the ultimate source of judgement

CALDERDALE
COLLEGE LIBRARY
HALIFAX

and values. Coleridge wanted to integrate the cultivation of feelings and experience with scientific progress, but also speculated on the desirability of a specific 'class' of people, endowed by the state, who would be responsible for the general 'cultivation' of society. J. S. Mill's 'humanitarian' liberal Utilitarianism recognised that cultivation of 'feelings' should be part of the total culture and stressed the importance of a much-improved national system of education, which would elevate the level of knowledge and information for all classes in society. He also argued that such a culture must allow for free development of individuality so that each individual could contribute better to the collective culture, based on the individual worth of each person. It was the cultural and political effects of this individualism in America which concerned de Tocqueville and still concerns American theorists like Bell, Sennett and Lasch (see Clecak, 1983). Mill's was still a Utilitarian notion of culture but assumed that democracy included the access of all individuals to the necessary and civilising influence of culture. The twentieth-century sociologist, Mannheim, has interestingly seen this civilising process, which is ideally part of democratisation, as one in which all individuals are able to broaden their 'existential perspective' (Mannheim, 1954, pp. 229ff).

Nineteenth-century sociological theorists sought to understand social processes because they were anxious and often pessimistic about the nature of the new industrial society and what would replace traditional sources of stability. We can see this same concern, in a slightly different form, in the discussion of culture. The theoretical search for mechanisms of social integration was paralleled by the search for the 'harmonious development' of human intellectual and cultural perfection (Coleridge, quoted in Williams, 1963, p. 121). For Matthew Arnold, whose ideas were widely applied to Britain and America, this development of 'culture' was the only alternative to 'anarchy', by which he meant lack of standards of morality, intellect and judgement. He defined culture as 'the study of perfection' in general, criticising those 'philistines' who believed that the ultimate value was wealth, success and technological efficiency (Williams, 1963, p. 124; Levine, 1988, pp. 223–4). Like Mill, Arnold thought a truly liberal educational system important in the process of ensuring the development of culture, but like de Tocqueville he distrusted the power which democracy might give to the 'raw and rough' working classes. He emphasised the importance of harmony in this search for perfection and the need for the state to coordinate, control and guarantee that the influence of the 'best' people should predominate. He was clearly arguing for culture as the means of ensuring a consensus of values and an élite or class to safeguard this consensus: 'without order there can be no society, and without society there can be no human perfection' (quoted in Williams, 1963, p. 132).

Culture as a way of life

It is useful to note some important similarities between the theories we have examined. Most of the nineteenth-century theories have a more or less explicit view of culture as the creation of a consensus over values and standards, a position remarkably similar to sociological structural-functionalism. In addition, since culture is seen to represent ultimate values, the best of which humanity is capable, all the theories have some notion, however vague, that the determination and dissemination of 'culture' must be associated with a particular class or élite. Finally, we must note that a fairly clear distinction is emerging in these theories, between the notion of 'society' and 'culture', and that culture is something which over-arches, reflects and ultimately has its own effect on the social.

We saw that modern anthropologists' approach to culture stresses the idea of culture *as a whole* and as a way of life. T. S. Eliot, the poet, writing on culture in the twentieth century combined this anthropological perspective with the nineteenth-century emphasis on the importance of a social élite in the preservation and transmission of culture. Like earlier (and later) writers, Eliot was pessimistic about the results of industrialisation and capitalism, the organisation of life by the profit motive and the exploitation of natural resources. His ideal was a Christian society 'in which the natural end of man – virtue and well-being in community – is acknowledged for all' and his theory of culture is part of this overall ideal (quoted in Williams, 1963, p. 225). He states that British culture includes

all the characteristic activities and interests of a people. Derby Day, Henley Regatta, Cowes, the twelfth of August, a cup final, the dog races, the pin table, the dartboard, Wensleydale cheese, boiled cabbage cut into sections, beetroot in vinegar, nineteenth-century Gothic churches, and the music of Elgar (Eliot, 1962, p. 31).

While this is a broader definition than that of say, Arnold, it is narrower than Eliot's emphasis on culture as a way of life would imply. Even ignoring its datedness in the 1990s, it still excludes much of our 'way of life': pop music, manufacturing, pornography, weddings, women's magazines, romantic love, race relations, motor bikes, watching television, technology, science. It is also specifically English. Williams comments that Eliot's description includes 'sport, food and a little art': he adds to the older concept of culture as 'the arts', a minimal definition of 'popular culture'. Put another way, Eliot's definition of culture excludes the dimensions of gender, class, and race and ethnicity. It also excludes science and scientific thought. Despite his claim that 'to understand the culture is to understand the people . . . it is lived' (Eliot, 1962 p. 41). Eliot slips into using culture in its meaning of an absolute standard of 'high' culture, the best, when he argues that at the time he is writing (1948) culture is in decline. There are other points in Eliot's formulation which emphasise both the 'lived' nature of culture and its complex patterning. He mentions that each industry has its own culture 'with its own form of festivity and observances' (Eliot, 1962, p. 16), and also that a flourishing culture is not unified, in the sense of homogeneity, but takes from and is enriched by regionalism and localism. This latter point is demonstrated by much twentieth-century writing on American culture with its emphasis on the local or ethnic community (e.g. Hartman (ed.) 1974).

Eliot points out that we need to distinguish between culture at the level of the individual, the group and society as a whole. The most contentious aspect of his theory is his argument concerning class and culture. In modern societies he states, there are levels of culture which correspond to the more differentiated functions of individuals and groups, that is, to social classes: 'the class itself possesses a function, that of maintaining that part of the total culture of the society which pertains to that class'. He continues by arguing 'that in a healthy society this maintenance of a particular level of culture is to the benefit, not merely of the class which maintains it, but of the society as a whole' (Eliot, 1962, p. 35). Each specific class culture 'nourishes' the others: there is a necessary interdependence between the culture of each class and culture is the creation of the society as a whole. The higher classes do not have more culture but a more conscious culture. Eliot justifies the greater power associated with the higher classes by their greater responsibility in society and this analysis seems remarkably similar to structural-functionalist analysis, where, as we saw, class is thought of in terms of stratification. However, Eliot conceptualises culture specifically as differentiated rather than uniform and also, in large part, operating at an unconscious level.

In formulating a relationship between the maintenance of culture and social class, Eliot is criticising theorists like Mannheim who argued that modern societies were becoming not class societies, but groupings of élites holding power and maintaining intellectual and cultural standards on the basis of education and specialisation of function. Eliot recognises the necessity for the existence of an élite, in the sense of those with special knowledge and skills, but sees it (or them) operating within the context of a class society. In arguing that culture is a function of class and that the highest classes will help to maintain their own culture and through diffusion and power, the culture of lower classes as well as the totality of society's culture, Eliot is emphasising not only the importance of 'high' culture, but also that of tradition and continuity. His stress on the essential relationship between class and culture and his criticism of 'élite theory' is closely tied to his notion of the ideal society: an 'organic structure' is necessary for the transmission of culture from generation to generation (Eliot, 1962, p. 15). A society based on stratification of élites and the resulting culture would lead to an 'atomic' society: one in which individuals were isolated from each other and where there was no organic and continuing tradition. In this sense, Eliot echoes Durkheim's views on the superiority of 'organic' social integration. Interestingly though, Eliot stresses that the total culture gains by the process of friction with other cultures and by class conflict and 'disintegrates' only when 'strata' become so separated that they develop totally distinctive and separate cultures.

Although Eliot's is essentially a conservative position, it contains insights and propositions and raises issues about the nature of culture which coincide with those of other theorists. In particular, we shall see the importance of the role of class in culture. Eliot's views are an updated version of the concern with the quality of communal life and culture which we find in the nineteenth-century thinkers we have mentioned and which is a continuing theme of American cultural critics in particular (Clecak, 1983; Bellah *et al*, 1985). Even Marx, whose 'ideal' society required the abolition of all the institutions thought by more conservative thinkers to be necessary, for human beings to realise their true humanity, allowed for the importance of tradition and continuity in the material and parallel cultural revolution which he thought inevitable, although he believed that the dialectical process of social change would ultimately bring about a new culture (see Chapter 2).

Williams listed as 'keywords' two phenomena which nineteenth-century social theorists regarded with both approval and concern – 'democracy' and 'class'. Alongside industrialisation went the increasing differentiation of society into social classes based on wealth and power, but also greater political participation of all classes. Eliot's 'functionalist' view of class acknowledges the importance and inevitabilities of class in modern societies but also an updated expression of fear of the 'masses' or the 'mob' in democratic societies, a fear going back to the French Revolution and its consequences, including the founding of an American Republic. Mill's espousal of universal education, for example, was a liberal expression of this. As the old traditional culture, based on aristocratic privilege and power was eroded (and in the case of liberals and radicals this was seen as progress) the lower classes, it was argued, were no longer constrained by tradition and custom and required education in order to participate in the development of the new 'civilisation', whether this was Britain, France or the United States.

Mass society and culture

Eliot's twentieth-century conservative, élitist view of culture and tradition and his fears concerning unregulated industrialism were rooted in the notion of 'mass society' and its concomitant, 'mass culture', which in turn derived from the nineteenth-century theories already examined and those of others, like de Tocqueville and Nietzsche. The notion of mass society 'developed out of nineteenth-century sociology in a direct line of continuity' and emphasises two major strands of thought in particular (Bramson, 1961, p. 31; see also Swingewood, 1977, p. 2ff). One is the belief that 'pre-industrial' societies were tightly knit, integrated, organic folk communities – what Tönnies called '*gemeinschaft*' – integrated through what Durkheim termed the 'conscience collective'. In these societies each individual had a place confirmed by tradition and custom and mostly operated on the level of the 'primary' group – the family, guild or village. In contrast, industrial society is governed by market, commercial relationships and characterised by 'atomised', isolated, alienated, disenchanted individuals without roots in the community and prey to the anomie (normlessness and chaos) of urban industrial life. However, Durkheim saw industrial society as having the potential for more organic integration, reconciling greater individuality with greater interdependence, a theme which constantly recurs in much American writing on the nature of modern American culture.

Both conservative and radical writers share a pessimistic view of twentieth-century society. They were pessimistic about the process of industrialisation, urbanisation, popular education, and the development of political democracy. Their most pessimistic theme argued a connection between the social conditions of mass society and the rise of totalitarian social and political movements. Again the image is that of human beings, rootless, lonely, directionless, and thus ready-made fodder for fascist parties. Common to all 'mass society' theorists, whatever their political alignment and differences, is an élitist view of society and culture and a rejection of individualist liberalism. Writers like Mannheim and the Frankfurt 'school', Ortega y Gasset, T. S. Eliot, F. R. Leavis and Dwight MacDonald, share the view that in order to reintegrate modern society and avoid the excesses of totalitarianism there must be an intellectual cultural and political 'élite' to ensure the transmission of a worthwhile and relatively autonomous culture. For writers like Nietzsche, Gasset, and Eliot it is the 'mediocre masses', including the new middle classes, who threaten the tradition of 'high culture'. As Bramson indicates, this theory about the nature of society and culture involves 'questions of fact structured by and saturated with values' and it 'is difficult to separate those aspects of mass society theory which are specifically cultural from those which are political' (Bramson, 1961, pp. 43 and 121).

We need to explore the concept of mass culture in more detail, but we shall leave further discussion of 'high culture' against which it is being judged, until Chapter 3. In his discussion of culture, Eliot

CALDERDALE
COLLEGE LIBRARY
HALIFAX

acknowledges his intellectual debt to the American, Dwight MacDonald (Eliot, 1962, p. 9) and it is worth looking in some detail at MacDonald's discussion of popular/mass culture which, despite its ultimate conservatism was influenced by the Frankfurt school theorists. It is also in essence, a popular theory: it is very much a 'commonsense' one, held by people other than sociologists and still an influential strand in writing on US culture. Although the beginnings of mass culture lie in the political and social changes of industrialisation, MacDonald emphasises the importance of technological developments leading to the creation of a whole new range of mass media including television and films, as well as mass production of books, records and so on. What distinguishes mass culture 'is that it is solely and directly an article for mass consumption, like chewing gum'. It is also, he argues, 'a parasitic, a cancerous growth on High Culture', by which he means that mass culture draws on the traditions and achievements of high culture. Mass culture integrates 'the masses into a debased form of high culture . . . It is fabricated by technicians hired by businessmen; its audiences are passive consumers, their participation limited to the choice between buying and not buying' (MacDonald, 1957, pp. 59–60).

A good modern example of this would be the way in which the conventions and forms of 'high' art are used directly and as *pastiche* in some advertisements to create a continuity between the traditions of high and mass culture (Berger, 1972). This is only possible because the techniques of mass production have made widely available good-quality reproductions of classical paintings as posters and books. The 'cultural needs' of the masses, MacDonald argues, are exploited in order to make commercial profits and to maintain the power of the ruling class, in both the United States and the Soviet Union. In discussing the latter, he argues that it is not the profit motive but the political obedience of the masses which is achieved by the imposition of mass culture. His designation of both the USA and the USSR as mass societies, ignores the enormous differences in technology and resources existing between the two countries in the 1950s.

MacDonald compares mass culture with 'folk art' which he sees as a spontaneous expression of 'the people' and quite clearly separated off from the high culture of the aristocracy prior to industrialisation. He patronisingly argues that it was perfectly legitimate for folk art to exist for 'the people' so long as the cultural élite maintained its own culture. He objects to the lack of separation of these different cultures and their merging together:

> Like nineteenth-century capitalism, Mass Culture is a dynamic, revolutionary force, breaking down the old barriers of class, tradition, taste, and dissolving all cultural distinctions. It mixes and scrambles everything together, producing what might be called homogenized culture . . . It thus destroys all values, since value judgements imply discrimination. Mass Culture is very, very democratic: it absolutely refuses to discriminate against, or between anything or anybody (MacDonald, p. 62).

Most striking about MacDonald's discussion is his certainty of the absolute nature of cultural 'taste' and values defined by high culture. He accepts that there is 'good' and 'bad' art, without indicating what standards he is using. He asserts, for example, that although Dickens's, work is popular it is high culture, whereas that of his contemporary, G.H. Henty is not, because Henty was 'an impersonal manufacturer of an impersonal commodity for the masses'. This is a circular argument, to say the least, and presents no criteria for judging between one literary work and another other than the apparent intentions of the author! Similarly, he dismisses as 'spurious High Culture' a whole list of painters, writers, architects and others, for example, Somerset Maugham and Arnold Bennett, on the ground that they have produced 'manufactured' items, no different from mass-produced cultural items of television, films and other forms of popular media. Part of MacDonald's objection to mass culture is in terms of its form and content – for example, comics and movie Westerns, which 'infantilise' adults. Conversely, children grow up too quickly because they have access to adult movies and television (it is interesting to note here the current concern over children's access to 'video nasties').

Because he is outspoken and uncompromising, not hesitating to give examples of 'good' and 'bad' culture, it is easy to caricature MacDonald's position, but in essence, his theory is typical of mass society theorists. Implicit in his work are assumptions about the production of culture and its relationship to the wider production process of capitalist society. He makes clear that there is a mass-culture industry and points to the high level of division of labour within magazine, radio and cinema industries, which he argues prevents truly spontaneous creation of art: 'Such art workers are as alienated from their brainwork as the industrial worker is from his handwork . . . Unity is essential in art; it cannot be achieved by a production line of specialists, however competent' (MacDonald, p. 65). MacDonald is pessimistic about the future because he argues that mass culture is a system against which individuals cannot be educated to fight, an 'engine' which cannot be stopped. Later American theorists echoed this view: 'I side with that earlier MacDonald who saw the masses (which is to say everybody) as victims of a merciless technological invasion that threatened to destroy their humanity' (Rosenberg, 'Mass Culture Revisited' in Rosenberg and White (eds) 1971).

It is the apparent powerlessness of the individual against the economic and technological forces and mass culture produced by capitalism which is the concern of 'critical theory' or the Frankfurt School. These theorists were radical pessimists in their views (in contrast to the conservative pessimism of, say, Eliot) with their roots in Hegelian Marxist thought. Although it is impossible to discuss here the many differences and contradictions between the individual theorists of this school, in general, their theories were an attempt to integrate Marx's emphasis on the class nature of society with the insights of psychoanalysis, into a modern humanistic analysis of society and culture. Their concern with the nature of mass culture and fear of totalitarianism, can be explained partly by the fact that many of these writers came into contact with American mass culture as refugees from the National Socialism of Nazi Germany (Bramson, 1961, pp. 121ff; Swingewood, 1977, pp. 10ff; Connerton, (ed.) 1976). It was the alienation and atomisation of the individual, they argued, which explained the acceptance of the ideology of National Socialism and the average American's satisfaction with mass culture.

Adorno, Horkheimer and Marcuse followed Fromm and Reich in accepting the centrality for Freudian theory of the socialisation role of the family; they saw psychological factors as mediating between social structure and behaviour (culture). This led them to argue both that the authoritarian and unloving family produced authoritarian and/or racially prejudiced individuals and that the breakdown of family authority in modern society allowed the 'culture industry' to play a major role in socialisation. The 'breakdown' of the family and the formation of the individual's ego by the peer-group and mass media means that everyone becomes simply one of the masses and less of an individual, 'other-directed' rather than 'inner-directed' (Riesman, 1953). The 'masses' consist of a passive majority, unable to perceive that their own freedom is threatened and the culture industry is the means by which any revolutionary potential of the masses (the proletariat) is destroyed.

Characteristic of the mass culture portrayed by the Frankfurt School are its lack of both autonomy and creativeness, aspects of traditional culture which these theorists see as vital to counteracting the economic and social values of capitalism. Traditional or high culture, like nineteenth-century bourgeois European culture, is seen as having a relatively autonomous critical and imaginative function completely absent from the 'wish fantasies' and 'aesthetic barbarity' of modern mass culture. The latter, because it is produced by the 'culture industry' simply reflects uncritically the values of the dominant order.

This mass culture debate has identified America in particular, as the society where traditional and folk culture is most endangered and the debate continues in various forms in American writing on culture (Dunn, 1986; Caughie, 1986). American 'liberal-pluralist' critics of the Frankfurt School and mass-society theories in general, for example, Shils and Bramson, argue that these have idealised pre-industrial society, its organic nature, and the possibility that human beings and human culture can reach a stage of perfection. Gans identifies the elitism of such theories: 'the mass society critique is an attack by one element in society against another: by the cultured against the uncultured, the educated against the uneducated, the sophisticated against the unsophisticated, the more affluent against the less affluent, and the cultural experts against the laity' (Gans, 1974, pp. 3–4). Such critics point to the advantages for the individual of pluralist political and social institutions, reflected in the choice and range available within mass culture and which they argue prevents the totalitarian power so feared by the Frankfurt School: 'Mass society has liberated the cognitive, appreciative, and moral capacities of individuals' (Shils, 1959, p. 3; Bramson, 1961, pp. 96ff). Gans argues that what he calls popular culture consists of 'taste cultures' which reflect the values of different groups – 'taste publics' – and that these cultures are shaped by the people themselves (Gans, 1974; see also White, in Rosenberg and White (eds) 1971). More controversially, Marshall McLuhan argues that the technological possibilities of the mass media will unite people in a 'global village' and that our views of culture are outdated: 'In the name of "progress", our official culture is striving to force the new media to do the work of the old' (McLuhan and Fiore, 1967).

We agree with part of these criticisms of mass society theories which are based on romantic and erroneous assumptions about the nature of pre-industrial society and also on élitist conceptions of what society and culture *should* be like. As we shall see in Chapter 9, they also contain a simplistic model of the way in which mass media affect individuals. Such theories do not adequately explain the existence of ethnic, regional or gendered cultures, the development of subcultures, or the specific content and appeal of popular culture (e.g. see Ross, 1989). However, we are also critical of the 'pluralist' notion of mass culture, which pays insufficient attention to the way that culture is produced or created and the structures of power and control involved in this process and to the consumption of culture. In using the term 'culture industry' to describe mass culture, the Frankfurt School and theorists like MacDonald are identifying a highly relevant point about culture in industrialised societies: it is commercialised and dependent on market forces. Cultural items like music, clothes, engagement rings, wedding ceremonies, sport, cult movies, literature, political campaigns, are commodities which are produced and consumed. The mass media are producers of a very sophisticated kind, producing not simply objects or items but values (including wants and desires) which influence behaviour and are part of 'lived' culture (also see Chapters 4 and 9). Something with which writers on the mass media are increasingly concerned, is the degree to which cultural consumers are simply an undiscriminating 'mass', or differentiated by class, gender, ethnicity and other factors such as age. The importance of some of these social divisions for the analysis and understanding of culture is the subject of later chapters.

Culture and modernity

While many American cultural theorists have rejected the pessimism of the mass-society thesis they have been critical of social and cultural changes of the twentieth century, displaying a continuing concern with the type of society which the United States is becoming (and by implication, other Western societies too). Some of these theories may be called loosely 'pluralist', but others are not

easily classified, containing implicit assumptions about the relationship of culture to the rest of society and positing a connection
between culture, personality structure and 'national character'.

Radical 'counter-culture' theorists of the 1960s were critical of
capitalism, bureaucracy and technology, as were many earlier post-
war writers and artists – for example, Jack Kerouac, Alan Ginsberg,
William Burroughs. In their place they pursued the ideal of personal
fulfilment, and it might be argued, revived many much older ideas
concerning the 'pursuit of meaning' in American life. Despite this
search for a new 'golden age', the counterculture utilised and
became absorbed by many of the processes of commercialised
popular/mass culture. It has been argued that this radical cultural
dissent signalled 'the end of WASP male cultural domination in
public spheres as well as in the minds and imaginations of citizens'
(Clecak, 1983, p. 213) and that US culture has become increasingly
syncretic, absorbing both ethnic, class and regional cultures
(Herberg's *Protestant, Catholic, Jew*, 1960, is an early comment on
this process). The US counter-cultural critique of the 1960s triggered
its own critique, as well as opposition from the establishment to its
political and social radicalism. Cultural critics like Lasch, Sennett,
Podhoretz and Rieff have argued that the counter-culture has
created a preoccupation with self-fulfilment, hedonism and priva-
tisation, to the exclusion of older American cultural values of
discipline and concern for collective and communal life: the culture
has become one of narcissism, selfishness and anomie (Lasch, 1978;
Sennett, 1977; Clecak, 1983). The sociologist Peter Berger comes to
similar conclusions but talks of the 'disintegration of mediating
structures' between the individual and the 'megastructures' of
modern societies (Berger, 1979, pp. 167ff).

Such generalisations concerning the nature of US American
cultural change and its effects on personality are hard to evaluate,
not least because they are not explicitly rooted in any specific
theoretical orientation. They appear to equate culture with
'tradition' and continually conflate notions of the cultural, social
and political, making it difficult for sociologists to explain the
precise relationship of the cultural changes discussed to the wider
structures of society. There is an unacknowledged neo-Weberian
flavour to much of this work, including the notion that cultural
changes have social effects (see Chapters 2 and 6). However, the
trends identified by these cultural critics have a certain commonsense

appeal and the recent sociological study by Bellah *et al.*, (1985) shows the ideas of 'individualism' and 'commitment' forming part of the beliefs and values of middle-class Americans.

In *The Cultural Contradictions of Capitalism* (1976, 1979) Daniel Bell comments critically on similar trends, but argues that the culture of 'self-realisation' is historically specific and part of the syncretism of the culture of modern capitalism. Bell's sociological model distinguishes culture from social structure and from the political realm, seeing each realm (or system?) as governed by a different 'axial' principle. While Bell argues, as Marx did, that social processes are dialectical and modern capitalism inherently contradictory, he gives a determining role to culture which is reminiscent of Parsons. Ultimately he sees modernity as disrupting the 'unity' and 'coherence' of culture. Return to such unity can come only through the development of a 'post-modern' culture in which religion will feature and provide answers 'to the existential predicaments, the awareness in men [sic] of their finiteness and the inexorable limits to their power . . . and the consequent effort to find a coherent answer to reconcile them to the human condition' (Bell, 1979, p. xxix). While Bell sees the cultural contradictions of capitalism as ultimately soluble through cultural change, he leaves unresolved many theoretical issues concerning the relationship of culture to capitalism. Like nineteenth-century sociological theorists, Bell is anxious to understand culture in society in order to change it. Like them and like modern 'mass-society' theorists he posits the necessity of unity or consensus of culture, which does not solve the issue of how we evaluate culture and how we decide on the values which are part of it (see also Chapter 10).

In the next chapter we shall pursue the notion that culture is produced, is related to structures of power and domination and also raises methodological problems for sociologists.

2 Theoretical and Methodological Issues in the Study of Culture

'Culture is not a neutral concept'

There is a danger that in retrospect theoretical developments are seen to occur more clearly and less ambiguously than they really do and in attempting to introduce and review such debates we oversimplify. For this reason our discussion of the variety of approaches to the concept of culture has not taken a strictly chronological form. Changes in ideas and theoretical orientations frequently develop in opposition to those current or dominant at the time, but several different theoretical positions may be in use at the same time as the basis of research and academic debate and oppositions are rarely clear-cut. In our discussion of theoretical work we have chosen what appears to us to have been most significant, for the development of later theory and/or in influencing ideas and attitudes to culture more generally: 'Culture is not a neutral concept; it is historical, specific and ideological' (Swinge-wood, 1977, p. 26).

As we have made clear, it is not only sociologists who have contributed to the development of a 'sociology of culture'. We have outlined some of the ways in which the concept of culture has been approached since the nineteenth century and the common assumptions underlying these approaches. Later in this book we shall point to the directions which we think the sociology of culture has taken most recently. Our immediate task is to discuss some of the most influential theoretical developments which have occurred in the last few decades, some of which have their roots in nineteenth-century theories. We shall indicate something of the range of contributions from differing disciplines and theoretical traditions.

21

CALDERDALE
COLLEGE LIBRARY
HALIFAX

At the same time that the Frankfurt School was making its critique of 'mass society', based largely on despair of the possibility of the proletarian revolution predicted by Marx and their experience of American culture, American (and British) sociologists were writing and have continued to write in a different vein, partly in opposition to the longer tradition of Marxist thought and influence in European social science. Much American sociology has been of the 'pluralist' kind, influenced by structural-functionalism and also by the distinctive historical development of the United States, strongly linked to but also outside European cultural and political traditions. It has rejected both the social and political implications of Marxism which have influenced much European and British sociology. A different strand of American sociological thought has been that of 'social interactionism', which has rejected the positivism of much European sociology and has roots in alternative philosophies: the interpretative position of Weber, the formalism of Simmel and the American pragmatists. We will discuss the contribution of this perspective to the sociology of culture later in this chapter (see also Chapter 5).

Given the importance of Marxist theory in Britain and Europe we shall look now at some aspects of this which have contributed to the sociology of culture. This task is complicated by the range of interpretations and we have not attempted to cover the whole variety of Marxist theories of culture (see Hall, 1981).

Marx on culture

The emphasis of anthropologists on culture as a uniquely human social activity, noted in the last chapter, is also found in Marx's social theory, where he argues that 'Men [*sic*] can be distinguished from animals by consciousness' and also by the fact that they 'produce their means of subsistence'. In Marx's theory it is the fact of human productive activity which is most fundamental for the organisation of social, political and cultural life. Marx's term 'consciousness' is important here; by this he seems to mean not simply the human species' capacity for thought, but the organisation and patterning of human thought and activity in a collective sense – something very close to anthropological definitions of culture examined in Chapter 1. But it is the relationship between consciousness and 'material life' –

the 'real' world created by human economic activity – which is Marx's concern and this is clearly stated in a frequently quoted passage: 'The mode of production of material life conditions the social, political and intellectual life process in general. It is not the consciousness of men that determines their being, but on the contrary, their social being determines their consciousness' (*Preface to the Critique of Political Economy*, p. 29: Marx, 1950).

In emphasising the importance of economic activity for the organisation of social life Marx is grounding or rooting human culture in what he considers to be the necessary activity of production, but he is not referring to economic activity in any simple sense:

> Rather it is a definite form of activity of . . . individuals, a definite form of expressing their life, a definite mode of life . . . . As individuals express their life, so they are. What they are, therefore, coincides with their production, both with what they produce and with how they produce (*German Ideology*, p. 7: in Marx and Engels, 1938).

These passages are often taken to illustrate Marx's 'economic determinism' and in *Preface to the Critique* there is a clear statement of the 'base and superstructure' model of society which can be interpreted in the same way:

> In the social production of their life, men [*sic*] enter into definite relations that are indispensable and independent of their will, relations of production which correspond to a definite stage of development of their material productive forces. The sum total of these relations of production constitutes the economic structure of society, the real foundation, on which rises a legal and political superstructure and to which correspond definite forms of social consciousness (pp. 328–9).

According to this model, then, culture is determined by or dependent on the economic base or infrastructure. Each type of historic economic structure – 'mode of production' – has a corresponding superstructure which includes social, political, legal and cultural institutions and customs. Culture is not simply an epiphenomenon but is produced by and integral to a particular type of economic system and dependent on the type of technology which prevails. So for example, the prevalence of bourgeois literary culture in the nineteenth century depended on the initial invention of the printing press in the fifteenth century and on the improved and cheap production and distribution of printed books in the nineteenth century. It can be argued that Marx's is a determinist theory of society and culture and also an evolutionary one – each mode of production emerges out of the previous one and represents a stage nearer a more ideal (classless) society. But he does not fall into the trap (which many nineteenth-century theorists did) of arguing that there is an even or simple relationship between the specific aspects of culture and the material base of society (which includes technology). He argues, for example, that although Greek culture developed in a specific set of social and economic circumstances (mode of production) which were unique, aspects of this art and culture remain and afford us artistic pleasure. The 'charm' of Greek art for us is not that it was 'in contradiction to the undeveloped stage of society on which it grew', but that it was unique: the social and economic conditions in which it flourished 'can never return', history cannot move backwards (*Grundrisse*, pp. 109–11: Marx, 1973). Although we might quarrel with Marx's assumption of the universal appeal of Greek art, and ultimately what can be seen as his economic determinism, his theory acknowledges the specific and unique aspects of culture and allows for their continuance from one mode of production to another.

Ideology and culture

So far, this elementary Marxist model of culture may seem rather abstract although it does encompass the idea of culture as something 'lived' and 'produced' in the course of social and economic activity. It is the exact nature of this culture and its relationship to the base/ superstructure model and material existence which has exercised modern Marxist theorists and their deliberations have focused on the crucial concepts of class and ideology. For Marx, social class is fundamental to the relations of production in most societies and class relations generate ideology:

> The ideas of the ruling class are in every age the ruling ideas: i.e the class which is the dominant material force of society, is at the same time its dominant intellectual force. The class which has the

means of material production at its disposal, has control at the same time over the means of mental production (*German Ideology*, p. 39: Marx and Engels, 1938).

On the basis of this model, it is difficult to see how culture and ideology are anything but *reflections* of class relations, with the content entirely determined by the ideas and beliefs of those with power. The implications of this for culture are that it is monolithic and homogeneous and cannot in itself produce effects.

Modern Marxist theorists of culture, however, have stressed the importance of some forms of culture as resistance against the power of the dominant class and emphasised culture as lived, as action. This is based on reinterpretations of Marx, most significantly by Antonio Gramsci and Louis Althusser. These reinterpretations have rejected crude economic determinist readings of Marx and recognised more subtlety in his thought, particularly in his view of the complexity in base/superstructure relationships. Althusser has conceptualised the 'social formation' in terms of levels or 'instances' which have some degree of autonomy, although the levels are causally interconnected and the whole has a coherence, a unity. The exact relationship between the levels — economic, political, ideological, varies historically, so that a level other than the economic may dominate a society's development. Nevertheless there are definite priorities in the causal relationships, the structure is a 'structure in dominance' and the priorities are determined in the 'last instance' by the character of the economy. It is this that gives the whole its unity (see Althusser, 1977, pp. 203 ff, and Althusser and Balibar, 1977b, pp. 108 and 319.)

We can see that Althusser's model allows for ideology to be a level or system of reality in its own right: it has considerable autonomy and can affect other areas of social structure including the economic. Ideology, in Althusser's re-reading of Marx is not a false representation of reality — false consciousness — but it is a structure of thought and consciousness in which we all think, act and experience the world and ourselves. 'Ideological state apparatuses', including religion, education, the family and mass media, develop and reproduce the values, beliefs and ideas which form our culture. Althusser conceptualises ideology as a system of symbolic representations through which we, as individuals are constituted as self-conscious 'subjects'.

Ideology is embedded in social practices which are governed by the rituals of ideological institutions. For example, being a Christian is not just a question of holding a set of beliefs. It involves behaving in particular ways, participating in certain practices: the ideas derive from the material practices rather than the reverse. A little child is taken to church and goes through the motions of prayer and so on, long before the rituals have any meaning. By the time the meanings are understood the practices are taken for granted, the beliefs are already instilled and the child recognises her/himself as a Christian. So ideology works by shaping the social identities of individuals, by forming them as subjects through internalisation of the system of symbolic representations and the practices in which these are embedded (for the similarity between the ideas of Althusser and Durkheim see Strawbridge, 1982). Althusser refers to this process as one of 'interpellation' or 'hailing'. As we are called by the terms we recognise ourselves as Christians, as daughters and sons, as British and so on. For the most part we experience these identities as freely chosen or at least natural. Subjects then are formed through ideologies and all societies have an ideological level.

We have identified ideology as a system of symbolic representations and Althusser has been criticised for having a 'dominant ideology thesis' (see Abercrombie, Hill and Turner, 1980). However, arguably, he sees ideologies as plural, articulating in complex ways. Later theorists certainly do so. It is also important to note here the slippage between the terms 'ideology' and 'culture'. Some theorists confine the term 'ideology' to those aspects of culture which are specifically identifiable with the process of reproducing the social relations of production whilst others use the term more generally.

Cultural hegemony

In his thinking about the complexity of base/superstructure relations Althusser was influenced by Gramsci. Those who see Althusser's theory as ultimately too structuralist and determinist have recently drawn more directly on Gramsci, whose notion of cultural or ideological hegemony has been particularly significant. This has allowed the theorisation of control by the dominant social class as a complex process with more room for the subject (individuals or groups) to be seen as an active force. In this theory moral and intellectual superiority is established in a variety of ways, including incorporation of oppositional ideas and styles and the 'saturation' of society, to the extent that ideology 'even constitutes the substance and limit of common sense for most people under its sway' ('Base and Superstructure in Marxist Cultural Theory', in Williams, 1980a, p. 37). This seems to allow for the heterogeneity of culture and cultural practices in any particular society, while maintaining the Marxian notion of culture as ultimately determined by the relations of production:

> For if ideology were merely some abstract, imposed set of notions, if our social and political and cultural ideas and assumptions and habits were merely the result of specific manipulation, of a kind of overt training which might be simply ended or withdrawn, then the society would be very much easier to move and to change than in practice it has ever been or is (Williams, 1980, p. 37).

Hegemony refers to the way in which the consent of the subordinate classes to their domination is achieved: this is both a struggle and a process and it is never permanent:

> It is a set of meanings and values which as they are experienced as practices appear as reciprocally confirming. It thus constitutes a sense of reality for most people in society, a sense of absolute because experienced reality beyond which it is very difficult for most members of the society to move, in most areas of their lives' (Williams, 1980, p. 38; see also Gramsci, 1971; Mouffe, in Bennett *et al.*, 1981; Bocock, 1986; Swingewood, 1977 pp. 30ff).

So, for example, we may argue that the idea of romantic love as the basis for psychological and sexual fulfilment is an ideological component of Western capitalism, while at the same time, ourselves, falling in love, feeling sexual jealousy if our partners are unfaithful and finding personal fulfilment in a stable marriage. Williams has usefully conceptualised the hegemonic process in terms of a contest between three dimensions or levels of culture. First, there is 'effective' dominant (hegemonic) culture. Second, there is 'residual' culture containing historical meanings and practices which may eventually become incorporated as part of dominant culture – for example, ideas and beliefs about Britain's imperial past. Finally, there is 'emergent' culture of new ideas, meanings, experiences,

CALDERDALE
COLLEGE LIBRARY
HALIFAX

styles which eventually become incorporated in some form, even
though initially they may constitute an oppositional or counter-
culture – for example, some feminist ideas; theories of 'self-
fulfilment; styles of dress and music, like punk, initially associated
with 'youth cultures'.

Cultural studies

A version of Marxian theory, drawing on both Althusser and
Gramsci, which emphasises consciousness and the importance of
superstructural concerns, and incorporates insights from structuralism and feminism (see Chapter 7), has informed and developed the
work of the Birmingham Centre for Contemporary Cultural
Studies (CCCS) in Britain, since the 1960s. Cultural studies has
become established as an academic field separate from literary
studies, sociology, anthropology and social history, all of which
contributed to the new synthesis (Hall, in Hall *et al.*, 1980). This
approach has been less influential in America, where resistance to the
importance of both 'popular' culture and Marxism have led to
different theoretical concerns (Dunn, 1986; Caughie, 1986; Buhle
(ed.), 1987).

Stuart Hall, a leading contributor to the CCCS has defined
culture as the 'lived practices which characterise a particular society,
class or group at a particular historical period'. It includes 'the
practical ideologies which enable a society, group or class to
experience, define, interpret and make sense of its conditions of
existence' (Hall, 1982, p. 7). Similarly, Bellah *et al.* define it as those
'patterns of meaning that any group or society uses to interpret and
evaluate itself and its situation' (Bellah *et al.*, 1985, (p. 333). While
the CCCS sees culture as concerned with the way in which social
groups develop distinct patterns of life and give expressive form to
their social and material life experience, Bellah *et al.* represent a
dominant American view, explicitly rejecting the view that culture
is 'to be explained by economic or political factors' (Bellah *et al.*,
1985, (p. 333; also see Bell, 1980, pp. 6–7). British cultural studies
became increasingly concerned with the problem of the 'relative
autonomy' of cultural practices, a radical move away from the older
base/superstructure model. This raised questions concerning the way
in which a particular arrangement and ordering of culture

developed, how a particular cultural order became dominant and 'How did the preferred cultural order help to sustain 'definite forms of life' in particular social formations?' (Hall, in Hall *et al.*, 1980, p. 27). Criticism of the way in which this group has conceptualised class in relationship to cultural practices is dealt with in Chapter 6.

Cultural studies in Britain developed initially out of debates around landmark texts: Hoggart's *The Uses of Literacy* (1957), Williams's *Culture and Society* (1958) and *The Long Revolution* (1961), and E. P. Thompson's *Making of the English Working Class* (1963), all of which challenged the élitist concept of 'Culture' as something fixed and immutable, or as collections of texts or artefacts (see Chapters 1 and 4), with a more anthropological and dialectical notion. Culture was perceived as created and experienced and emphasis placed on the empirical details of specifically working-class culture (see Hall, in Hall *et al.*, 1980, for important differences between these works). Further development within cultural studies continued through rejection of the dominant structural-functionalist positivist paradigm in sociology and its accompanying emphasis on 'scientific' methods (already challenged from within sociology itself) for the hermeneutic, interpretative approach of Weber and Schutz and American 'social interactionism'.

Culture unfolding

Symbolic interactionism is a synthetic yet fragmented theoretical approach whose basic tenets remain largely implicit. It is not 'grand theory' in the way that Marxism or Parsonian structural-functional-ism are and its roots lie in the belief expounded by Weber, amongst others, that sociology does not have any special claim to truth, given the complexity and and inexhaustible nature of social reality. At best, using the *verstehen* approach, sociology can describe or reconstruct the social reality of culture so that we can understand it in a way that also makes sense to its participants. Drawing from the ideas of Simmel and American Pragmatists like John Dewey and George Herbert Mead, symbolic interactionism has emphasised the fluid and emergent character of social processes and the way in which symbolic worlds are constructed by participants. In this sense, culture is not a structure but a continual process of 'becoming' (Rock, 1979). Central to symbolic interactionism has been the method of participant observation as the way of understanding the creation and unfolding of culture from the point of view of its participants.

A criticism of the interactionist approach from 'orthodox' sociology has been that it neglects – in fact denies – the existence of social structures and their consequences for cultural processes. But the complex work of Erving Goffman and also the studies of ethnomethodologists, drawing on the ideas of symbolic interactionists, show social participants themselves creating such structures. It is more important here to acknowledge the richness and number of empirical studies of American culture produced in this 'microsociological' vein, including the 'Chicago School' studies of 'subcultural' and other communities. Focus on the group and the community in social interactionism have combined with the emphasis in American sociology on Weberian concepts of power, status and stratification to produce community studies like those of the Lynds, Dollard, Bensman and Vidich, and Lloyd Warner, which are in part, studies of local, regional or ethnic cultures (for example, see Merrill, 1961, pp. 146ff; see also Chapter 5). Interestingly, some of these studies also use theoretical insights from other traditions too. For example, part of the classic Yankee City study by W. Lloyd Warner is *The Living and the Dead: A Study of the Symbolic Life of Americans*, which follows Durkheim and Radcliffe-Brown in emphasising the creation and maintenance of symbol systems, looking at popular American cultural symbols like 'Biggy Muldoon'.

The ethnography of culture

In the 1960s American 'Chicago School' writers, like Becker, had already highlighted the use of ethnographic methods (for example, Becker, 1963) and in Britain cultural studies developed a concern with methodological issues surrounding the study of culture. Unlike social interactionism, however, cultural studies has attempted to link the ethnographic and particular aspects of culture to the wider structural issues identified by Marxian theories.

The concern of the CCCS with the structural/material nature of culture and ideology and its production and reproduction gave rise to the criticism that some of the work of this group was over-theoretical. Although this may be a valid criticism, the group has produced and inspired a considerable range of studies of particular cultures and cultural groups, including the seminal volume, *Resistance Through Rituals: Youth Subcultures in Post-War Britain* (1976) and later the work of Paul Willis – *Learning to Labour* (1977) and *Profane Culture* (1978). These studies use ethnographic and documentary methods, including participant observation, as most appropriate for studying cultures which are *lived* and must be understood both at the level of practice and the level of meaning for the participant, the subject. But the studies attempt to overcome criticism of the phenomenological and interactionist use of such methods, which is that they ignore social structural factors and are divorced from theoretical concerns (see essays by Pearson and Twohig; Roberts; and Butters 1976). In discussing the relationship between cultural theory and ethnographic methods Willis argues that we need to distinguish between the 'indexical' (the 'facts' and details) and 'homological' (the relationships between these details) levels of culture, examples of which, respectively, might be how long, where and when a group of young people listen to pop music, and how far such music parallels and reflects 'the structure, style, typical concerns, attitudes and feelings of the social group' (Willis, 1978, p. 191). 'Homological' analysis involves more interpretation by the researcher than 'indexical' analysis, but both involve participant observation backed up by documentary and other evidence. Willis's view of the nature of society relates directly to the methods of studying it which he advocates:

> I do not see society as a series of disconnected individuals living out their particular lives, but as a structured whole within which individuals and groups live under differing degrees of domination, expressing *and reproducing* in different degrees through symbolic patterns and cultural practices a sense of *positionality* within and perhaps resistance to the hidden, misunderstood or unseen overarching structures which limit their field of choices and help to constitute them in the first place (Willis, 1978, p. 193).

He is concerned then, not with individuals as subjects, but with the '*subjectivity* of symbolic systems, actions and values', so research must be done 'in the natural situation of the actors' (ibid, pp. 194–5). While the researcher must be flexible, not allowing theories to 'get

in the way' of experiencing the subjective aspects of a culture and .
cross-checking material collected through participant observation,
with other sources and participants, the process must also be self-
reflexive, critical. This includes recognition of points of contact
between the theories of the researcher and the subjectivities and
values of the groups and individuals being studied. Willis argues that
far from being a problem, the process of analysing the intersection
between the 'social paradigms' of the researcher and of the research
subjects is one of the strengths of the critical ethnographic method
(see also Giddens, 1984, on social actors as social theorists). Willis
also identifies a third level for the analysis of culture, the 'integral',
which is concerned with the generation of homologies (for example,
the motor bike as a symbol of 'macho' maleness) and how they
develop in specific historical circumstances.

Culture, language and symbolic order

Discussion of the relationship between theory and interpretative
methods in the study of culture, emphasises another important
point: the symbolic nature of culture. Sociological emphasis on the
symbolic nature of the social and cultural has a long history cutting
across differing theoretical traditions. We have already seen its
influence in the Marxist and symbolic interactionist traditions, the
latter, as we have seen, drawing on the work of Weber. Durkheim
too, saw society as a structured system consisting of institutions,
established patterns of behaviour and a shared language which shape
our lives. Without 'collective representations' individual thinking
would not be possible at all. Persons or 'souls' are essentially social,
we are formed as social beings:

> It is quite true that the elements which serve to form the idea of
> the soul . . . come from and express society . . . . But whatever
> we receive from society, we hold in common with our
> companions. So it is not at all true that we are more personal as
> we are more individualised (*The Elementary Forms of the Religious
> Life*, pp. 271–2: Durkheim, 1971).

Fundamental to social reality for Durkheim are classification
systems, ways of ordering, arranging and making sense of things.
He was particularly interested in dichotomies or binary concepts.

For example the 'sacred' is what the 'profane' (the everyday) is not, women are what men are not, cold is the opposite to hot, and so on.

Lévi-Strauss, a modern anthropologist who has influenced work on culture in both Marxist and Durkheimian traditions, claims that all cultures (and languages) contain a whole range of binary concepts. In the same way that language (of any kind) has rules, Lévi-Strauss argues, so do the basic components of culture: he is concerned with the universals of culture such as myth and kinship rules. Human culture consists of the way in which we classify, categorise and organise 'nature', the most basic example being the way we cook food and distinguish it from raw things – cooked being the opposite of raw (see Lévi-Strauss, 1970). Situations and occasions on which we eat particular kinds of foods and the type of cooking regarded as appropriate are not important in themselves, but signify something about the cultural order. Children in any culture learn social conventions concerning what to eat, what not to eat, what can be eaten raw, what should be cooked and the foods which are appropriate to specific social occasions. It is the homology between a type and order of food and the rest of the cultural system that Lévi-Strauss is trying to indicate (Lévi-Strauss, 1970; Leach, 1974; Sperber, 1979). A modern example here would be the concern in Western societies with health foods, food additives and contamination, nutrition and the condemnation of processed and 'fast food'. It is arguable that a processed or 'fast food' diet is less wholesome than that eaten by humans for thousands of years, but the significance of our concern is that the preparation and eating of food at home in a family setting is being displaced. It could be argued that this concern reflects a deeper anxiety about the place of the family and traditional values in modern life than about health.

Mary Douglas has done interesting work on the symbols, rituals and activities involved in the construction of everyday social reality, particularly such down-to-earth aspects of social life as dirt, bodies, food, material possessions, jokes and speech. Her work draws on that of Lévi-Strauss and she has been most strongly influenced by Durkheim, particularly his work with Mauss on classification. Trained as a cultural anthropologist, Douglas draws on traditional cultures to illustrate general processes. Her interest centres on the ordering of social life – 'the moral order'. Dirt, deviance and other things regarded as pollution reveal important things about systems and rules of classification, particularly in relation to the symbolic

granted' world of everyday reality out of unorganised meaningless experience, simultaneously constructs our value system. Being dirty or clean is not just a matter of fact: there is a moral dimension to reality that makes classification and misclassification, being in place and out of place, a question of right and wrong.

The act of re-establishing order is one means of re-establishing society. Sorting, tidying up, cleaning and putting things in their place are ways of reinforcing both the structure of social reality and our moral sentiments. Douglas argues that modern hygienic practices are just as symbolic and ritualistic as purity rituals in traditional societies – 'we kill germs, they ward off spirits'. The modern practice of identifying pollution rituals with hygiene reflects our use of scientific and medical conceptions of reality to justify social order. Dirt and disorder are made possible by the system of order and from this point of view crime and deviance are the same as dirt. Whereas dirt is matter out of place deviance is behaviour which is out of order. Order is re-established by ritual action, dirt (and crime) are cleaned up and this serves to reaffirm the moral order. Deviance and dirt are normal and functional: our reaction to them is one of the basic mechanisms which renews and defines social rules and boundaries. Our ideas about what things are, and what is right and wrong are established on a day-to-day basis by our own and other people's reactions to violations of social rules.

In *Natural Symbols* (1970, 1978b) Douglas develops the idea of rituals, drawing on Bernstein's earlier sociolinguistic work (collected in Bernstein, 1974). She argues that it is useful to understand rituals as forms of communication. They communicate social information and help renew collective sentiments. Thus, rituals should be treated in much the same way as speech, as transmitters of culture. Like Bernstein, Douglas considers culture to be transmitted mainly through the internalisation of speech. We are created as social beings, adopting the socially defined roles which form our identities and are embedded in our language, as we learn to speak. She adopts Bernstein's distinction between an 'elaborated' and a 'restricted' code. A restricted code is a form of speech which arises in small-scale, local, social situations where participants share the same basic assumptions. What is spoken is essentially already known to all members. Its function is to reaffirm the group's solidarity, in much the same way as Durkheim saw religious ritual functioning in traditional societies. When an individual uses a restricted code she or

CALDERDALE
COLLEGE LIBRARY
HALIFAX

he is performing a linguistic ritual which acts to renew common ideas and values at the same time as reinforcing the individual's social identity. Elaborated codes, on the other hand, are employed in situations where speakers do not necessarily know or accept each other's fundamental assumptions. In this case speech has the primary function of making viewpoints explicit.

Linking ritual and social solidarity in this way, allows Douglas to examine the relationship between changes in group life and the amount of ritual activity. She utilises the concepts of 'grid' and 'group' from Bernstein's work on the school curriculum: 'grid' referring to rules which govern interactions between individuals, 'group', to collective identity. The terms may refer to whole societies or to subgroups within societies. The stronger the 'group' the more collective reality there is, shared beliefs and values are strong, boundaries separating it from other groups are clearly drawn and there is more ritual to reaffirm the collective sentiments. Strong 'grid' organisations are those in which individuals have clearly defined roles: 'The grid is visible in the segregated places and times and physical signs of discriminated rank, such as clothing and food' (Douglas, 1982, p. 192). As grid gets weaker role definitions become weaker, there is greater ambiguity in relationships and less well-defined criteria for judging status and what is decent and indecent.

By linking ritual and language we can treat in the same way a great variety of symbolic systems which communicate social information. Douglas has written on music, art and food in this vein (see, for example, 'Deciphering a Meal', in Douglas, 1978a, pp. 249–75). Wuthnow *et al.* (1984) use this approach to analyse Black American music from slavery to the 1960s, showing that there was a strong collective identity amongst slaves 'which accordingly generated restricted musical codes, like spirituals' (p. 107), using biblical images to symbolise relations between blacks and whites, and a musical structure suitable for group singing. Later 'blues' and jazz emphasised a more individualistic approach, reflecting the decline of black solidarity and migration to the north. With the renewed solidarity of the Civil Rights movement in the 1960s, it is argued, the more restricted codes of 'soul' music developed.

Douglas's work over-emphasises the local and small-scale application of notions of grid, group and restricted codes (see Wuthnow *et al.*, 1984, pp. 105 and 122–5). For instance, group would seem to apply also to larger-scale modern political communities: collective sentiments are certainly represented by images of 'the People', 'the Nation', 'Democracy' and 'Socialism'. Other writers in the Durkheimian tradition have shown how modern 'witch-hunts' reaffirm group identity in times of tension and uncertainty (for examples, see Thompson, 1986).

We can see that sociologists and cultural anthropologists, Durkheimians and some Marxists, all look to language in their search for a key to understanding social life. The twentieth-century philosopher, Wittgenstein, argued that 'the limits of my language means the limits of my world' and in his later work he developed a powerful view of social reality as a range of 'language games' with distinct sets of rules. Social theorists of many persuasions have utilised Wittgenstein's concept of language games. For example, in his anthropological work, Geertz sees culture consisting of clusters of rule-governed forms of life, a multiplicity of cultural systems. Culture is 'conducted in the context of systems of communication, using symbols linguistic, material and behavioural' (Austin-Broos, 1987, p. 149. Geertz and other theorists have also drawn on the insights and analytical tools furnished by the structural linguistics of Saussure.

He argued that language is a system, a code of signs: a sign is something which stands for – is a symbol of – something else. For signs to be recognised their meaning must be shared by a group because the connections between signs and the objects and ideas which they signify are arbitrary (Saussure, 1959; Harland, 1987; Culler, in Bennett *et al.*, 1981). So, for example, the variety of words in different languages which mean 'woman' have nothing intrinsic in them to indicate a person of the female sex, it is only historical cultural usage that gives these words meaning. But language is not simply a set of labels which we learn: it is a coherent system of interdependent terms. The word 'woman' in English only has meaning in the context of a whole system of words – man, girl, child, boy, baby: the relationship between words and what they signify is not arbitrary *within* a language because it is a structure of concepts, a code specifying the relationship between objects, not simply the objects themselves. The term 'engagement ring' can only be understood by knowing that this object is worn by a woman in Western societies who is either signifying her intention to marry a specific man, or, if she is also wearing a wedding ring, is married. It can only be fully understood in the context that a man does not wear such rings but buys them for the woman he intends to marry, a fact signifying something about the different relationship of males and females within the social institution of marriage.

It is the sets of relationships signified in language which classify and give meaning to our experience. English, German, Chinese and Hebrew and so on, exist as languages in this sense and their existence is not dependent on their use by particular speakers. Quite the reverse, our ability to speak, to understand and be understood depends on the existence of languages as systems. Structuralists make an important distinction between a language as a system – what Saussure termed *la langue* – and particular bits of linguistic behaviour – *la parole*. More recently Chomsky has distinguished linguistic 'competence' from 'performance'. It is our knowledge of a language, our competence which makes performance possible. Although speakers of a language must have knowledge of the system, or 'competence' in order to use it in linguistic performances, they are not consciously aware of their knowledge. Whilst, for example, they might be unable to explain the rules for producing sentences, they can, nevertheless, produce perfectly comprehensible sentences. This insight helps us to understand the way in which individuals produce comprehensible and acceptable social behaviour, even though the overall system of social relationships constituting their society is obscure to them. Moreover, the structuralist model allows us to understand how language is a level of material reality: it exists as a structured system of symbolic representations which carries cultural meanings and values. It is not dependent upon individual consciousnesses although it works through consciousness. It shapes the consciousness of subjects and thus forms individuals into social beings. The 'subject' is 'de-centred'. These themes are echoed in structural Marxist, Durkheimian and post-structuralist writings on culture where other symbolic systems are treated as languages (or texts).

The semiotics of culture

Modern semiotic forms of cultural analysis have developed directly from the structuralist model of language (Sturrock (ed.) 1979). 'What semiotics has discovered . . . is that the *law governing*, or, if one prefers, the *major constraint* affecting any social practice lies in the fact that it signifies; i.e. it is articulated like a language' (Kristeva, 1973). Like Douglas and Geertz, semiotic theorists see cultural practices – gestures, dress, music, and so on – in terms of a process of communication. They identify a sender and a recipient, and the 'message' as a 'text', which may or may not be 'read', understood, in the way that the sender intends. A simple example here would be the sending of flowers to a woman by a man intending simply to thank her for dinner the previous evening, but which is read by the woman as indicating – because they are red roses – that he is interested in a romantic relationship. Specific cultures or subcultures may be studied as texts in this sense. The esoteric signs and symbols involved may be read in one way by those individuals involved in the group or culture and another way by those outside it. In his study of the music and style of youth subcultures – punk, rastafarianism, glam rock and others – Hebdige argues that these groups deliberately cultivate a 'style', of dress, music, behaviour, which is esoteric, shared only within the group and antagonistic to or subversive of mainstream culture. So, for example, punks used the swastika as an emblem to signify their alienation from society, detaching the signifier – the swastika – from what it normally signified – fascism – thus offending and shocking older members of society (Hebdige, 1979).

Hebdige's semiotic analysis of youth subcultures is based on the work of the CCCS, and we saw that Willis's discussion of ethnographic analysis includes recognition of the importance of understanding the symbolic nature of cultural practices. Cultural texts do not have simply literal (denotative) meanings and the work of the semiotician Barthes, shows the way in which the literal meaning and its expression produce yet another level of meaning. Barthes's starting point is the way in which we take so much of our culture for-granted, as 'natural': we assume things are as they are because they are natural. There is a similarity here between Barthes' concept of 'mythology' – the ideas and explanations we have for the way things are – and Gramsci's point that ideology works and operates even at the level of 'common sense'. A similar point is made by Hall: he argues that ideology works in part through shaping our perceptions of social and political institutions (such as 'the market') as 'natural' and inevitable (Hall, in Curran *et al.*, 1977). Barthes uses semiotics to explain the way in which levels of cultural meanings are created through the use of symbols. For example, tea-drinking in

England and wine-drinking in France indicate more than relaxation, goodness; they symbolise something about the collective nature of each society, about nationality, likeness; there is nothing more British/French – natural – than drinking tea/wine – *being* British/French (Culler, 1983, p. 34; Barthes, 1973). It is the strength of such myths which in turn allows subcultures or oppositional cultures to develop on the basis of overturning or subverting the myths.

Culture as discourse

Earlier structuralist linguistics tended to portray languages as unitary systems. All speakers of say, French, were seen as speaking the same language, and it can be seen that if culture is viewed as inextricably bound up in such a language system we can quickly be led to assume a common culture or a 'dominant ideology', ignoring any notion of a complex articulation of cultures within a society. More recent 'post-structuralist' discourse theories avoid this unitary view. In contrast to structural linguistics, discourse theories emphasise that linguistic performances or utterances occur in specific social situations (Harland, 1987). Competence is practical competence, or the ability to produce appropriate utterances in particular situations. For example, when asked how we are, we do not normally reply with a detailed account of our aches and pains, unless we happen to be talking to a doctor. On most occasions we recognise the question as a polite greeting and reply in like manner. We are able to apply the appropriate rules of social interaction as well as the linguistic rules. (Ethnomethodologists have attempted to show how social life would become chaotic if we ceased to observe the rules of specific discourses, while arguing that it is we who create these rules, for example, see Garfinkel, 1967).

Discourses are essentially dialogues and they vary according to the kinds of social institutions and practices within which they take place. Far from being a single unitary system, a language like French or English must be seen as consisting of a whole range of smaller systems or discourses: there are dialects, patois, professional jargons, slangs, technical languages and so on. Words and expressions used and their meanings alter from one discourse to another and in relation to the social positions of those using them. It is argued that it is not a language as a whole that gives words their meanings, but rather the specific discourses in which they are located. Moreover, discourses are produced in struggles between classes and other groups and relate to conflicting ideological positions. Consequently, power struggles can manifest themselves as contests over meaning. Shop-floor speech differs from boardroom speech and managerial discourse defines problems and situations differently from trade-union discourse. We might consider, for example, the conflicting discourses centring on the idea of an 'uneconomic pit' in the 1984 miners' strike. Management discourse defined this as a central issue and it became a site of ideological struggle. An uneconomic pit was defined quite differently within the discourse of the miners' union and the management's meaning was contested in the attempt to resist pit closures.

Paralleling the notion of linguistic competence, which we discussed earlier, the rules of a discourse, which allow utterances to be comprehensible, are not consciously known and followed by speakers. The rules operate, as it were, 'behind their backs'. Discourse analysis aims to discover these rules, just as the structural analysis of a language aims to discover the rules that constitute competence. Discourse theory breaks with the notion of a language as a unitary system but retains the decentred view of the human subject. Subjects are now viewed as being formed by discourses which embody conflict and contradictions and assert power. As Diane Macdonell points out, discourse theory does not just interest itself in class relations and overt political struggles. It has also become concerned with the relationship between language and power in what appear to be politically 'neutral' areas, particularly those areas of culture defined as 'knowledge', such as medicine:

> The speech of a hospital patient concerning his or her body differs from that of the doctor. In any institution, there is a distribution and a hierarchy of discourses. Where a pregnant woman wants her childbirth to be natural, her statements and the concepts in which she thinks may conflict with those of the doctor. The field of discourse within an institution is not uniform; and not all the statements made about the woman's pregnancy may be accepted as 'knowledge': the woman may find that her words carry little weight (Macdonell, 1986, p. 2).

Ann Oakley has also shown how gender may be an important issue of power in the discourse of doctor and patient (Oakley, 1981).

Much of the work of Michel Foucault has focused on the way different 'knowledges' have developed in the course of history. What counted as knowledge in the eighteenth century was different from what counts as knowledge today. Then, it was possible to 'know', for example, about 'madness' and 'folly'; now we can 'know' about 'mental illness'. It is usual to see this as a progression from pre-scientific to modern ideas and more adequate scientific forms of understanding. Like Douglas, however, Foucault questions this view of the progress of knowledge. He argues that knowledges are forms of social control, they exert power as can be seen in the above illustration, and new knowledges develop with new forms of power. Foucault has been particularly interested in the development of the knowledges of the human sciences and the ways in which they have constructed our views of 'normality'. These concepts of normality apply to all sorts of ideas we have about ourselves and for which we set standards: 'a healthy body'; 'a stable personality'; 'sanity'; 'a normal family'; 'a proper man or woman', and so on. Moreover, they institute new ways of exercising power through disciplinary mechanisms linked to the notions of normality and deviance. These disciplinary devices differ from those in the past which focused on the body and physical punishment (Foucault, 1977). They are more psychological in character and operate through schoolrooms, welfare offices, hospitals, mental institutions, prisons, families and workplaces, through the cultural practices of teachers, welfare workers and others.

The human sciences are involved in constructing us as subjects, they are aspects of our culture. By tracing the ways in which they have become knowledges, Foucault is attempting to question the taken-for-grantedness of their views of normality and the forms of social discipline they impose. He shows that the formation of the controlling discourses of normality can also make possible 'reverse' or oppositional discourses. Psychology and psychiatry have played a part in constructing ideas of perversion. For example, Foucault argues that the category of homosexuality appeared as a 'psychological, psychiatric, medical category' around the 1870s. The homosexual 'became a personage, a past, a case history, and a childhood, in addition to being a type of life, a life form' (Foucault, 1979, pp. 43–4). Later in the same book he suggests that this very construction of a homosexual identity made it possible for homosexuality to begin to speak on its own behalf. Only when homosexuality existed as a form of personal identity, a category of subject, could demands be made that it is a natural and legitimate form of identity, rather than a perversion to be punished or cured. We might add here, that it is only then that we could begin to talk of homosexual culture (see Weeks, 1977; Humphries, 1985; and Chapter 7).

We can see how Foucault's work relates to and develops themes found in Althusser's theory of ideology (White, 1979). In any society there will be a whole range of systems of ideologies. These are embodied in complexes of discourses; structures which rule our ways of speaking, thinking and acting and which operate by forming us into subjects. There will be discourses governing all aspects of our social lives involving, for example, conceptions of health and disease, madness and sanity, sexuality, justice and punishment. Some of these ideologies will have the status of knowledges and will command a good deal of power. Others, such as the discourses of oppressed groups: the working class; women; blacks, and gays, will oppose these dominating conceptions. Foucault does not distinguish knowledge from ideology, and what is truth is defined by the rules of each particular and separate discourse. He thus takes up an extreme cultural relativist position, with regard to knowledge claims, with all the problems that this entails. He also rejects Althusser's stress on the ultimately determining powers of the base and with this he loses any conception of an overall unity in the structure of a society and why one group rather than another is in a position to impose its truth.

In this chapter we have outlined some significant themes and issues that have emerged in the study of culture and these will recur in later chapters which examine particular aspects of culture. With Foucault and discourse theory we have also begun to touch on the themes of our final chapter which explores the breakdown of some of the distinctions – structure/culture, objective reality/subjective experience, culture/knowledge – which have been considered useful analytical tools in the study of culture.

CALDERDALE
COLLEGE LIBRARY
HALIFAX

3   'High' Culture, Art and Aesthetics

'High' cultural production

Some studies of the media which examine the processes by which culture is produced and the ways in which 'society' and 'culture' relate to each other, frequently employ the terms 'high', 'popular' and 'mass' culture, in an attempt to clarify those processes. Often, the argument rests on the concept of culture as a commodity which is consumed according to the class structures and groupings which dominate within a society. One of the problems which arises out of this approach is that assumptions and values behind each of these terms are ignored and instead they are taken to be objective descriptions of different types of culture. This confusion of the subjective and objective is not restricted to the Frankfurt School, Marxian cultural studies and American sociologists (see Chapter 1). It is apparent in Leavis's, Gasset's, Zeraffa's and Scruton's writings on culture and its debasement (Leavis and Thompson, 1933; Gasset, 1932, 1961; Scruton, 1974; Zeraffa, 1976). At their heart lies the argument that modern industrial societies have produced populations with the physical abilities to consume culture, but devoid of the intellectual capacity to discriminate or select. Within the academic world, 'mass' retains the pejorative connotations which it was first given by the Frankfurt School; 'popular' has become the focus of Marxian cultural studies and some American cultural theory, and 'high' remains the central concern of cultural critics in academic and other institutions. These divisions are not clear-cut, however and American usage of 'mass' and 'popular' overlaps (see discussion in Chapter 6; also Caughie, 1986; Dunn, 1986; Gans, 1974).

The idea of culture as something which is consumed, is linked to the existence of specific 'consumer' groups with shared interests, defined by gender, class or intellectual standing (for example, see Bourdieu, 1986). Cultural production is defined in terms of the scale on which it takes place and ranked accordingly: a hierarchy or pyramid, with the unique work of art at the apex. Below that is small-scale artistic production in which profit is not anticipated – the small poetry print run, the art cinema circuit. Next would be the ambivalent layer, of the novel, for example, or Channel 4, which may reach a wider audience and if marketed efficiently make a profit. At the base of the pyramid is large-scale cultural production, intended to make large profits, for example, paperback-book publication aimed at the bestseller list, films on major release, Hallmark greetings cards. This ranking is based solely on the criterion of the volume of production at each level (see Frith 1986; Bourdieu, 1986, pp. 16–17; and Gans, 1974, for different and sociological formulations).

Here, of course, lies the fundamental issue in the way that cultural production and consumption are considered: the issue of quality. Just as 'high', 'popular' and 'mass' have become understood as objective descriptive terms, so the criteria by which cultural products are placed in any particular layer of the pyramid, or move between them, are seen not in economic terms, nor as being related to the interests of dominant groups, but in qualitative terms. They are given relative value depending on their position in the pyramid, and more quantitatively, always means worse qualitatively. But cultural products also have other qualities ascribed to them and it is necessary to examine these and what is implied by them (Bourdieu, 1986).

Beginning with the qualities themselves, it is vital to understand that these are not inherent in the cultural products: to the sociologist there are no qualities which we can attach to cultural products, which lie outside culture, or which are not relative to it. Mannheim has argued that with the 'democratisation' of Western societies goes the attempt to articulate aesthetic values more clearly and to relate them to 'objective' standards (Mannheim, 1956, pp. 174ff). Certainly, until the 1790s in Britain, Europe and America there was little attempt to examine the social meaning of such qualities. All investigation was aimed at an understanding of some inexpressible intrinsic qualities in the external world by which cultural

products could be ranked (Elliott, 1986, pp. 7–10). At the beginning
of the nineteenth century the aim was rather to establish a theory of
aesthetics which was outside history, but which lay within the
senses, in the aquisition of perception and illustrated particularly
through the arts, which as we saw in Chapter 1 were seen as the
essential component of a transcendent 'culture'. This position has
been challenged by Marxian theories, but can still be found and
different strands in the study of aesthetics will be taken up later in
this chapter. The alternative and more sociological position is that
within each society hierarchies of qualities can be discerned which
are historically specific and linked to the socio-economic structure of
that society. The sociologist Mannheim, uses Simmel's notion of
'social distance', seeing the process of what he calls 'distantiation' of
cultural objects – the creation of evaluative distance between them –
as a fundamental social process relating to the social distance
between groups (Mannheim, 1956, pp. 206ff). He argues too that
the social distance between 'high' and 'low' becomes less with
increasing democratisation (see also Gans, 1974). Weber's notion of
the increasing 'rationalisation' of the Western world also includes a
theory of aesthetics which relates to wider social changes (for
example, see Gerth and Mills (eds) 1948, pp. 340ff; Runciman
(ed.) 1978, pp. 94ff). As societies alter through time, there is an
accumulation of qualities, frequently from disparate sources, which
becomes melded into an apparently coherent whole. As we saw in
Chapter 1, culture is socially produced and the way in which such
cultural evaluations are made requires explanation.

Using Britain as an example, it can be seen that after the Norman
conquest, the variety of languages and culture of the indigenous
peoples was devalued, to be displaced by Latin and Norman French.
Music, poetry, stories, all related to the cultural traditions and values
previously established on the continent. Celtic and Anglo-Saxon
traditions were marginalised by being rejected within the Norman
court and Saxon texts were literally erased and written over
(becoming what are called palimpsests). High culture, the culture
of the ruling group, was the repository of those past forms which
had been assimilated by the ruling élite. As feudalism gave way to
mercantilism and emergent capitalism, so values shifted. English was
used as a language, the English that had evolved through the
accommodation of everyday (demotic) speech within the admin-
istrative structure – a synthesis in which social distinctions could be

identified through the language people used. The individual hero emerged as the centre of interest in stories, music and so on, his success determined not by birth, but by personal endeavour. The reality of these distinctions lay in the alliances of economic and more direct repressive power operated by the dominant group at each phase in British history. Similarly, Levine (1988) has shown the creation of 'high' cultural traditions in nineteenth century America, linking this to 'the shifting landscape of modernity' (p. 229), industrialisation and an increasingly differentiated class system.

Another example of the way that specific aspects of culture are produced is that of the paintings of Renaissance Italy (itself a cultural definition). Here patronage came predominantly from the two main power groups, the mercantilists and the church. In each case the consequent requirements of the patron were clear, and historically specific. In religious work conventions of colour, dress and appearance had to be observed, since they conveyed the symbolic and theological content of the work. In secular paintings, sumptuary laws, social hierarchies, symbols of wealth and the use of classical mythology to denote the education of the patron, again produced the vocabulary available to the artist, mindful of his patron's power. The qualities to be perceived in these works of art, were directly related to the society in which they were produced and dependent on the system of power which ensured that only certain types of paintings were produced.

However, the more cultural products are seen to refer directly to contemporary social circumstances, or 'real life', the less likely they are to be accepted immediately into the 'canon' of high culture (for example, see Bourdieu, 1986). Instead, a reverse argument is applied, so that the quality of products forming high culture is seen to be self-evident, natural, universal, and from these products criteria are established, on the basis of which other works can be judged. Institutionalised within universities, academies and so on, critical practice establishes those aspects of style and content which are to be seen as significant – the form is taken-for-granted as being appropriate to high culture. In this way, the sonnet and oil painting, in a particular time and society might be seen automatically as superior forms, but their subject matter and the way in which this is conveyed would be the elements scrutinised. The concept of 'the canon' can best be summarised as those cultural works which are by general consent perceived to possess the qualities which it has been agreed will be worthy of praise as superior to other qualities. But as we have shown, these qualities are themselves part of the processes of culture.

Raymond Williams discusses the operation of the 'selective tradition', as the construction of history, including cultural history. It is 'in part the emphasis of works of general value, in part the use of past work in terms of our own growth' (Williams, 1965, pp. 67–76). This is how works can be assigned to the 'canon' by society's cultural pundits, for qualities they were not seen originally to possess. Dickens's novels are frequently quoted as examples of this process. Retrospective selection occurs, of cultural products from the past which fit the value framework of the present. A cultural symbolic past is created, which in the case of Britain in the nineteenth century included ancient Greece and Rome, but not India or Egypt, in order to establish and legitimate the Imperial tradition. Eco discusses the Western idea of what the Middle Ages were in similar terms (Eco, 1986, pp. 61–85). For America, the tradition of European culture was seen as superior to newly developing 'native' American cultures (for example, see the novels of Henry James). Individual elements of the canon are not permanent and the canon is seen as flexible. Nevertheless, at any point in time, it is assumed to be definitive and universal.

The canon is used not only as an anterior justification of that cultural production which is most highly esteemed (if not necessarily preferred) by the dominant élite, but also as a critical benchmark for further evaluative and legitimating activity. New or newly discovered work will be compared for subject matter, technique and form with work already included in the canon. Its authenticity as a cultural product will be related to the tradition selected. The canon provides the standard which Ortega Y Gasset (1932, 1961) summarised as 'the principles on which culture rests'. Without these standards, this final court of appeal, according to this argument, there could be no culture. In this way, women's fiction with a domestic subject has been rejected as failing to achieve 'greatness' and not allowed to enter the canon in Britain, however proper its form, because its content failed those principles. This process serves another function: the reinforcement of high culture (for example, see Gans, 1974, pp. 77–81; Bourdieu, 1986). It makes possible the maintenance of a distinction between cultural products. Assessment of prescribed qualities distinguishes between those products which are to be detached from the specific circumstances of their production and consumption (de-historicised), and those cultural products whose clear relation to their production and consumption means that they will be seen as deficient in praised qualities (for example, the artwork in an advertising poster). This process enables the dominant group to accommodate potentially oppositional cultural production, a process important in maintaining cultural hegemony. Not only the residue of the past but the work of the potentially critical or disruptive avant-garde can be encompassed in the 'ahistoric present' of high culture. E. M. Forster expressed this when, speaking of literary genius and inspiration, he proposed the motto 'History develops, Art stands still' (Forster, 1962, p. 28).

Aesthetics and culture – 'One instinctively knows'

Williams traces the history of the word 'aesthetic', through Baumgarten and Kant in eighteenth-century Germany, to the present, as being both subjective 'sense activity' and as a science of sensual perception – an implied objectivity. Each usage related to the attempt to define beauty and as Williams points out, the emphasis which has emerged has been on individual valuation rather than the social (Williams, 1983, pp. 31–2; and see Gerth and Mills (eds), p. 342). Similarly, we saw in Chapter 1 how definitions of culture moved from the literal and metaphorical to an overlapping and ambiguous range of evaluative meanings. In each case, the words convey specific 'commonsense' meaning but resist conclusive definition. They incorporate meanings about the personal, intuitive, qualitative, subjective and universal.

The paths of social criticism are littered with attempts to provide explanations of what makes works of art works of 'art', although not all discard so totally as Forster did, the relevance of the social and temporal. For Roger Fry it is a synthesis of four visions:

- biological;
- curiosity;
- aesthetic – the apprehension that a cultural object is the 'outcome of a particular feeling . . . . Our apprehension is unconditioned by considerations of space or time', Fry, 1937, p. 48);
- creative, which is 'detached and impassioned'.

Aesthetic quality becomes 'significant form . . . the outcome of an endeavour to express an idea rather than to create a pleasing object' (Fry, 1937, pp. 236–7). The sociologist Simmel, too, stressed this aspect of the aesthetic (Lawrence, 1976, pp. 223ff). Aesthetic emotion appears to be inexpressible but of infinite importance. But here again, the concept of timelessness obscures the socially determined elements in the discussion of aesthetic judgements (Bourdieu, 1986, pp. 28ff).

Not all attempts at articulating aesthetic theory have been so tenuous or amorphous. One conceptual force in aesthetics which has persistently re-emerged in the West, both to determine and explain awareness of mutually agreeable 'rightness', of evidently harmonious composition, is Platonism and neo-Platonism which developed specifically within music and architecture, although during the Renaissance they were also applied to drawing. It is this type of 'technical rationality' which Weber saw as increasingly characteristic of Western culture (for example, see Runciman (ed.), 1978, pp. 94ff). The principles underlying this concept can be summarised crudely as the mathematical explanation of harmony, both acoustic and visual. Geometry was held to be the key and through the principal geometric forms, humanity and the universe were united. Wittkower (1949, 1973) explores the development and application of this concept during the Renaissance, emphasising the metaphysical basis of this unity – that its effectiveness lay in the philosophical, rather than in the physical world. He notes that to interpreters of the writing of Vitruvius (c.30 BC) on architectural principles, like Alberti (c.1450) and those who followed, 'the harmonic perfection of the geometrical scheme represents an absolute value, independent of our subjective and transitory perception' (Wittkower, 1949, 1973, p. 8). It is this geometrical explanation of cosmology which Leonardo da Vinci illustrated in his famous drawing of the Vitruvian figure of Man in circle and square, which retains sufficient force to be included in space probes as potential communication with other sentient beings. The classical tradition in aesthetics in England, particularly important in British and American architecture, can be traced back to these ideas, through Inigo Jones, Lord Burlington and William Kent, and Isaac Newton in mathematics. Newton's theories of colour and the laws of number are in this tradition rather than the new material relativism expressed by David Hume and Edmund Burke. The temporary resurgence of neo-Platonism in the eighteenth century was in clear contrast to the combination of the rational and aesthetics as subjective experience, which became dominant later.

The idea of aesthetics in the West is thus bound up with both metaphysics (ideas on the nature of the world) and continuing investigations into the nature of creativity, which encompass philosophy and psychology – those 'depths of mysticism' which brought Roger Fry's investigations to a halt (Fry, 1937, p. 237). We have seen the ethnocentric views of early anthropologists in Chapter 1. Before the 1950s most anthropological studies which discussed aesthetics at all viewed it from the point of cultural absolutism: the art of small-scale, pre-literate societies was considered primitive by definition and thus devoid of aesthetic value. Since then there has been a move towards ethnographic relativism: universal standards are no longer assumed in the methodological framework which shapes the studies undertaken. As a consequence, the enormous variation in aesthetic views and values which exists between societies has been revealed.

Much of this more recent work stems from a development of Durkheim's theories exploring the relation between social and spatial organisation. As Fernandez points out:

> The relevance of these facts of social and spatial organisation to aesthetic problems should be clear, for aesthetics, after all, has as one of its primary concerns the manner in which values, whether color [*sic*] or tones or even words for the poet, are formally arranged in space (Fernandez, 1971, p. 54).

There is an increasing acceptance that decoration in 'primitive' society has an aesthetic as well as a ritual motive. That aesthetic criteria differ between societies emerges to some extent, even in those studies which appear to indicate a high level of transcultural agreement (see, for example, Child and Siroto, 1971). It has proved impossible to identify a universal correlation between value-orientations and artistic style. The indications then, are that whilst the processes by which individuals formulate aesthetic judgements may well be universal, the criteria on which individuals draw are culture-specific, and socially determined (Kavolis, in Jopling (ed.) 1971; also see Lévi-Strauss in Chapter 2 above).

In the West, since the rise of the mercantile classes, aesthetic sensibility has been linked to both class and education. The tastes of

CALDERDALE
COLLEGE LIBRARY
HALIFAX

the peasantry and later the urban mob have been categorised as savage and debased, from Bartholomew Fair onward. For Matthew Arnold and Walter Pater in the nineteenth century and the Leavisite school in the twentieth, the inculcation of the necessary sensitivity to make such judgements could only meet with limited success, since the capacity itself was perceived as limited within a society (also compare the 'Black Papers' debate in education, see Chapter 8). Just as Altick (1957) distinguishes between mechanical literacy and discriminating reading, in the seventeenth century, so Ortega Y Gasset distinguishes between the intellectual élite and modern mass-man, who tends 'to consider and affirm as good everything he finds within himself; opinions, appetites, preferences, tastes. Why not, if . . . nothing and nobody force him to realise that he is a second-class man . . .'. Because people live in a mass society 'the basic texture of their soul is wrought of hermeticism and indocility; they are from birth deficient in the faculty of giving attention to what is outside themselves . . . They will want to listen and discover they are deaf' (Gasset, 1961, pp. 47 and 50).

Aesthetics, then, can be seen as the rulebook of a society's culture, the evaluative process by which high culture can be recognised and appreciated, similar to the more general processes of social categorisation and classification discussed by Mary Douglas (see Chapter 2). Gans argues that 'high' culture is dominated by 'creators' or those who adopt the aesthetic standards and orientations of artistic practitioners.

'The arts' and genre

Initially, we need to identify some of the cultural conventions which hold good by general consensus in Western societies. Other chapters will provide further illumination on the way that consensus is achieved (including the consensus on what constitutes 'knowledge', see Chapter 8). For the time being, we can argue that it is consequent upon the operation of ideology and its production and reproduction within society (see especially Chapters 2, 6 and 9). It is impossible here to provide examples from every available form of cultural production, and we have indicated the applicability of cultural analysis across specific forms, at a particular time.

In Western societies 'the arts' are seen as separate but related disciplines within the humanities, requiring the practice of identifiable communicable and expressive skills on the part of the practitioner, and observation and recognition of these skills by the critic. In order that these skills should be exercised without interminable repetition, the rules which are applied have some flexibility. Within each discipline they are more or less detailed and explicit. Between disciplines, however, there is no acknowledged common ground. Each art is perceived as being uniquely governed by rules relative only to that art.

At the present time, the rules of harmony and counterpoint will be taught to the aspiring music composer who will then work either within or against them. The poet may be taught the patterns of rhyme and rhythm, but more likely will be encouraged to move forward by trial and error to 'individual' expression, no less rule-governed than music, when comparisons of individual poems are made. The composer's music will be assessed on what the individual has produced, the quality of perfomance and appropriateness of venue. The poem on the other hand will not be judged on the paper, typeface or binding or the publication in which it appears. The play which explores the predictability of social existence for a given individual will be criticised, the novel which does the same may equally be praised. The painting which offers a version of the rural idyll will not encounter the scorn which would greet its literary equivalent.

None of these responses is permanent. The rules which govern production within disciplines, the evaluation of material within each discipline and its subsequent categorisation, can be adapted as circumstances alter. Genre is the concept which provides the framework for this process, being at the same time both prescriptively definitive and amorphous. To the extent that the concept of genre is now used for the analysis of cultural products from the bottom of our pyramid of cultural products outlined above – 'popular' culture – the distinctions between 'high' and 'low' culture begin to break down. Genre theory has been developed extensively over the past twenty years in a variety of ways which reflect the diversity of its antecedents. In its earlier form, genre was used as a means of categorising works of art, literature and music according to their subject matter and the extent to which rules were applied and formulaic convention adhered to within each work.

Genre was (and is) the mechanism which defined boundaries, beyond which works could not be included in a specific category. Thus, arbitrary divisions in literature were recognised, whereby within the genre of poetry, the lyric, the epic, the ballad, the sonnet and the narrative poem could be distinguished and a new work in each genre judged by precedent (Abrams, 1957).

In Europe in the eighteenth century there was a clear categorisation of artists' work in which the painter was expected to choose to study and then produce work related only to that genre. The status of high culture was confirmed through the establishment of institutions with royal patronage and support, which sought to maintain rigid classification of their discipline. In the case of the Royal Academy in England, for example, this rigidity was backed by a theory which dictated appropriate style and subject matter, and confirmed the hierarchical status of specific genres in art. Any painting aspiring to the category of high art had to employ a classic or mythic theme, executed in oils and constructed in accordance with specific geometric norms. These rules were sufficiently rigid for Benjamin West's painting, in 1770, of the death of the British hero General Wolfe, depicting Wolfe in contemporary costume, to be found shocking in its overturning of established theory and categorised as historic genre painting rather than high art, a decision which ruined West's career.

Other recognised genres at the time were those of portrait painting and landscapes. Genre painting in Britain in the nineteeth century was understood as painting dealing with the everyday rather than great historic events (Chesneau, 1887). Although this attitude has relaxed, it has not disappeared. In this way genres continue to serve both as boundaries of expertise and of relative status. However, this tends to make them sound like purely functional classifications. But as Andrew Tudor amongst others, has pointed out, they depend on shared sets of meanings and conventions within a culture (Tudor, 1976). Genre classifications order discourse rather than the world. They offer a symbolic system, but they affect our world view as they establish the terms on which we can perceive the world (Jordin, 1984, p. 70). They can be beneficial to both producers and audiences because they serve to mobilise expectations and enable selection, with an enhancement of pleasure which comes from prior knowledge (Tudor, 1976; also see Chapter 9). Readers of science fiction, viewers of *film noir*, anticipate the pleasure of the experience in the knowledge of what a new product within the genre will offer. This is not a permanent state, however. As expectations are confounded by parody or by a disruption of the conventions of the genres themselves, so changes occur and so, too, the status given to various genres alters. These changes can be observed in science fiction, for example, where the growth of feminist writing has significantly altered the scope of writing which explores alternative possible worlds (see also Chapter 8). The active relationship between the reader or groups of readers and the product implied in genre theory indicates a much more complex relationship between cultural products and their users than mass society theorists allowed (see Chapter 2; also Gans, 1974).

'Telltale signs'

While it is important to recognise the impermanence of responses to cultural products, and thus the impermanence of the boundaries between 'high' and 'low' culture, it is equally important to be aware that within each discipline, none of these responses is consistent. The relation between the cultural product and the society from which it stems is frequently reduced to volatile and fragmented contradictions in the everyday world, yet these contradictions are accommodated within culture. Popular women's magazines include the poetry of Patience Strong and her followers, but also interview or profile classical actors and opera singers. These apparently random phenomena can be understood through the application of cultural theory. The visible practitioners of culture – the 'ordinary people' with special qualities, who can be represented as artisans through their work as performers – can be discussed by magazines in the same terms as other successful businesswomen. The high profile which is necessary to them in their work is also what makes them suitable subjects for journalism – their success and skill is conspicuous. The material with which they work remains largely untouched as a mystical area of culture, irrelevant to its practice. The process of mediation rather than the matter mediated is significant (see Chapter 9). Those forms of cultural expression where the production of matter is the central activity do not hold the same attraction. Unless there is a framework which would make sense of the product and its production and valuation, by relating it to the everyday world, including class, politics and economics, popular journalism leaves the generators of culture and the material they generate largely alone. If there is no sexual deviation, no colossal expense or price, no explicit appeal to a class minority, then high art is held to be of little interest or relevance to the popular reader. In the same way, the 'quality' papers (in October 1989) featured Francis Bacon at 80 as an interesting personality. His role as a producer of high art is at the same time taken for granted and subordinated to his status as elderly *enfant terrible*. In each case, the reader's willing consent to the status of the generator as star is assumed, but the art itself is not examined. The high art will be reviewed in the appropriate section of a specific media form (for instance, a journal or programme) as a minority interest.

A similar standpoint can be observed in the views expressed by cultural critics of the right in Britain and America, as one of their reasons for rejecting the 'mass'. In a tradition which stems from Matthew Arnold, Richards, Eliot and Leavis concentrated on the individual response to or immunity from high culture as determining cultural development. Understanding of the 'good' in culture was to be seen as a moral achievement. The ability to analyse the ingredients of cultural products on the other hand was simply to be seen as a learnable skill, which did not imply the development of superior aesthetic appreciation. No bridge between the two was offered: empirical connections between them were recognised, but the existence of a body of cultural theory which could offer a viable explanation of the relationship between class, ideology, society and culture was emphatically denied. Since culture lay outside time and society, the explanation for apparent disparities must lie in congenital rather than social differences. Northrop Frye spoke for this tradition when he argued that 'the real values of literature' were being misread by sociologists of literature as stemming from society (Frye, 1976, pp. 24–5).

This approach makes it necessary to look for the existence of discrete strict critical disciplines which justify, after the event, the status of genres and of works within them. This is implicit in Leavis's commitment to the transparency of words and meaning in literary texts: 'it is necessary to have a strict literary criticism somewhere and to vindicate literary criticism as a distinct and separate discipline' (Leavis, 1937, pp. 59–70). Critical judgement then is dependent upon the refinement of the critic's skills within the discipline. It may not be possible to express the telltale signs in words, but we must trust to the sensibility of the critic to recognise their presence on our behalf and to communicate their existence to us.

However, as we have already seen, the status given to particular genres and cultural products at any one time is not constant and the explanations of the Arnoldian cultural critics are inadequate to explain this process. To provide a fuller answer we need to go back to the idea of hierarchies of quality, and the establishment and maintenance of high culture as part of the power structure of a society.

High culture, class and the market

If we refer to T. S. Eliot's apologia for the continuation of an upper class as a stable repository of cultural values, we find confirmation of the structural Marxist position of the processes which occur (Eliot, 1948, 1962; and see Chapter 1). Eliot illustrates the concept of ideology in action, without identifying it as such. He demonstrates how the remains of that culture which confirmed the status and authority of the dominant group at an earlier stage, continues to influence what is received as high culture in the present, which is influenced in turn by what emerges in alternative, marginal or oppositional practices. For Eliot class 'gives the background for those producing group-culture' – it provides the infrastructure upon which high culture can be maintained. The history, beliefs and values maintained by the highest class, are those which also ensure the continuation of high culture. Without them there is nothing but 'fragments shored against ruin'. For some sociologists of culture this is an explanation of how the 'best' comes to be regarded as intrinsic and natural, rather than recognised as an aspect of the assertion of the dominant ideology.

The status afforded to privileged cultural products does not depend solely on the ideological superstructure, however, but on the support of evidence of its economic value. Literature is at first sight an exception, in that the publication of poetry, for instance, is not a profitable activity. However, its status as a privileged product (confirmed in Britain by the Laureateship) is sufficient to provide kudos for publishers in the days of conglomerates, supported by more profitable branches of enterprise. On the other hand, the publicity and 'hype' afforded to the deliberations of literary juries and the awarding of prizes has made the publication of the fiction of high culture profitable. But even in the case of literature, demonstration of status comes through the limitation of available production, with initial print-runs on a much smaller scale than anticipated popular paperback best sellers.

This happens through the operation of the market in two main ways. Producers of culture must gain access to their consumers through the gatekeepers and entrepreneurs of culture, publishers' readers, art-gallery directors, impresarios and critics, both formal and popular, who help to determine not only acceptance of current products, but also the future selection of what is to be produced. Their capacity to pass on cultural products is much less than the quantity of material available to them. This too has its limitations. Writing, sculpting, composing and so on, all take time and space not available to all those with the skill to produce. Art schools will train and offer facilities to those already defined as artists in embryo. Who becomes an artist, writer, poet is partly determined by processes outside the institutional culture-producing structure – that is, by the operation of structures of class, gender and race (Wolff, 1981, pp. 42–3).

The concepts of authorship and authenticity, too, restrict what can be offered, since group production undermines that idea of the artist as a uniquely skilled producer upon which the status of cultural production depends. 'Authorship' within capitalist societies also serves to confirm the status of cultural products as individual properties. Ideas can be owned and ownership transferred or leased within economic transactions, governed by copyright. Finally, 'Art' is frequently presented within the media not in terms of content, but of the structure or institutions which contain it – the Tate Gallery, the Guggenheim, La Scala, the Barbican, and so on.

So there are limits to what can be produced and offered to the would-be consumer, as a consequence of the form of the culture industry itself. There is also a further limitation, which relates to the broader economic structure of society.

'A joy forever'

The economic value of cultural products is not based on the time or effort spent in labour by their producers, but on the demand created for them. The laws of supply and demand operate as stringently in the culture industry as in any other area of a capitalist society. This in turn requires some categorisation of what Ruskin termed the non-utilitarian commodity.

We have seen how entrepreneurial activity restricts the supply of 'high culture' goods and demand is fostered by emphasis on the uniqueness of the product. The work of the uniquely gifted author from whom no more is forthcoming has a greater market value than the work of an author still producing, whose unique qualities have not yet been established in the market. Thus, the 'best' authors are dead authors, preferably unrecognised or undervalued in their own lifetime and working in highly visible and usually non-perishable media. In this context unique works have a market value sustained by the competition to own. The auctioning of Van Gogh's painting *Sunflowers* in 1987 and other subsequent international auctions of works by major dead artists simply provide exaggerated examples of this. The more bizarre possibilities of this evaluation are explored in fiction by Joseph Heller (Heller, 1988).

Haug explains this phenomenon by identifying aesthetics as a commodity in capitalist society, where use-value has been superseded by exchange-value. Luxury itself being a powerful sensual stimulus, there is 'creation and control of a need for luxury' through competition for consumption and luxury (Haug, 1986, p. 21). Capital, with art at its disposal, not only shows off as a connoisseur and admirer of fine art but also, in its esoteric interests, adopts the lofty illusion that 'it is the highest creations of the human spirit, and not profit, which is its determining aim' (Haug, 1986, p. 129). Commodity aesthetics then, appears to solve the contradiction between private interest and the concerns of society. It expropriates 'high culture' and creates style, in art and architecture, as a manifestation of luxury consumption.

Less dramatically, production of limited editions in art and literature, the award of prestigious prizes and presentation of music and drama with restricted access – concentrating on those cultural products which display the prerequisite qualities to classify them aesthetically as high art – serve the same function as the cultural

CALDERDALE
COLLEGE LIBRARY
HALIFAX

auctions. They confirm the status of the products within high culture and define the audience or 'readership' in economic terms. The position of any item within the pyramid of culture described earlier in this chapter is clearly granted not by aesthetics, but by scarcity. This readership, whilst materially defined primarily in economic terms, is ideologically constructed within society's super-structures, which provide and sustain the value-systems which in turn define high culture. Educational institutions accept and teach the cultural canon, the recognised components of high culture, and the formal skills of applying critical analysis to cultural products as discrete disciplines. The consumers who form the readership, however, are those perceived as responding intuitively to the aesthetic refinement of the 'best' in high culture: in other words, those who share the particular sets of meaning of the cultural élite (for example, see Gans, 1974).

In the published version of his Manchester lectures in 1877, Ruskin explored the concept of value in art. He concluded that the non-utilitarian commodity was not a luxury, but 'the only kind [of property] which a man [*sic*] can truly be said to "possess"' (Ruskin, 1877, p. 171). Because their real value lay in the intellectual or emotional pleasure they gave, not in their price as luxuries, in his scheme books were not to be obtained too cheaply. At the same time, paintings should be much more widely and cheaply available through reproductions. At no point should the economic worth of a work of art be so small that there should be no real (but proportionate) cost to the purchaser. Duplication and reproduction would obviate the establishment of relative value based on scarcity and excess demand.

This dichotomy of the two sorts of value – aesthetic non-utilitarian, and scarcity but also non-utilitarian – has not been resolved, since we can see that cultural products are categorised according to an amalgam of commercial and intellectual value, established and maintained both in the economic infrastructure and the ideological superstructure of society. While Marxist theory accepts the social nature of value, this dimension has been somewhat neglected in writings on art and culture, in favour of philosophical and analytical investigation of social production (Haug, 1986). This discussion of aesthetic values does not help us either, to clarify the place and importance of popular 'mass' culture and its relationship to high culture. The huge demand for popular culture commodities does not make them more expensive, but facilitates mass production and reduces costs. The philosophy and economy of culture are intermeshed and it is this dialectic, the tension within the balance, which provides the categories of art at any one time. Ruskin demanded intellectual goodness – necessary to produce the lovely – as well as power, to produce the most skilled. Which returns us to the currently unanswerable problem of how we arrive at aesthetic judgement.

Categorisation of 'art' through genre has been discussed, but the way in which distinctions are made between art, craft, and popular art also requires consideration. Broadly speaking, craft is understood as 'applied' art, skill displayed beyond the functional requirements of objects. Mere fitness for purpose would require a beaker to be heatproof, hollow, watertight and suitable to drink out of. This could be achieved cheaply by mass production in basic unadorned material with minimal human intervention. But as craft, beaker-making would be labour-intensive and require some form of ornamentation either in variety of shape, or decoration. Produced by an artist of the acknowleged calibre of Lucy Rie, or Bernard Leach, the *function* of the beaker is minimised and merely provides the discipline within which the craftsperson works. The item would not normally be purchased as something to drink out of, but as an example of a particular artist's work. (In Japan, the status of such artists is confirmed by their being created 'living national monuments'.)

This implies that there is an agreed progression from the solely functional to the high-art object but this is not the case. Hierarchies of aesthetic value are social values applied between as well as within cultures. It is this process which placed the work of Western artists above the artefacts of African societies, by assuming universal valuations and aesthetics in which the 'civilised' always stood above the 'primitive'. A relativist approach provides more illumination. Crowley (in Jopling (ed.), 1971), examining Chokwe art and aesthetics, bases his study on Chokwe evaluations rather than his own, in an area where he observed 'objects decorated beyond function' in every home. He concluded that the division between fine and applied art was not universal and that art and aesthetic judgement were more central to Chokwe than to American society. Western assumptions about the 'fetishistic' rather than aesthetic role of art objects in Africa was contradicted by his and other fieldwork.

The division that we make between art and craft is culturally specific and appears to be a phenomenon of industrial societies.

Allied to this is the predominantly Western perspective on the mass-produced object as an aesthetic object. Lowenthal offers the most extreme attitude, when he dismisses the possibility of aesthetic content in popular culture on the grounds that it is a commodity production and *therefore* not art, a view rooted in the theories of mass culture discussed in Chapter 2 (Lowenthal, 1957). The two are seen as mutually exclusive, although as Gans points out, each type of culture has its own aesthetic values (Gans, 1974, pp. 67ff). Less clear-cut, but no different in perception, is the concept of 'kitsch'. Here, work which reproduces the subjects and forms of high culture in popular and usually (but not exclusively) mass-produced versions is assumed to have less value to the innocent (or ignorant) viewer. A miniature plastic Venus de Milo as the centrepiece of a plastic table-fountain, or a small three-dimensional rendering in plaster of Leonardo da Vinci's fresco, *The Last Supper*, can be defined as kitsch. The concept serves to exemplify the different but synchronous shared meanings in a society and at the same time ranks them in terms of ultimate aesthetic value (Wolff, 1981, Conclusion).

In Britain, the desire to distinguish between art and skill and the problems which arise in categorising specific activities accordingly, was given recent stimulus by the success of the ice-skating pair, Torville and Dean, in international ice-dance. Something which had been perceived only as skilful athleticism was redefined by many critics as possessing an aesthetic quality, equal to ballet, which made it art. On the other hand, there were those who dismissed these claims as pretentious. The music, context and narrative were all involved in categorising ice-dance as intrinsically inferior to art, whereas, for example, nineteenth-century opera, down to the last absurd twist in an absurd plot, is categorised as art! The popularity of synchronised swimming has posed similar questions. The skill and coordination required for this activity were unquestioned, but the costume and presentation, and here, the lack of narrative, are enough to deny it the name of art. It is difficult to reconcile this with recent developments in modern dance which are abstract and have encompassed the use of water as a medium, other than by concluding that what emerges from popular culture is by definition only categorised as athletic skill. There is an interesting contradiction here: for the ancient Greek philosophers the aesthetic content of athletics was of paramount importance, but for Western societies who claim the cultural ancestry of Greece, it is marginal.

Alternative theories

There is a strong tradition of Marxist aesthetic theory which attempts to relate social recognition of what constitutes the good and beautiful in the arts, with the economic nature of the society in which this occurs. More problematic have been the ventures to construct a universal Marxist aesthetic beyond ideology, in which the 'real' relations of humans to 'real' conditions are expressed, but aligning this with 'the aesthetic dimension' as Marcuse expressed it (Marcuse, 1978). The role of aesthetic forms, in which the distortion of perceptions in real life can be overcome in art, is central to this discussion. Brecht and Benjamin both saw form as essential to the truth or validity of the cultural product (Brecht, 1977; Benjamin, 1970). Marcuse's work is perhaps the most accessible critique of recent Marxist aesthetics, by virtue of its brevity, although tending toward the mystical on occasion. Nevertheless, he does point to the significant omission in earlier Marxist aesthetic theory of the individual subject, in the desire to place stress on the social. This is an area in which debate continues, particularly in response to post-structuralism, and to the development of feminist aesthetic theory. Because Marxist aesthetic theory still seemed to be taking for granted a universal hierarchy of forms, largely replicating a male view of society, there has recently been a blossoming of Marxist–feminist theory, in which not only the economic but also the gendered structure of culture has been challenged (Kristeva, 1973; Mulvey, 1975; Wolff, 1981). Taking up the question of aesthetic form, these women explore the nature of pleasure in aesthetics. As Terry Lovell says, 'Aesthetic sensibilities are class- and sex-linked, and the politics of aesthetic pleasure will depend on the particular ways in which that sensibility has been appropriated and developed along lines of sex and class' (Lovell, 1980, p. 95).

4 Culture and Imperialism

Imperial cultures

The notion of culture in general, and cultural changes within Western societies in particular has been discussed in Chapters 1 and 2. In one sense, the whole of history is about cultural change. Theories of cultural diffusion stress the evolutionary potential of cultural items as the reason for their adoption, sometimes linking these, as Parsons does, in his concept of evolutionary universals, to other social structural changes. However, such theories tend to ignore the economics and politics of cultural change which the concept of imperialism emphasises. 'No society can successfully dominate another without the diffusion of its cultural patterns and social institutions, nor can any society successfully diffuse all or most of its cultural patterns and institutions without some degree of domination' (Hoogvelt, 1978, p. 109).

On a global scale, much cultural change, development, diffusion and conflict has been due to the imperialism of dominant societies, particularly the dominance of Western societies over 'Third World' or 'developing' societies and indeed, imperialism is still a crucial factor in broad-scale cultural changes. But 'imperialism' is yet another concept which needs to be more clearly defined before more detailed discussion of its relationship to culture can take place. A useful start can be made with the connotations of imperialism provided by Raymond Williams in *Keywords* (1983). Williams identifies two divergent definitions of the word, which lie behind the work of social anthropologists and others concerned with cultural change. Although there is general agreement that inevitably imperialism carries with it cultural baggage which is left behind, even when the personnel who brought it have departed, debate centres on the nature of this imperial cultural legacy. On the one hand, Williams states, imperialism has been defined as a socio-political system of government and control from the centre, which aims at the spread of Western-style democratic institutions. Imperialism in this sense is seen as having a 'civilising' role, an assumption based on nineteenth-century ideas about the nature of social development, which we mentioned in Chapter 1. Defined in this way, once independence has been granted to former colonies, imperialism can be said to end. On the other hand, imperialism can be defined more narrowly, as an economic system of investment and control, which is not dependent on direct political control and in which, it is argued, explicit cultural and social change are not sought by the imperial power. However, these two definitions are not exclusive, since there is a strong economic element in the first, and a strong socio-political element in the second: both Marx and Weber stressed the interconnected nature of the economic, social and political aspects of society.

Regardless of whether or not we wish to argue that colonial societies benefited from the process and regardless of the form which imperialism took, during the eighteenth and nineteenth centuries the imperial nations of the West imposed their own culture on colonial societies when they took socio-political and economic control of their empires. They used a combination of political, social and economic strategies to establish and maintain their dominance. For Western societies in the eighteenth and nineteenth centuries, the purpose of 'civilisation' was to achieve social order and refinement, and these were seen as absolute rather than relative concepts. The imperial nations had a moral duty to civilise their empires, since civilisation and culture went hand in hand (Williams, 1983; also see Chapter 1). Also, since high culture, defined exclusively in Western terms (see Chapter 3), was the prerogative of the most highly civilised, the dominant societies, there were no qualms about pre-existing socio-political structures in non-Western societies. We must remember here, that the 'tribal' or 'small-scale' societies of Africa, Asia, Australasia and other areas were often relatively undiffer-entiated in structure, with economic systems closely bound up with kinship structures, these in turn creating a complex political culture, frequently misunderstood or ignored by colonial administrators. We might argue that the culture of such societies was so embedded in framework. The institutions were staffed by clergy and others whose education, values and attitudes accorded with their own ethnocentric culture. Textbooks, therefore, were those produced by the publishing houses of the imperial power, students showing academic ability sat the examinations set by the examining boards of the 'mother' country. As bureaucratic structures grew, an inspectorate system developed, but in no cases did this involve a revision of the substance of the educational process. Education, then, with its promise of entry into the colonial, if not the imperial, élite, was not a process of the acquisition of neutral knowledge, but included the assimilation of the cultural values of the imperial power (see Chapters 3 and 8 for cultural definitions of knowledge and aesthetic and artistic values).

It becomes clear then, that cultural imperialism is inevitable within any type of imperial structure. The 'best' novels, plays, paintings, produced in any colonial society will be those which most successfully emulate the characteristics of cultural products already within the canon of the dominant high culture (for an analysis of the 'post-colonial' response to this see Ashcroft *et al.*, 1989.) Indigenous material may be used as a source, but it undergoes a transmogrification, fitted to the rules of Western aesthetics, before it becomes art rather than native 'craft'. (If you doubt this, ask those around you aged between 40 and 60 to name a piece of African music: if anything is forthcoming, it is likely to be *Missa Luba*, the African Mass setting used by Lindsey Anderson on the soundtrack of the film *If*). The cultures of colonial societies have been subordinated to the mainstream of Western culture, and moreover, incorporated into a class structure and cultural disadvantage which reflects the imperial power. This process encourages more of culture than the arts, as the British example shows. Firmly established amongst the English middle classes and within their patronage, cricket was exported throughout the Empire as a way of founding team spirit and healthy occupation, whilst polo, discovered as the game of the moghul aristocracy (in India), was appropriated by the imperial aristocracy and the officer class. The economic dominance of the imperial power, together with this control of cultural institutions, left very limited potential for any sustained tradition of alternative cultural production.

A similar subordination of indigenous values occurred in social, value- and belief-systems as occurred in the artistic aspects of culture. Colonial political, religious, economic and educational systems were all intended to supplant indigenous ones which were seen at best, as inefficient, at worst as primitive and barbaric. To give one example: many traditional African societies had complex land-ownership and agricultural systems through which women maintained a degree of economic independence (Rogers, 1980, p. 122). From the end of the nineteenth century, the growth of cash crops for export on a large scale was encouraged by colonial governments, but subsidies, payment, teaching of new agricultural techniques and knowledge of new crops, all concentrated on the male heads of families, regardless of previous practice. Women were left to produce subsistence crops and barter any surplus. At the same time, there was a huge expansion in the use of migrant labour in other economic enterprises, so that women also took on responsibility for cash crops, but without the recognition and rights they had traditionally possessed. The consequences of this colonial agricultural policy were not only agricultural: they affected economic, social and gender relations and altered culture 'as a way of life'. This can be instanced in Gambia, Kenya, Botswana, Zambia (Rogers, 1980, pp. 168–74). Henn provides a variety of examples from different African societies, with a cautious note as to historical assumptions (Henn, 1984).

The anthropological inheritance

Within the imperial and colonial context, which offered unrivalled access and support, in exchange for information gathered, the discipline of social anthropology developed. However, despite their claims to the status of objective observers, gathering scientific field notes, anthropologists' interpretations were highly coloured by their own culture.

> As they took the colonial system for granted, often capitalizing on it and sometimes actively supporting it, they did not perceive that colonialism created a colonial people – 'the native peoples' – under the economic, political and spiritual domination of an alien power which possessed and ruthlessly used . . . violence against them. Instead, they chose to see colonial peoples in terms of a

(1966) and Henrietta Moore (1986). American cultural anthropology has emphasised the complexities of specific cultures. If the relationship between human perception and the environment, on a social rather than an individual level, is the primary concern, then studies of culture become relative rather than comparative (as Geertz has argued, see Chapter 2). This is a move away from the older unidimensional view of 'primitive' societies as 'living ancestors', with their artefacts, language and social structures providing stereotypes which have parallels in ethology rather than ethnology. It is a move to study those cultural formations – of language, myths, kinship and power – which determine the nature of any society at any particular time. In this approach cultural production does not consist of a multiplication of images which are really totemic metaphors, natural symbols representing the societal function and value of something (and according to some anthropologists, indicating the essentially irrational nature of 'primitive' cultures). To the structuralist, cultural production represents expressions, or even critiques, of aspects of relations within a society and between it and the natural world, which are understandable only in terms of their context, thus they are metonyms. Lévi-Strauss was an exponent of this approach, examining myths and beliefs as illuminating world-views because they expressed structures of thought (see Chapter 2 above and Leach, 1974).

This distinction between structural-functionalist and structuralist anthropology relates directly to how we think about culture in societies under imperial or colonial influence. If we see imperialism as purely functional, then with independence those functions cease, but if we see it as structural, then the sets of relations established do not automatically cease with the granting of political autonomy. If 'savage' art is functional and totemic, it can only have a curiosity value in the valuation of a 'superior' culture, but if it is metonymic, then, for instance the cubist movement in art can 'discover' and employ the devices of some African carvings, however 'exotic', by exploring the relationships they express, on whatever level of comprehension. If we accept that the cultural products of other cultures are indeed metonymic, we have to abandon long-held beliefs in their comparative worth and the universality of aesthetic values, in favour of an acceptance of relative and contextual worth. It is in this area particularly, that semiotics has been helpful, in explaining the social operation of metonym, as creating that mythical language which then becomes taken for granted and natural. Successive connotations produce metonyms by which the ideological appears logical and 'natural' (Eco, 1979).

Some writers have stressed the importance of culture at a psychological level, since art and artefacts can also be read as expressions of the 'social unconscious'. Jungian psychology in particular has developed the notion of historically specific conditions and interpretations of psychological states, rather than the universalised assumptions of Freud. Following from this, we would expect the 'social unconscious' of imperialism and colonialism to have a different content from other types of society. The psychological synthesis developed by Franz Fanon, the black writer, to explain the psychological/cultural effects of colonialism drew on the existentialism of Sartre, on sociology, and on the ideas of British 'anti-psychiatrists' or phenomenologists in the 1960s, like R. D. Laing.

Fanon believed that millions of black people lived in misery, directly caused by the socio-economic changes of colonialism and that the internal psychological structure of the colonised individual and the structures of neocolonialism were equally oppressive and bound together. Fanon argued that the concept of *négritude* (originally part of a literary movement and meaning 'essential blackness' or 'negro-ness') was not simply a cultural legacy from colonialism, but a necessary antidote for black people to the cultural domination of colonialism: 'After the conflict [for liberation] there is not only the disappearance of colonialism but also the disappearance of the colonized man' (Fanon, 1967, p. 198). Essentially, Fanon was pointing to the damaged cultural identity of black people at a psychological level, created by Western colonial cultures which emphasised the inferiority of 'black' cultures. The popular slogan of the 1960s and 1970s amongst 'black liberationists' in Europe and America – 'black is beautiful' – sprang from the application of Fanon's ideas to all 'oppressed' black groups. Fanon summarises the position of other cultural and social critics of imperialism: 'Liberation is the total destruction of the colonial system, from the pre-eminence of the language of the oppressor and "departmentalisation", to the customs union that in reality maintains the former colonized in the meshes of the culture, of the fashion, and of the images of the colonist' (Fanon, 1969 p. 105).

At the same time that the first colonial field-workers, anthropologists and social philosophers were collecting data, other cultural

CALDERDALE
COLLEGE LIBRARY
HALIFAX

material was accumulating as a result of explorations in 'savage territories'. The Pitt-Rivers collection in Oxford was only one example of many, in which tools and artefacts of indigenous peoples of the expanding empires became available to satisfy the curiosity of the civilised world. By the end of the nineteenth century these were usually no longer haphazard trophy collections, but arranged in accord with the ahistorical and ethnocentric view of other cultures still prevailing into the 1930s. This placed cultures on an evolutionary scale ranging from 'the primitive, the barbaric and the orientally civilized' (for example, see Gott and Cameron, 1932, p. 148). The systematic accumulation of Third World art objects started with the first missionary expeditions, but a tradition of collection was established earlier, with 'cabinets of curiosities' for view built up by scholars and reinforced during the eighteenth century, by the gentlemanly acquisition of souvenirs from the Grand Tour, to fill up the country houses, *châteaux* and *schlosses* of Europe.

The new discipline of anthropology gave another focus to the collecting habit and museums provided repositories for overflowing collections. This development took place in Britain over the period 1750 to 1850. Montague House in Bloomsbury was purchased in 1753 to establish the British Museum, with Hans Sloane's collection of antiquities, curiosities and pictures intended to inspire as its core. The first Museum Act (1845) encouraged the establishment of museums, by empowering boroughs with more than 10 000 people to impose a ½d rate to set up public museums. Thus, educational and moral improvement went hand in hand with the demonstration of cultural superiority and the hegemony of high culture. Museums reinforced the dominant view of the lineage of civilisation, confirming the mainstream of Western culture and providing evidence of its absence in imperial territories.

There is debate surrounding the role of museums in contemporary Western societies. Argument centres on the detachment and isolation from everyday life of objects of high culture, and the presentation of material from other cultures. The morality and appropriateness of the possession of cultural objects is also questioned, which depending on one's perspective, were either 'looted' or 'rescued' from other countries. We need to ask the question, do museums and institutions such as the Commonwealth Institute and the Museum of Mankind [*sic*] (in Britain) provide a starting-point for appreciation and understanding of other cultures and a relative perspective on our own, or do they reinforce the attitudes and values of the dominant cultures, the cultures of colonialism and neo-colonialism, at the expense of the Third World?

The colonial legacy

Social anthropological studies of the later colonial and post-colonial period show the impact of colonialism on the culture of traditional societies and the way in which changes such as urbanisation speed up cultural change. Although continuing in the empirical style of classical anthropology, many of these studies show how older kinship, tribal or regional identities alter with modernisation and that emergent cultures contain elements of pre-colonial, colonial and post-colonial societies (for examples see Wilson, 1941, Gluckman, 1960, Little, 1974). A more radical and critical vein of social anthropology stems from feminist reappraisals of anthropology and sociology and emphasises the impact of colonisation and its distortion and destruction of traditional cultures (for example, see Oppong, 1983; Rogers 1988; Rosaldo, 1980; Moore, 1986). There is a danger, however, that a critique of the cultural consequences of colonialism leads us to view traditional societies as more stable and egalitarian cultural wholes than they really were. Acceptance of the point that all cultures are relative to others does not provide answers to questions of morality and values around cultural practices such as abortion, female infibulation, capital punishment, purdah, ECT treatment for depression, institutionalised violence and so on.

Work on cultural production in post-colonial or neocolonial societies has taken place within the area of cultural studies more generally, encompassing particularly literature, mass media and economics. Within literature, there have been two particular areas of study: first, the ahistorical essentialist approach to the 'other' expressed within the cultural products of the West, explored especially by Edward Said and Talal Asad, examining literature as a post-structuralist anthropologist (Said, 1978; Asad (ed.) 1973). Second, the ideological content of industrially produced fiction and the consequences of its 'secret education' upon views of imperialism held by the Third and First Worlds have been explored, especially by Dorfman and Mattelart (Dorfman and Mattelart, 1973;

Dorfman, 1983). In each case the links between the economic, political and cultural have been demonstrated, and it is clear that cultural production relies upon capital investment and returns. Imperialist ideologies mediate between both historical and present actualities and the Western image of the Third World. Said shows how the ideology of orientalism, the movement to territorial acquisition, the socio-political content of administration, all served to provide a 'confirmation' of attitude from which alternative cultural values were excluded (Said, 1978). But as areas without large capital resources for investment in culture, the Third World, and indeed much of the First World, relies on the supply of cultural products and technology from the United States. The solution has been to superimpose upon a selective, censored, mediated and restructured signification of the indigenous cultures, an imperial culture whose universality is implicit, and which permeates the educational and the recreational fabric. Mattelart in particular, has identified some of the more recent operations of this process in Europe, where transnationalism dominates national culture, especially in television productions (Mattelart *et al.*, 1984).

Much emphasis has been laid on the role of the mass media in the issue of cultural imperialism and this has been the arena for much recent international debate between the 'left' and 'right'. On the one hand, for instance UNESCO can be viewed as an enabling body, facilitating training and production within the Third World to increase the potential for cultural independence. On the other hand, there is the 'free market' view expressed by William Randolf Hearst, jnr:

> The threat hanging over the free press today is virtually world-wide, through a vast international conspiracy directed by UNESCO. The latter is one of the anti-democratic agencies commanded by Moscow, although it operates in Paris under the flag of the UN. (Mattelart *et al.*, 1984, p. 61).

The potential power of the mass media as a cultural force is acknowledged on all sides, both as an instrument of overt political power, and with regard to the hegemony of concepts within the dominant culture (see Chapters 2 and 9). Here, the link between culture and economics is inescapable. The stance of the former or neo-imperial powers (including the USA) has been to help with training and production within the media for so long as the propositions of the Third World are acceptable, an attitude which led, for example, to the withdrawal of both Britain and the USA from UNESCO. The function of this attitude for the maintenance of neo-imperialist ideology was perceived by Fanon in the 1950s, as we have seen, and also by Paulo Freire and Amilcar Cabral, both radical theorists interested in the ideological power of imperialism in all its aspects (Freire, 1972; see also Chapter 8).

Cultural imperialism

In one sense, there is a single Third World view of cultural imperialism, whatever the political complexion of individual Third World countries. They share common problems of competing with already-existing systems of 'mass' cultural production in the West, which have no serious shortage of resources, and also of needing to use systems which were themselves set up by the West. Initial work on media imperialism indicated a simple unidirectional model of dependency, whereby developing countries relied on the educational and technical resources of the colonial powers in order to establish cultural and media institutions of their own on the same model, becoming in the process enlarged markets for the cultural products of those powers (Boyd-Barrett, 1977).

Whatever the ideal attitude to cultural imperialism held in the Third World, it is tempered by pragmatic considerations and decisions are determined by politics, economics, the percentage literacy rate (varying between 15 and 80 per cent depending on country), type of media already operating, availability of an acceptable indigenous language, accessibility of non-imperial models and traditions, and their chances in international markets. All the ex-colonial Third World countries have experienced media as propaganda in some form, (for example see the British view of film in its African colonies and in India in Notcutt and Latham, 1937, Appendix G). It is recognition of this that motivates many Third World countries – for example, Mozambique (formerly Portugese), Zanzibar (formerly British) and Bourkina Faso (formerly French) to avoid media imperialism. Although they do not want to repeat the dependency model, at the same time their lack of foreign exchange makes them potentially vulnerable to the ready availablility of cheap material from the neocolonial states. For other former colonies, like India, which has a huge market and can provide all its own training, the only 'problem' is in the context of production, where occasional extra finance is required for the importation of newsprint and paper.

Widely divergent views of cultural imperialism, are indicated by the different solutions taken by Third World countries, ranging from control by multinationals, as with TV GLOBO in Brazil, the frank dependency of Guam, the almost-total free-market situation in Hong Kong, total state control together with slow independent development in Zanzibar and a mixture of all these, as in South Korea. Given these differences, as well as differing imperial approaches – for example, France and Portugal encouraged a division between culture and technology whilst Britain was setting up models of its own cultural system – it is important to remember that even technology transfer is not value-free, and certainly has economic implications. Apparent cultural independence is in fact very limited when mechanical and technical supply, processing and maintenance remain in the hands of the West, and even more so when organisation is based in multinational companies.

At the same time, the significance of various media differs from society to society – where Mozambique emphasises film, much of South America emphasises the role of radio, and countries with high literacy rates emphasise books and newspapers. The context of consumption also varies, as does the role assigned to media culture. In some cases media culture is regarded as shared and social, part of the community experience and the educational process and therefore also part of the rural, peasant world. In other cases it is regarded as individual, directed at private ownership and therefore largely at the urban middle class. Such choices obviously relate closely to the socioeconomic complexion of each country, but other factors are also involved in the choice of medium. Film encounters processing problems and the cost of filming, but is easy to take round rural areas with a screen and a dynamo; video and TV have editing and sound problems and require sets, electricity, a centralised network, and there are also equipment maintenance problems; radio is vulnerable to foreign beaming from neighbouring hostile countries or commercial stations, so it can prove counterproductive and destabilising (as could satellite TV transmission); print demands a reasonable literacy rate.

In each case, modern media can either promote indigenous cultural forms, or swamp them, especially when linked to the multinational producing companies. Even rejecting the languages of imperialism is not always an easy choice, in the knowledge of the consequences and ideological implications which follow. No language chosen can be too parochial, for this limits its uniting ability, so in a country like Nigeria, with many languages in currency, the choice is between a dominant indigenous one, which may emphasise tribal or regional divisions, and a version of English, the language of imperialism.

Media imperialism

Some specific problems of cultural imperialism can be identified if we look at the operation of particular media. Radio is often under national control, so that news, music and so on, with a national focus is provided, but frequently there is more time than material, and Western radio or commercial channels belonging to the multinationals, or missionary-run stations are drawn on. Also, although radio is a cheap medium, the relative range of the transmitter determines the size and accessibility of the audience. In African societies, radio is mainly state-run; this is also the case in South America, but without a licensing system, and output is dominated by commercial stations.

For the Third World press, newsprint and paper often have to be imported, depleting foreign-currency reserves. The choice then is whether to have a small national organisation, or to be part of an international conglomerate. Many Third World countries insist on local ownership, which then buys into the multinationals. There is also the problem of where to obtain news from, since the news agencies are dominated by American, French, British and Soviet world agencies. Third World societies often cannot compete with these, given the lack of an organisational structure and the huge financial backing required for technological development. Third World publishing has involved the development of entrepreneurial skill rather than the growth of indigenous firms, but as international conglomerates pull out because of falling profit margins, more opportunities are created. Education systems are at last being freed from a dependence on First World books, but to make use of new technology would mean massive capital investment.

In the world of television, there is an international belief that quantity *produces* quality through expertise; production criteria have been established which hold sway internationally. A reference-frame of Western genres has developed, which are interdependent and this minimises the opportunity for Third-World genres to emerge, or to compete. There are also international requirements regarding the structure of programmes – time (both in the sense of actual length and as temporal convention in narratives) is defined by American practice and by the provision of advertising space, so a narrative structure is imposed before content is even considered. It is also far cheaper (and often more popular with audience and advertisers) to buy in Western programmes and production than to set up indigenous production. Video raises problems of technical choices, as 'international quality' means greater expense for productions, and the better technical quality of American imports initiates demands from local customers and renders earlier equipment obsolete (see papers presented to the African Television Conference, Commonwealth Institute, November 1984).

The main exporters of film to the Third World are the USA, the UK, France, Italy, India and Hong Kong. Where there is international cooperation in production, this involves an international division of labour, in which the Third World benefits from the training of technicians and more work for its professionals. But the production structures are rarely balanced and local rates for jobs are disrupted. Film is recognised as having a significant cultural role, particularly in South America and Africa, but there remains the problem of distribution, still largely controlled by multinationals, which can determine availability. Even advertisements, the economic underpinning of most of the media mentioned, are made in the West, advertising the products of multinational conglomerates, increasing the outflow of money from the Third World and creating demand for the products of Western culture (see Gabriel, 1982).

Looking in detail at the role and consequences of media imperialism, the link, the dialectical relationship, between culture and economy is made clear, especially since the Western media are increasingly in the hands of multinational or intranational companies rather than individual nations, a fact which does nothing to lessen their ideological and cultural impact. The processes may not be so obvious in other cultural forms, but nevertheless they occur (see also Chapter 9 for other comments on the ideological role of media). The consequences of cultural imperialism can then be summarised as follows: there is a marginalisation of local cultural forms and products which do not conform, or reach the same 'standards', whether these are the production values of *Dallas* or the stylistic conventions of the novel; there is a failure to develop independent cultural forms and media; there is an outflow of foreign exchange on imported software and hardware through advertising, and through failure of the multinationals to employ local skills; wants and expectations are created at the expense of local cultural values. Sociologists have recently been emphasising the idea of 'global culture' which transcends the nation-state, following the processes of imperialism we have discussed (Featherstone, 1990).

Cultural imperialism now lies as much in the hands of transnational organisations as with Western nations, but in areas of both content and structure, there is an unequal relationship based on an economic and political imbalance. As Freire says:

> Cultural conquest leads to the cultural inauthenticity of those who are invaded; they begin to respond to the values, the standards, and the goals of the invaders . . . For cultural invasion to succeed, it is essential that those invaded become convinced of their intrinsic inferiority . . . Cultural invasion is on the one hand an *instrument* of domination, and on the other, the *result* of domination. Thus, cultural action of a dominating character, in addition to being deliberate and planned, is in another sense simply a product of oppressive reality (Freire, 1972, pp. 122–3).

The purpose of this chapter has been to demonstrate the extent to which the relationship between culture and society is not simply hermetic and domestic, but is tied to national and economic expansion on an international level and that the dominant culture has power beyond the perceptions and interests of the dominant groups. Post-modernist writers are emphasising 'the diversity, variety and richness of popular and local discourses, codes and practices' and see the 'globalisation' of culture, partly as the result of imperialism, leading both to 'cultural homogeneity and cultural disorder' (Featherstone, 1990; and see Chapter 10). This post-modern emphasis is partially explored in other chapters which

5 Race, Ethnicity and Culture

'Race' as ideology

It can be argued that cultural studies has been ethnocentric and allowed 'race' to be invisible (Gilroy, 1987, p. 12). A slightly different criticism is that of unintended intellectual racism of some of this work:

> Non-English readers may feel at times . . . the constriction and airlessness of a certain parochialism, a preoccupation with figures and issues that seem, under a different sky, less momentous than we would make them. They should remind themselves that we are living out the dotage of an imperial culture, and that our dreams are peopled by ghosts. But from that culture we have inherited other habits too, towards which no indulgence can be extended; for the 'common politics' which . . . gives some kind of coherence to . . . cultural analyses and critiques . . . brings with it a uniformity of a more negative kind: its virtual blindness to questions of race (Batsleer *et al.*, 1985, p. 10).

Whether or not these criticisms are valid, in our discussion of culture so far, race and ethnicity have been left as implicit concepts. Further sociological discussion of culture must take cognisance of the material and ideological existence of race and ethnicity and their importance for defining, studying and understanding cultural change.

Since first attempts to categorise and theorise the morphological differences (e.g. skin colour, hair, shape of skull) between peoples,

81

CALDERDALE
COLLEGE LIBRARY
HALIFAX

observed as explorers and anthropologists expanded the social world and differentiated it from the natural world (see Chapter 4), the concept of race has exerted a powerful hold on Western thought. Arising out of specific historical circumstances, the concept is still treated as a 'scientific' phenomenon. Race is a cultural – 'an ideological construct, not an empirical social category; as such it signifies a set of imaginary properties of inheritance which fix and legitimate real positions of social domination or subordination in terms of genealogies of generic difference' (Cohen, 1988 p. 23). Pre-capitalist concepts of race were based on theological explanations of human genesis and myths about non-human species, but drew on much earlier representations of 'the Other, images and beliefs which categorise people in terms of real or attributed differences when compared with Self'. These were modified to accommodate the demands of the hierarchy of class and culture which developed with capitalist society (Miles, 1989, pp. 11 and 13ff).

As an ideological construct, arising out of and reflecting social structural arrangements, race has a cultural dimension. The categorisation of humankind into races went alongside the process of cultural imperialism examined in Chapter 4. Embedded in eighteenth- and nineteenth-century concepts of race there was a notion of culture as a way of life. Cultures associated with 'savage' or 'primitive' races were viewed as ratifications of the Eurocentric hierarchy of races. There was little understanding of such cultures as 'Art' or 'Culture': it was recognised that 'savage' tribes had graphic or craft facility, but this was understood by Europeans as having a solely instrumental technical function. Primitive races were considered without aesthetic or historical dimensions (see Chapter 4): Darwin characterised them as liking 'hideous ornaments and equally hideous music' (Strawbridge, 1988, p. 109). It was recognised that the myths of such peoples could be incorporated into painting, story and music, a complex set of referents established and technical ability identified, but none of these established the existence of aesthetic awareness. Racial characteristics of primitive people supposedly included a genetically transmitted sense of rhythm, or story-telling ability – natural aptitudes not to be confused with the intellectual capacity of the European races, which made possible that artistic development, refinement and appreciation which was European 'Culture'. There is a sense in which this view parallels the élitist view that people of lowly social origins and little education were incapable of appreciating 'high' culture (see Chapters 3 and 6).

Robinson Crusoe's fictional 'civilising' of the black man, Friday, an early example of the complex playing-out of the Euro-centric concept of race, is sufficiently potent to be used as a modern advertising motif. The impact of Enlightenment thought on this concept of race simply broadened its scope. Both the 'brutish savage' and the 'noble savage' of eighteenth- and nineteenth-century thought were defined as primitive and without rationality. Whether the savage was seen as living in primeval innocence or original sin, debate centred on the feasibility of civilising the non-European through the imposition of exogenous culture (see Chapter 4).

This is not to deny changes in theories of race and culture since their first articulation. In the eighteenth century no distinction was made between anthropology and the taxonomy of racial difference; physical attributes were identified, social patterns described and artefacts collected, all evaluated by comparison with the European norm. In the second half of the nineteenth century, evolutionary theory reinforced the cultural and ideological components of a concept already resting on belief in the innate superiority of the European race, and which was ideal as a rationale of imperialist expansion (see Chapters 2 and 4). Eugenics, influential as a popular social theory until the Second World War, after which it was discredited by association with Nazism, proposed the deliberate employment of genetic factors for the further development of races through selective breeding. Race was seen as a grouping of distinct physical and mental characteristics attributable to biological causes (phenotypical). In this form, the concept is now largely discredited (except in the propaganda of racist organisations like the National Front). But elements of some of its tenets, in more sophisticated form, can still be found in the work of sociobiologists such as van den Berghe who propounds 'an interactive gene-culture co-evolution' (van den Berghe, 1988, p. 254). In its popular form, sociobiology is a reductionist theory utilising concepts like the 'naked ape', to explain aspects of human cultural behaviour, including racism and sexism (see Rose, Kamin and Lewontin, 1984).

There have been studies of racial groupings in Britain and America – Frazier (1932), Cayton and Drake (1946), Little (1948), Richmond (1955) are some of the earlier ones – which, while questioning the attitudes and prejudices which the concept of race produces (racism), nevertheless accept *de facto* the concept itself (see Miles, 1989, ch. 1).

Britain's imperial history also encompasses extensive contact with Islamic and oriental societies – for example, Persia, India, China, Japan. Here, racist notions of the 'Other' were tempered with recognition that such societies were powerful, with empires of their own. Their cultures were the object of curiosity and sometimes valued or appropriated in various ways, largely through trade. From the seventeenth century, aspects of oriental cultures, for example, were appropriated for their aesthetic value: 'the English . . . are generally pleased with everything that comes from China . . . They have filled their houses with our furniture, their public gardens with our fireworks, and their very ponds with our fish' (Goldsmith, Letter CX, [1762] 1966, pp. 425–6). Despite such appropriation, missionaries – who were part of diplomatic and trading missions to such societies – reported the 'barbaric customs' they found, although by the nineteenth century such societies were classified on the scale of cultural evolution much nearer to European civilisation than 'tribal' societies (Said, 1985). But it is important to remember that oriental and Islamic societies were also the source of more racist stereotypes – opium-eating 'fiendish' orientals and mysterious harem-keeping Arabs.

If the discourse of 'race' is the result of social categorisations and representations of human groups as 'Other' on the basis of biological evidence of phenotypes – blood groups, bone structure, facial planes, skin pigmentation, or any combination of these – then clearly culture, whether as way of life, or as art, has merely secondary significance. Race becomes an externally imposed category, which need not refer to the experiences and perceptions of a group, or of the members within it. That there may be a match between the external representation and the subjective identification, is a psychological and cultural phenomenon, rather than evidence for the scientific validity of 'race'. The significance of 'race' lies in the social perceptions of the societies in which the concept has developed and the consequences of this.

Cultural roots of racism

Cohen discusses the complexity and diversity of racism, dependent
on the structural, functional and historical factors which give rise to
it (Cohen, 1988, ch. 1). Wolpe defines it as referring to 'discrim-
inatory practices in which a socially constructed notion of 'race' is
implicated' (Wolpe, 1988, p. 110). It has been used in the formation
of nationalism, as justification for oppression and explanation for
imperialism (for example, see Samuel (ed.) 1989; Mason, 1970).
Nationalism can be seen as an ideology which legitimates the
cultural boundaries created by imperialism and similar contacts
between different societies. Miles argues that racism is exclusively an
ideological phenomenon. 'Racialisation' refers to social relations
'structured by the signification of human biological characteristics in
such a way as to define and construct differentiated social
collectivities' (Miles, 1989, p. 75). Social and cultural boundaries
are established and maintained through racism:

> Racism is not a side issue in contemporary Britain; it is not a
> peripheral, minority affair. Britain is undergoing the critical phase
> of its post-colonial period. This crisis is not simply economic or
> political. It is a crisis of the whole culture, of the society's entire
> sense of itself (Rushdie, 1982, p. 417).

To understand this crisis of culture it is useful to examine the
historical cultural roots of racist attitudes and beliefs in Britain. The
historical 'moment' for the evolution of these ideas is usually taken
to be the slave trade and colonialisation (for example, Walvin (ed.)
1982; but see Miles, 1989, who argues that racist ideas existed much
earlier).

The same arguments and fears that exist today were part of
'white' reaction to 'blacks' hundreds of years ago:

> To a large extent certain fears about employment, black
> immigration and miscegenation, are common throughout.
> Racialism is thus not solely a product of modern capitalist
> society. There is a legacy of English racial attitudes towards the
> Negro, the roots of which go deep into the age of European
> expansion in the sixteenth and seventeenth centuries and find their

origins in misunderstandings, fears and commercial exploitation (Walvin, 1971, p. 5).

Authority for whites' treatment of their 'racial inferiors' could be found in the Bible and in the accounts provided by travellers (Banton, 1970, p. 14). Explorers' reports pictured the black man as a savage, as lazy and lustful (see Walvin, 1973, p. 162). Such ideas provided a justification for slavery and imperialist expansion in Africa, Asia and the West Indies, as 'civilising missions'.

Stereotypes and caricatures of black people were part of European cultural heritage, reinforced by the influence of Darwin and the later pseudoscience of social Darwinism. Cultural availability of ideas and symbols about other 'races' was a factor in the emergence of both racism and slavery. The contrast between black and white had acquired certain cultural connations before the advent of either capitalism or slavery and established a symbolic order for the propagation of race prejudice to a full blown racist ideology (see Giddens, 1989; Cohen and Bains (eds) 1988; Fryer, 1984, pp. 133–90; and Miles, 1989).

The colonial and imperialist history of Britain supplied the necessary breeding-ground for a racist ideology which, if not 'official' state ideology nevertheless forms an important part of the English way of looking at the world, of English culture, illustrated in this verse by Kipling:

> Take up the White Man's burden –
>   Send forth the best ye breed –
> Go bind your sons to exile,
>   To serve your captives' need;
>
> To wait in heavy harness,
>   On fettered folk and wild –
> Your new-caught, sullen peoples,
>   Half-devil and half-child   (quoted in Cox, 1959, p. 345).

In Britain and America by the twentieth-century, racist ideology became 'common-sense', to use Gramsci's term. Though Britain has lost its 'civilising' role, many of the attitudes of that political position have survived. The position of ethnic and racial minorities in Britain and America today is not one of slavery or 'colonials', yet many aspects of our colonial and slave-owning past have continued into the dominant cultural figurations, which reflect and reproduce the structure of racial inequality and discrimination.

Race and ethnicity in the melting pot

Although sociologists have tried to evade the problems involved in the term 'race', by extending the concept of 'ethnicity', this too is an ideological construct with a specific history. Given the importance of generations of immigrant settlers or 'non-native' peoples in the formation and development of the USA it is not surprising that we find the term first used systematically in the work of American social scientists. Generally the term is used to refer to a part or section of a society whose members are thought by themselves or others to share a common origin and important elements of a common culture and who participate in activities which uphold this culture. Smith defines ethnic units as 'subdivisions of some single racial stock, differentiated in the beliefs of those who do and those who do not belong to them by real or putative community of descent and cultural practice' (Smith, 1981, pp. 188–9). Ethnicity depends on the social construction of difference, in which biological factors may be a part (Wallman, 1988, p. 229). 'Race' is deterministic as used within sociology, while 'ethnicity' contains an element of choice (see Cohen, 1988; Rex, 1986, ch. 5). Sociological studies of ethnic groups, undertaken in Western Europe and America have concentrated on the ethnic group itself, its self-definition and regulation, the boundaries between ethnic groups and the relationship of the group to the society in which it exists (Banton, 1970; Rex, 1986). Early work in America used the concept of ethnicity to study those 'groups of distinctive national origin or language viewed as foreign minorities, such as the Irish, the Hungarians, or the Italians' (Abramson, 1980). But there is confusion in the early sociological literature over whether or not religious distinctiveness – a significant factor in American social and cultural development – was an aspect of ethnicity. There was also confusion and overlap between the term ethnicity and the concept of 'race', American Indians (indigenous Americans) and 'Negroes' (Afro-Americans) usually being regarded as 'races', but Jews often described as a 'race' as well as a culturally distinctive ethnic group.

More important than this conceptual fuzziness are the theories and ideologies implicit in the idea of ethnicity. Modern criticism of notions of assimilation and cultural pluralism, which have been part of ethnicity as an analytical category, has ignored the emphasis on cultural processes so central to American social scientists writing from the 1920s to the 1950s. Their concern with processes of cultural contact and collision, particularly within an urban setting, marked a move away from biological determinist theories of race. They did this in part by emphasising 'the fact that the situation of the European immigrant in the United States can be defined in terms that imply its logical relation to that of the Negro' (Park, 1950, pp. 198–9).

Using techniques of observation borrowed from anthropologists, the studies of the 'Chicago School' stressed the interaction of ethnicity with a variety of other cultural factors. Their 'ecological' interactionist approach focused on the urban area as a community and 'melting-pot', rather than on the economic and political processes which modern theorists argue underly these cultural processes (see Chapter 2 and Madge, 1963, pp. 88–125). In the work of Robert Park, for example, we find acknowledgement of the role of racism and racial prejudice in creating racial and ethnic conflict, together with assumptions about the cultural processes involved in interactions between dominant and minority cultures. While acknowledging the importance of the stability and order in social and cultural life emphasised by classical sociologists like Durkheim, Park's ideas owed more to Simmel's 'phenomenology of everyday life'.

Park thought that in all situations of contact between different ethnic groups conflict developed once the minority group began to express discontent with its inferior status, but that this was an intermediate stage in a process which, through accommodation, eventually led to assimilation and some form of cultural integration. The cultural devices of American immigrant groups, like the churches and foreign-language press, while creating an 'ethnic' culture and community were also part of the assimilation process in that they familiarised ethnic-group members with wider aspects of American life (Matthews, 1977, ch. 6). Chicago School sociology had close links with social psychology and stressed the psychological functions of ethnic cultural institutions for immigrants (Matthews, 1977, p. 166; also see Rose (ed.) 1962; and Lal, 1988; for a similar psychological view see Erikson, 1966, pp. 145ff.). Work on urbanism and traditional cultures in African societies has shown a similar process (for example, see Little, 1965). It is interesting to note here, that the Chicago School's view of the city stressed its developing and varied cultural structures and communities in contrast to the pessimistic views of 'mass society' theorists (see Chapter 2).

Park's pioneering studies inspired later work, for example by Cayton and Drake, whose monumental *Black Metropolis* (1946) provided details of 'the social system existing among northern urban negroes' (ibid, p. 770). This demonstrated the contradictory pulls experienced within a subordinate culture, of being accommodated within the dominant white society, while at the same time resisting the denial of a separate and valued culture which was at least potentially, and at times actually, in opposition to the dominant culture. In popular terms the idea of ethnic assimilation in the melting-pot of the American (or any other) city has seemed to mean cultural absorption or incorporation into the 'host' culture and therefore denial or loss of distinct ethnic minority cultures. While Park believed that some form of 'common culture' is necessary, he thought the process of cultural change brought about by conflict between ethnic and racial groups to be one in which both subordinate and dominant groups changed. He also argued that the process of assimilation was more problematic for groups like American Negroes and 'Orientals', where the 'host' culture included prejudiced racialist beliefs. He pointed out that the type of initial contact between cultures affected the type of conflict which resulted (Matthews, 1977, p. 170). Similarly, the modern British theorist of race relations, John Rex, points to the cultural and psychological shock suffered by slaves transported to America. He argues that low or unfree status is part of the ethnic cultural tradition of blacks in many societies and an important factor in subsequent relations between blacks and whites (Rex, 1983, pp. 42ff; also see Blauner, 1976; Gilroy, 1987; and Franklin, 1965, pp. 899ff).

Ethnic studies and cultural pluralism

In the 1950s and early 1960s the American civil rights movement, with its objective of 'racial equality' for American blacks, resulted in many structural studies of racial discrimination. Implicit in these studies there was a debate concerning the nature of Negro culture and whether or not 'desegregation' and 'integration' of blacks would mean assimilation and the loss of a distinctive Negro culture, or a move towards more cultural pluralism. Commenting on this debate Ralph Ellison stated:

> One thing that is not quite clear to me is the implication that Negroes have come together and decided that we want to lose our identity . . . Glazer [for example, in *Beyond the Melting Pot*, 1963] makes this assumption and follows it up with the rather frightening picture that all other immigrant and minority groups . . . in this country have somehow worked out an accommodation which respects the group identities of other peoples, but that Negroes are running wild . . . that we would like a total homogenization of the society . . . that Negroes have no culture . . . But I, as a novelist looking at Negro life in terms of its ceremonies, its rituals, and its rather complicated assertions and denials of identity, feel that there are many, many things we would fight to preserve ('American Academy Conference on the Negro American – 14–16 May 1965; in *Daedalus*, 1966, p. 408).

Today, black novelists like Maya Angelou and Toni Morrison write about the variety and distinctiveness of American black culture. It is significant that Ellison as a black American writer should have put forward this view of black culture at a Conference in which participants were mainly white male academics. One of the few to take up Ellison's point, was the sociologist, Talcott Parsons, who saw Negro culture and the resolution of racial conflict as essentially part of a pluralistic society (Parsons, pp. 411–12; also see Parsons, 1966, pp. 1009–54). 'Integration' and 'cultural pluralism', never defined very clearly, were part of the ideology of structural-functionalist sociology and the same liberal-pluralism which dominated discussions of the mass media and culture (for example, see Chapters 2 and 9; also Coser, 1965, pp. 251–62; also see Wolff, Moore and Marcuse, 1969).

In Britain emphasis on ethnicity and race as aspects of social and cultural relationships incorporated the immigrant-host model in response to increasing migration from commonwealth countries. The classic British study using this approach is Sheila Patterson's *Dark Strangers* (1963 and 1965), based on research carried out in the 1950s. This analysed the relationship between West Indian migrants and the indigenous population of Brixton. Using the concept of 'accommodation' she argued that, given the correct policies, black people would eventually be assimilated and absorbed.

Patterson's argument was that though what she called an 'immigrant situation' was undoubtedly complicated by the factor of skin-colour the esssential point was the fact that they were migrants and their problems different, but only by a degree from those facing any other group of migrants. This new group of migrants was simply experiencing the same kind of process of cultural assimilation formerly experienced by the Jews and the Irish. She neglected to consider the fact that many Irish coming to London during the 1950s and early 1960s were confronted with signs saying 'No Irish, No Coloured, No Dogs' (Cohen, 1988; Miles, 1982). For Patterson, West Indians needed to adapt to the 'host' country and undergo re-socialisation and acculturation into British ways, while the receiving society learned not to discriminate. The optimism of this study is based on the idea that there are no insuperable barriers or structural blocks to impede the process of cultural assimilation.

Banton (1970) challenged many assumptions of this model, especially that assimilation is a natural or desirable goal. The implication is that migrants will wish to take on the culture of the host-country. It ignores the contribution which other cultures might make to the total culture. For example, Parekh wrote of the dominant culture in Britain and whilst commenting favourably on certain aspects of the British way of life, also pointed to the cold, drab and highly individualistic quality of social relationships, in contrast to the characteristics of Indian culture (Parekh, 1974, pp. 41–85). Assimilationist notions assume essentially an exclusive and racist view of nationality, nationhood and culture (Gilroy, 1987, pp. 60ff.). A recent and well-publicised example of such views is the comment by the Tory politician, Norman Tebbit, on British Asians and Afro-Caribbeans who do not cheer for the English team during cricket matches and who therefore are 'not really integrated' into British society (*The Times*, 21 April 1990, p. 1). As several writers have pointed out, the idea of the British 'nation' does not yet include minority cultures based on 'race' (for example, see Gilroy, 1987, pp. 59ff; and Samuel (ed.) 1989, vol. 2).

However, the move in academic circles towards ethnic studies has produced a literature detailing the cultural differences of the various migrant groups in Britain, a good example of which is *Between Two*

CALDERDALE
COLLEGE LIBRARY
HALIFAX

Cultures (Watson (ed.) 1977). The merit of these studies is that emphasis moves from viewing black people as a homogeneous mass and seeks to explore not only different cultural backgrounds, but also the upsurge in cultural activities by black minorities in this country. For example, the importance of Rastafarianism for young black people of Afro-Caribbean origins has been examined, showing the ways in which this cultural base is used as a platform from which to resist and rebel against a dominant racist culture (Cashmore, 1979). Ethnic studies in America have stressed the importance of ethnic cultures for the psychological identity of individuals and some British studies similarly (for example, see Pryce, 1979; Open University, 1982; Husband (ed.) 1982, contains essays on both structural race relations and ethnicity). At some stage in the late 1960s or early 1970s, in Britain and America the abandonment of the term 'Negro' in favour of the term 'black' reflected the growing awareness by non-white Americans and British immigrants of their own, distinctive cultural identity. Similarly, documentary photography in Asian communities in Britain is an attempt to re-establish a sense of ethnic difference (Parmar, 1989).

Criticisms of the concept of ethnicity have focused on the extent to which it emphasises cultural pluralism and 'integration' at the expense of recognising unequal structural power relationships which underly dominant and minority cultures, power relationships which other theories identify as racism. It can also be argued that the consequence of ethnic studies is to attach ultimate 'blame' to ethnic minorities themselves, for their disadvantaged or subordinate position, because this approach focuses on 'migrants' and their cultural peculiarities (for example, see Open University, 1982). From this perspective it is only a short step to 'blaming the victim' and identifying minority and black people as a 'problem', with high crime-rates; weak, or alternatively oppressive, family structures, the 'wrong' educational attitudes and so on. At the level of popular culture, the musical *West Side Story*, featuring Puerto Ricans and Italians in America, is a good example of 'problematising' ethnic minorities and portraying their problems as being due to lack of assimilation. Similarly, emphasis on conflict within British Asian families over arranged marriages, pathologises these families and fails to point to the range of conflicts existing in indigenous British families (Lawrence, 1982). Critics of ethnic studies and the concept of ethnicity claim that this perspective deflects attention from the racism of the 'host' country and the institutionalised racism of the State (see Richardson and Lambert, 1985; Amos and Parmar, 1984; Lawrence, 1982). However, we can also argue that at their best ethnic studies emphasise the relational nature of ethnicity as a cultural and social process involving accommodation and assimilation as well as resistance and separateness (for example, see Lal, 1988).

Racism: structure and culture

In Britain the host-immigrant model of ethnicity was undermined by events of the 1960s and 1970s: not only was assimilation not occurring, but migrants and increasingly British-born black people were defending many elements of their own cultures. This is not the place for lengthy discussion of theories of racism but we need to look at their effect on the way that we view the cultural configurations of race and ethnicity. The argument that the roots of racism lie in the need of European economies for the cheap labour which earlier slaves and now migrants provide, is linked to a particular kind of Marxian theory concerned with the analysis of the relationship between the dominant class and the operation of the capitalist State. Race, like class, becomes a fundamental division within society. An early statement of this type of theory is by Cox, 'it is probable that without capitalism, a chance cultural occurrence among whites, the world might never have experienced race prejudice' (Cox, 1959, p. 345); the productive relations of capitalism harbour conflicts and tensions which create the necessity for racism. Such a Marxist approach addresses itself to the 'initial production' of racism by the capitalist system but also to ways in which racist ideologies are reproduced and transformed, as capitalism itself changes and alters. Accounts like Cox's, and at times, Sivanandan's (1976), assume that economic forces and conflicts are the main causes of racism, which performs vital functions for the capitalist system, in which the all-powerful State represents the economic interests of the dominant class, regulates the migration of labour and manipulates popular racism according to the needs of the system. Racism then is analysed simply as a reflection of the economic system and its cultural, ethnic and political dimensions marginalised.

More structuralist versions of Marxism concentrate on the 'system' needs of capitalism. For example, the work of Castles and Kosack (1973) argues that racism functions to divide the working class, reducing its revolutionary potential. Racism allows scapegoating to occur which acts as a 'safe' outlet for frustrations with the organisation of society. There are a number of problems with this explanation, the most damning of which is that it is a self-fulfilling prophesy. Whatever occurs – immigration Acts or 'race relations' legislation – can be argued to be in the interests of the capitalist system (see Miles, 1982, and Solomos, 1988). (Such circularity is remarkably like structural-functionalism.) Recognising some of these problems, writers such as Hall (1980) and Gilroy (1987) insist on the 'relative autonomy' of the economic, political and ideological spheres but this too tends to lead to statements about the complex interrelations of these three areas and little analysis of the ways in which the areas actually relate or where autonomy stops (also see Chapter 2).

Miles and Phizacklea (1984) attempt a reinterpretation of some of the issues, arguing that 'race relations' is not a legitimate area of study and that for sociologists to give 'race' analytical status is dangerous because it becomes part of the process whereby the ideology of 'race' persists. As we saw earlier, Miles defines racism as ideology, but he tries to distinguish his use of ideology from, for example, that in the work of the Birmingham Centre for Contemporary Cultural Studies (CCCS, 1982; Gilroy, 1987; and see Chapter 2). Miles accepts that the ideology of racism is a material force giving rise to certain social practices and ways of behaving. Racism as an ideology is not constructed simply and purposely to justify colonial exploitation and/or to divide the working class. Rather, once these ideas become a central element in the world view of bourgeois culture, they begin to have real material effects. However, he argues against the notion of 'race' as an ideological construct being treated as if it had an independent force – a 'life' – which can influence and determine events. He states that an emphasis by the CCCS on cultural relations, rather than on production relations, ignores the material and political basis of racism (Solomos, 1988, p. 101). Despite his concern with the 'production and reproduction of meanings' which constitute racism Miles fails to produce an analysis of the cultural and economic articulation of racism (Miles, 1989, p. 97).

The other main structuralist approach to issues of race is broadly Weberian and the most prominent writer in this tradition is John Rex. The focus in his writings is essentially on social status, social meanings and the ways in which meanings direct social action. Essentially he sees race as a dimension of social stratification and as indicated earlier, race relations as arising out of specific historical circumstances of contact between races. Although Rex does not write much about culture as such, his work stresses the importance of belief systems and ideologies in race relations, while arguing that cultural differences in themselves do not determine race and ethnic relations (Rex, 1983, 1986, and 1988).

Structure or culture? Multiculturalism and education

To understand the diversity and complexity of 'race' and ethnicity as elements in culture we need to be clear about both of these concepts, the ways they are used within cultures themselves and that both have structural as well as cultural components. Recent debates on the issue of 'multicultural' education in Britain highlight many of these issues. In Chapter 8 we shall see that what is considered as education has a range of political, social, cultural and ideological implications. In general, educational policy in Britain has taken a consensual, non-confrontational stance to racial and ethnic matters, or adopted policies which can be seen to benefit all, rather than the ethnic minorities themselves (Kirp, 1985). Such policies, it can be argued, have also tended 'to foster the cultural subordination and political neutralization of blacks' (Mullard, 1985).

Initially, the aim of educational policies to tackle the 'immigrant problem' identified in Britain in the early 1960s was assimilationist, to which the only alternative was segregation – as had occurred in the southern states of America and more brutally under apartheid in South Africa – since immigrants were concentrated in particular areas and schools. Educationalists identified language and cultural 'problems' amongst children of immigrant parents and aimed at 'helping' such children overcome these 'handicaps'. Assimilationist policies were often interpreted by teachers into attempts to insist that immigrant children ate English food or behaved in other ways which conflicted with their religious, cultural and social mores. While English language teaching might undoubtedly enable such children to benefit from English schooling, at the same .time it effectively undermined the specificity of their ethnic culture. Underlying this attempt to assimilate immigrant children into English culture was a fear of the 'disruption' which might be caused by allowing alternative cultures to develop within schools: fear that the dominant culture might be threatened. Since the immigrants were also black, part of the rationalisation for these fears was a set of racist beliefs such as we outlined earlier.

By the late 1960s this relatively crude assimilationist policy had given way to integrationist policies, allowing ostensibly for cultural diversity. However, Mullard amongst others has argued that integrationist policies differed little from earlier assimilationist ones and that 'cultural diversity is tolerable so long as it neither impedes progress to political integration nor explicitly challenges the cultural assumptions of our Anglocentric society' (Mullard, 1985, p. 45). He also argues that the current policy of cultural pluralism or 'multicultural' education in practice is merely a refinement of all the previous models and assumes that it is black pupils, not white culture, which will change (also see Verma, 1986).

Multicultural education cannot be a reality in a society in which there is a dominant, white culture and subordinate, black or ethnic cultures – a society 'structured in dominance'. Such a situation indicates that there is structural inequality based on race and/or ethnicity which is justified by an ideology of racism. We can see here the importance of structural theories of racism stressing ideology and also those which see race and ethnicity as an aspect of structure like class (see Chapter 6 for the relationship between class and culture).

Gramsci's concept of hegemony, discussed in Chapter 2, allows us to recognise the ways in which ideology, economic and political structures and culture are constantly involved in a process of creation, resistance, reproduction and innovation, contradiction and negotiation (not only around the issue of 'race' and ethnicity but also gender and class). Putting the concept of 'hegemony' into operation means presenting a rich and complex account of the national/popular culture of a particular nation state. A recent article attempts such a study, arguing that we need a theory:

which not only allows racist discourses to 'speak' at a number of different levels, but helps pinpoint their changing principles of articulation, as these are governed by particular contexts and conjunctures (Cohen, 1988, p. 99).

Such a theory, for example, needs to explain the differences and similarities between anti-Semitism and colour prejudice, working-class racism and the relationships between class and ethnic hegemony (also see Gilroy, 1987).

Ethnicity, 'race' and cultural change

Unlike 'race', the concept of 'ethnicity' has a large intrinsic cultural component, since its major referent is not biology. But we need also to take into account that there are consequences for culture of belief systems which include the ideology of race and result in racism (see Gilroy, 1987). It is some of the complexity of the cultural consequences of ethnicity and race that we shall examine in this section.

The flexibility of ethnicity makes it possible for the group or individual to shift boundaries, within already-established para-meters. For example, you may choose to identify yourself as Scottish: your name may not indicate this if you have taken a non-Scottish husband's surname; your accent may provide no indication of upbringing; you may live outside Scotland; you may not conform to any tenuous physical stereotype of Scottishness. What then defines your Scottishness? Your genealogy indicates a father whose ancestors for 200 years have been identifiable Scots who bore a Highland clan name, yet he could not have represented Scotland in international sport, since he was born in Brighton, where his parents were on holiday! You can only 'be' a Scot by disregarding the other half of your ancestry and by identifying with specific political and/or cultural interests and positions. On the other hand, once you have declared your ethnicity, any moodiness, taciturnity or caution with money can be firmly identified by others as '[stereo]typically Scottish'. This element of choice, although with weightier consequences (because of racism), exists, for instance, for someone who has thirty-one white great-great-great-grandparents, and one black one. She may choose to 'be' black, espousing cultural and political activities recognised as Afro-Caribbean (or Afro-American). The bars to this process are those maintained at the boundaries of 'superior' ethnic groups, which depend on perceived physical or biological evidence. An individual with only one *white* great-great-great grandparent could not credibly assert membership of a white ethnic group because s/he would be physically identified as black. Ethnic choice then, can be limited by culturally determined factors, which need not be consistent, may disregard physical reality and are based on power relationships (see Rex, 1986, ch. 5).

The processes of accommodation of subordinate ethnic groups at a cultural level have been documented by Derek Scott. He places the adoption of Burns's and Moore's ballads as Scottish and Irish national anthems in the historical context of the subjugation and pacification of both countries, pointing out that

> These anthems illustrate classic hegemonic compromise: some acknowledgement of autonomy is demanded by Scotland and Ireland, yet their independence is recognized only in the context of a romantic and shadowy past. Of more recent date, the Welsh national anthem . . . conforms to the same pattern, and here the possession of an ancient independent language becomes a symbol of the country's relative autonomy (Scott, 1989, p. 25).

The marginalisation and partial assimilation of Gaelic culture during the nineteenth century is also charted as being directly related to the undermining of the socioeconomic basis of Gaelic communities.

In those cases where there has been effective opposition to the dominant group, even retrospectively, as with the Inuit and indigenous Americans recently, a reassertion of ethnic identity becomes meaningful. Whilst the possession of an independent language is in itself no guarantee of a viable ethnic alternative, it is at least an irritant to the cultural and educational hegemony of the host society, and one which, if the argument of the power of language to shape thought is valid, should not be underestimated (see Chapter 2 and also below).

Derek Scott also discusses the appropriation and mediation of black culture in America as a complex process of both assimilation and ranking in the development of a 'specifically American form of culture' (Scott, 1989, pp. 82ff). He shows how some aspects of black musical culture were incorporated into the dominant popular culture. 'Blackface' musicians or minstrels – white men 'blacked up' and playing so-called 'nigger minstrel' songs – became popular amongst whites. But this white pastiche of black music 'diluted' the original black culture and the phenomenon occurred of Negroes themselves as 'blackface minstrels'!

Another example of the complex cultural processes which operate between dominant and subordinate cultures is the way in which Christianity introduced by European missionaries into traditional African societies underwent a syncretistic change. By the twentieth century new black African messianic movements – such as Kimbanguism in the Belgian Congo – which believed in the imminent appearance of a black messiah who would rescue believers from the regime of the white man, had developed. Drawing on the importance of religion in their traditional cultures and attempting to harness what appeared to be the superior powers of the white man's God, such movements were forms of resistance against colonialism and often incorporated into the explicitly political independence movements (Wilson, 1973). Early prophetic and messianic cults amongst American Indians – for example the Ghost Dance – reflected 'the yearning of the Indians for the recovery of their own culture, which was rapidly declining' (Lanternari, 1963, p. 101). Similarly, 'cargo' cults in Melanesia linked traditional beliefs in the power of ancestral spirits to the technological superiority of the white man and his 'trade goods' encountered through colonisation (Wilson, 1973).

Resistance and accommodation are processes which occur together where cultures are placed in opposition and conflict: both processes are reactions of the 'host' or dominant culture as well as of the subordinate ethnic group. Racism is a reaction by the dominant group and includes the idea of other and subordinate cultures as alien (for example, see CCCS, 1982, p. 81). But it may also be utilised by a subordinate group, as Gilroy instances in his discussion of the demand by black social workers that black children be placed with black families (Gilroy, 1987, pp. 64–7). Mac an Ghaill (1988) shows the variety of cultural political strategies used by black teenagers to deal with the racism they face in British schools. A group of girls of Afro-Caribbean and Asian origin – the 'Black Sisters' – saw success in the school system as a strategy for survival and a symbol of pride in their blackness. In contrast, a group of Afro-Caribbean boys – 'Rasta Heads' – rejected white schooling. A group of Asian boys – the 'Warriors' – did likewise, while remaining less visibly antagonistic in teachers' eyes.

The language used, developed and changed by Afro-Caribbeans in Britain reflects their specific cultural history and experience, that of Rasta in particular being part of a culture which includes an 'ethnic' music and poetry (Sutcliffe and Wong, 1986). Gilroy and others have pointed to the syncretistic processes of black culture in Britain. Gilroy in particular stresses the importance of a diaspora, a dispersal of blacks from a variety of indigenous cultures, which has created a black culture which to some extent transcends ethnic divisions. He points too, to the way in which this black culture of music, dress and language has affected white, especially 'youth' culture (Gilroy, 1987; see also Jones, 1988). Less convincingly, Gilroy sees expressive black music and dance cultures as having a 'hidden' political dimension (similar to white male subcultures, see Chapter 6). Although this is undoubtedly true to some extent, the commercialisation of such cultures is part of the hegemonic process and ensures at least an uneasy incorporation and legitimation. As we showed in our example of syncretistic colonial religious movements, such cultural 'political' expressions require translation into more conventional politics to be effective.

Increasingly, self-defined ethnic groups within larger dominant groups have been studied as sources and repositories of alternative or subordinate cultures (Ballard and Ballard, in Watson (ed.), 1977; Cashmore, 1979; Smith, 1981) whilst at the present time we see a surge of sociopolitical activity amongst minority ethnic groups in Turkey, Lebanon, Iran, India and the USSR. Ethnicity in many countries has become most dramatically a culture of resistance, rather than the sterile preservation of a minority culture within a larger society. However, it is the combination of social, economic and cultural factors, and not the statement of cultural difference alone, which provides the impetus for these groups to challenge the dominant group. It may be flawed, as Richardson and Lambert (1985) point out, both as a descriptive and explanatory concept, but currently ethnicity is very much a dynamic force in societies throughout the world, and should provide much material for further study. Finally, ethnicity as a cultural phenomenon needs to be seen in articulation with the social, economic, political and ideological structures of racism and other structural and cultural forms of inequality and oppression, particularly class and gender (Ramazanoglu, 1989, chs 6 and 7).

6 Class and Culture

Class and consensus

In many of the theories of culture we have examined the relationship of culture to class has been an important issue, but it has also shown many contradictions, confusions and discontinuities. As we saw in Chapters 1 and 2, historically the main thrust of theoretical developments in the sociological study of culture took place within sets of paradigms emphasising a whole range of other issues. Within these, initially, culture was simply 'given' by the nature of the class structure itself. Alternatively, within the structural-functionalist paradigm, class was seen as contributing to an overall cultural consensus. From the radical perspective of theorists of the Frankfurt School, as well as more conservative 'mass society' theorists, class and class-based culture were seen as ultimately giving way to a consensus mass culture based on classlessness. The distinction between 'high' and 'low' or popular culture in many theories, hinges implicitly or explicitly on some notion of class, although the term 'élite' often fudges the issue.

Within Marxist theories of culture and ideology, deriving from economic relationships, class is seen as the major vehicle of both social change and cultural reproduction, although there is considerable debate concerning these processes (see Chapter 2) and the nature of class itself. An important part of Weber's work, too, theorises a relationship between the 'cultural' and the 'economic'. He is particularly concerned with the development of a specific culture in relation to an emergent class. In *The Protestant Ethic and the Spirit of Capitalism*, Weber traces the effect of a particular set of religious beliefs, customs, practices, values, on the social actions of members of a society, including their art, morals, laws and economic life. Weber's examination of the 'elective affinity' between Protestantism and capitalism is a study of a modernising culture which emphasises rationality in all spheres (see Chapter 10 for more recent development of these ideas). Weber's work is important, because not only did he provide a study of culture as lived, subjective experience but he also put forward an analysis of the dynamics of cultural change and class formation. But for Weber, class was only one aspect of social stratification and he also looked at status groups as 'carriers' of culture, an aspect of the study of culture which American sociologists in particular have continued.

Within social science more generally, the period immediately following the Second World War in Western societies was labelled 'the age of consensus', or 'affluence', as well as heralding the 'end of ideology'. Commentators – of the left and right – argued that technological change, government policy, divorce of ownership and control of industrial capital, the shift from production of goods to production of services and the growth of bureaucracy had created, in effect, a new form of society, in which the old debates about class and ideology were increasingly irrelevant (see Kumar, 1978). Essentially the argument was that:

> The years since the early 1950s have echoed with the claim that the old class structure of capitalism is steadily dissolving. The labels attached to that new order of society which is believed to be emerging from the ruins of the old – the 'welfare state', the 'affluent society the 'home-centred society', the 'mass society', 'post-capitalism', and so on have become the clichés of contemporary debate (Westergaard, 1972, p. 119).

Westergaard and other British writers disputed this view and in Britain and the USA 'rediscovery' of class (and poverty), the debunking of the notion of the affluent society and the '*embourgeoisement* thesis', challenged the idea of a 'classless' society and the dominant structural-functionalist perspective in sociology. This encouraged serious reconsideration of the theorisation of class, particularly from within a newly revived Marxist theory, and ultimately this was an important development for the study of class and culture. In American sociology, where Marxist conceptions of class have always been less influential the civil rights movement and subsequent developments ensured that the 'race question' and ethnicity were important in writing on culture. But American theorists like Bell, (Bell, 1980, p. 208) and Gouldner (1979) have also written on the continuing importance of class.

Class and cultural studies

Fundamental to Marxist theory is the notion that the dominant class both produces and controls the 'dominant' ideas, values and beliefs of a society, which in turn legitimise the *status quo* by ensuring that the population as a whole accepts the inequalities of wealth and power as being justified and proper. It can be argued from this that the subordinate class is ideologically deluded or 'mystified' into conforming with a social order which runs counter to its 'true interests'. So, for example, attempts by sections of the media to persuade us that strikes are irresponsible and 'bad for the country' could be viewed as the media taking on an ideological role and operating on behalf of the interests of the dominant class. But such a crude conspiratorial understanding of what ideology (and culture) is and how it works has been much criticised (see Chapters 2 and 9). In particular, the Althusserian concept of ideology (see Chapter 2) has important implications for a more sophisticated theorisation of class and culture. Althusser argues that ideology is a structure within which we think and act. As such, it cannot be described simply as. something propagated by a cynical ruling class to deceive the working class, for the ruling class too, think within this structure. If ideology is not seen as 'false consciousness', false knowledge, an incorrect way of viewing the world, then it points to the way in which the framework we use to understand the world, the culture that we inhabit, has been shaped and moulded by a specific set of interests which are allied with a specific class, the ruling class, but not in any simple or conspiratorial way.

Earlier we discussed the development of cultural studies in Britain (see Chapter 2), which has also influenced the study of culture in America. The interrelationship between ideology, culture and class has been central to the work of the Birmingham CCCS and featured in a series of studies conducted during the 1970s. Research at the Centre pivoted on the following series of questions:

What were the processes by means of which a dominant cultural order came to be 'preferred'? Who preferred this order rather than that? What were the effects of a particular ordering of the cultures of a social formation on the other hierarchized social arrangements? . . . How and why did societies come to be culturally 'structured in dominance'? (Hall, 1980a, p. 27).

The CCCS researchers worked with a definition of culture which attempts, on one hand, to hold on to the idea of culture as being created and re-created by classes and, on the other, to the idea of culture as structured (determined) by the class relations of capitalism. The tension between these ideas gave rise to the debate between 'culturalists' and 'structuralists' which centred on the question of how to go about the job of researching culture and class. Culturalists, like Raymond Williams and E. P. Thompson are more concerned with explaining culture and ideology with reference to its roots in a social grouping – for example, some shared ideas of what it means to be working class – whereas the stress within structuralism falls on calculating the political consequences or effects that might be attributed to particular ideologies or cultural forms in terms of the impact they might be expected to have on the consciousness of those who are exposed to or influenced by them (also see Chapter 9) .

Defining class

This 'problematic' in the study of culture – which is really another problem in determining what culture *is* – has not yet been fully resolved and indeed, becomes even more puzzling when we consider the fact that in many of the studies on class and culture, the notion of class is itself problematic. The failure to define and conceptualise class adequately has been identified as an omission of writers, like those attached to the CCCS, in their attempt to examine the relationship between culture and class (see Connell, 1983, pp. 222–30). As part of an attempt to 'construct a genre of working-class cultural studies' Critcher gives a list of earlier studies on working-class culture in his essay 'Sociology, cultural studies and the post-war working class' (in Clarke *et al.*, (eds) 1979), but in this we find that 'the working class' is treated as a ready-made unit of study, that is, as an agreed and easily identified class. The Birmingham Centre writers, while providing a critique of these earlier studies, fail to define their object of study. They do not appear to address the difficulty of defining class or relate their work to recent theoretical issues in the study of class (Clarke *et al.*, (eds) 1979). Recent CCCS studies appear to work with a definition of class culled from their earlier work, *Resistance Through Rituals*, which states:

> In modern societies, the most fundamental groups are the social classes, and the major cultural configurations will be, in a fundamental though often mediated way, 'class cultures'. Relative to these cultural-class configurations, subcultures are subsets – smaller, more localised and differentiated structures, within one or other of the larger cultural networks. We must, first, see subcultures in terms of their relation to the wider class-cultural networks of which they form a distinctive part. When we examine this relationship between a subculture and the 'culture' of which it is a part, we call the latter the 'parent' culture (Clarke *et al.* in Hall and Jefferson (eds) 1976, p. 13).

In their writings the CCCS group make a series of moves from class to culture to subcultures, which lead to inconsistencies and incoherences in their analysis of class cultures. In attempting to operationalise the concept of class in relation to culture, in terms of resistance, subordination, conflict and dominance, we need to begin by being clear about why class is important. A whole series of questions flow from confronting this issue. For example, is a class perspective the only way we can understand the structure of advanced societies, or indeed of any society? Was an analysis of class important at one stage of capitalist development but no longer, as some American theorists have tended to argue? We also need to address the question of how other social divisions, particularly gender, race and ethnicity, articulate with class.

Historians as well as sociologists have been and are grappling with the theoretical difficulties surrounding the definition of class and its relationship to the development of a new type of society – industrial society – with new cultural forms. For example, E.P. Thompson (1968) is concerned to show that the English working class 'made themselves', in the years between 1780 and 1832. He claims that it was during this period that 'most English working people came to feel an identity of interests between themselves, and against their rulers and employers'. He argues that there existed a working class 'in itself and for itself', that this class became a fully conscious working class in the Marxist sense, and that an aspect of this consciousness was a distinctive working-class culture. Another historian, Harold Perkin (1969), claims that distinctive social classes emerged in England in the years 1815–20, explaining this 'birth of class' by arguing that pre-industrial England was 'classless': the aristocratic rulers took a paternalistic interest in the condition of the lower orders. With industrialisation they abdicated their traditional responsibilities and concern, the old order changed and hostility between different groups resulted in the development of a class society in which each class was conscious of its own loyalties and conflicting interests with those of other classes. What is important about both Thompson's and Perkin's formulations, for our discussion of culture, is that each posits a distinctive consciousness and culture based on mutually antagonistic class positions and interests. In America too, 'the emergence of the new middle and upper classes, created by rapid industrialisation . . . seems to have accelerated rather than inhibited the growing distinctions between élite and mass culture' (Levine, 1988, pp. 225–6).

'New' class theories

CCCS work attempts to hold on to definitions of class which encompass those dimensions concerning shared interests. Following the classic Marxist formulation, they conceptualise it as being about groups in a similar relationship to the means of production and therefore see classes as antagonistic in relation to other classes. Such a formulation does not differentiate between the economic, political and ideological dimensions of class. This approach also fails to locate these ideas on class and culture in relation to what other theorists have argued is the changing class structure of modern or post-modern societies.

There are many criticisms to be made of modern class theorists which are outside the scope of this book, but, whether Weberian or Marxist in their orientation, they have argued that the classic theories of class developed in the context of a particular form of capitalism are inadequate to explain the changes which have occurred in modern 'post-' or 'late' capitalist societies (for example, Giddens, 1973; Bell, 1980, pp. 204ff. and 239–40). The rise of what is termed the 'intermediate strata' – consisting of white-collar, professional and non-manual workers of several kinds – is the major development, and theoretical debate is focused on the issue of how this new strata relates to other classes and how it alters the way in which class 'works', including, presumably, its relation to culture. 'New' class theories stress that the industrial, occupational and economic changes of late capitalism have resulted in major transformations in class structure, in a greater diversity of class groups and considerable mobility between them. Such changes have implications for our analysis of culture: for example, if the working class is conceptualised as no longer homogeneous, then we cannot study 'working-class' culture. Similarly we might need to ask whether the 'dominant culture' is a class culture. It is interesting to note here the trend towards fragmentation and breaking-down of rigid conceptualisations which we discuss later as post-modernist theories (see Chapter 10).

Writing within an Althusserian structuralist framework, Poulantzas stresses the relative autonomy of the political and ideological dimensions of class as well as the economic level. He also emphasises the importance of differentiation *within* classes, in terms of class fractions and strata (Poulantzas, 1973). In various parts of this book we look at culture as something which is produced, a commodity (see especially Chapters 3 and 9). It is interesting to speculate here then, whether those individuals involved in the production of both popular and 'high' culture, form part of the increasingly large group whose labour, according to Poulantzas, is not productive (does not produce 'surplus value', in the classic Marxist formulation), or whether production of cultural commodities can be seen as productive. In his analysis of class, Poulantzas is not concerned with culture as such, but emphasises that one of the ways in which the contradictions (antagonisms) between social classes are expressed is through the ideological apparatus of the state, including education and the media, which we have identified as being part of the way in which culture is produced and reproduced (see Chapters 2, 8 and 9).

Erik Olin Wright's attempt to overcome the problems of Poulantzas's analysis appears relevant here. Wright formulates the idea of 'contradictory class locations' and analyses class in terms of a number of processes underlying the social relations of production in advanced capitalism. He is particularly concerned then, with the relationships between and within classes:

> It is important to understand the precise sense in which these class locations are 'contradictory' locations within class relations. They are not contradictory simply because they cannot be neatly pigeon-holed in any of the basic classes . . . Rather they are contradictory locations because they simultaneously share the relational characteristics of two distinct classes. As a result, they share class interests with two different classes but have interests identical to neither. It is in this sense that they can be viewed as being objectively torn between class locations (Wright, 1980, p. 331).

The existence of class fractions and differentiation within classes would seem to point towards a complexity and duality of cultures and subcultures, which does not accord with the limited notion of class used in most of the studies of class and class culture to date. In a different vein we have already noted the comments of the American liberal, Daniel Bell, on the 'cultural contradictions of capitalism' (see Chapter 1). His notion of the increasing disjunction between social structure – which includes the economy – and culture, implies both that class is less important in modern societies and that class and culture have a less direct relationship than they did. Although in his neo-Weberian analysis he specifically states that a class must have 'a cultural outlook providing a coherent view, a common consciousness' (Bell, 1980, p. 155), he has difficulty in identifying the common basis of class interests and therefore, presumably culture (ibid, pp. 156–64).

Another American sociologist, Alvin Gouldner explicitly links modern class changes to cultural change. Gouldner argues the rise of a 'new class', in terms containing resonances (some acknowledged) from earlier theories concerning the development of modern society and culture. He sees this new class as the most progressive force in modern society because it possesses 'cultural capital' in the form of the 'culture of critical discourse'. Using Bourdieu's notion of cultural capital (see Chapter 8) Gouldner describes the new class as 'a new *cultural* bourgeoisie whose capital is not its money but its control over valuable cultures' (Gouldner, 1979, p. 21). Education

Lilienfeld, 1973; Beynon, 1984; Bulmer (ed.) 1975). Even the notion that 'class consciousness' is not synonymous with 'social consciousness', does not help us much (Davis, 1979). The work of Paul Willis seems to move into more fertile terrain, but fails to draw any generalised conclusions on the interrelationship between class, class consciousness and cultural formations (see Connell, 1983, pp. 220–30). He fails to discuss the issue posed by Mann in his study of working-class consciousness, which is that the Western working class is unlikely to reach the stage of being a 'class in itself and for itself' (Mann, 1973, pp. 68–73; also see Bell, 1980, pp. 203–4). Mann also posed the question whether the action of the working class is limited by the lack of a concept of any alternative to the present system. The lack of any clear discussion on these and related questions points up some of the problems of continuing to use a structuralist analysis of class. However, some of the early work of the CCCS on subcultures was an attempt to discuss forms of 'alternative' working-class consciousness, although such an analysis leaves unanswered many questions and has been criticised as an 'over-reading', an exaggeration of the class significance of minority cultural styles and forms (for example, see Cohen, 1980, pp. i–xxxiii).

Another major criticism, as we shall see in Chapter 7, is that such studies deal only with male culture. It is relevant to note here that with few exceptions, class consciousness has been implicitly conceptualised and studied in terms of men (but see Porter, 1982; Purcell, 1988; Hunt, 1980; Pollert, 1981; Abbott and Sapsford, 1987). This gender-blindness stems largely from the assumed relationship between men's work and class consciousness and the fact that, as we shall see, women's work is less clearly differentiated from their leisure activities – what we have characterised in terms of women's private and men's public culture (see Chapter 7). There seems to be a hidden assumption too, that because women's activities are more 'private', they are also more trivial, less 'political' and therefore not part of 'class consciousness'.

Other criticisms have been made of the CCCS approach: 'The structuralist conception of class translates into the CCCS analyses as an assumption that behind the superficial complexity of everyday life, there is a fundamental class situation which is the same for everyone in that class' (Connell, 1983, p. 224). As Connell then goes on to point out, when this notion of class is used in connection with an unresolved concept of culture then the result is that 'the concept of a separate culture becomes simply a necessary part of the concept of class. The approach obliterates the question of whether there actually is a distinctive culture possessed by the working class at a given time and place . . .' (ibid, p. 226); and, we might add here, whether this culture is shared between men and women, or between ethnic groups. These problems reappear throughout the Birmingham Centre studies, despite the many excellent discussions of these issues (for example, Richard Johnson's 'Three Problematics: Elements of a Theory of Working-Class Culture' in Clarke *et al.*, 1979).

Middle-class or bourgeois culture?

There is a tendency in the literature on culture and class to conflate the category of the dominant culture with that of the middle class, rather than for example, to use the category of the bourgeoisie. As Juliet Mitchell wrote:

> Each class has aspects of its own culture, which are relatively autonomous. This fact is illustrated by such phrases as 'working-class culture', 'ghetto culture', 'immigrant culture', etc., and by the absent phrase – 'middle-class culture'. We talk of middle-class mores: manners and habits . . . but not of a whole 'culture'. We don't think of 'middle-class culture' as something separate – it simply is the overall culture, within which are inserted these isolable other cultures. However, this cultural hegemony by bourgeois thought is not on an absolute par with the domination within the economy by the capitalist class (Mitchell, 1971, p. 33–4).

Use of two different terms – middle class and bourgeoisie – also indicates the confusions we have discussed over how we define class.

We saw in Chapter 3 that there are several critical disciplines dealing with 'high' culture, and that this culture is associated with the most powerful groups in Western societies. But the class structure of these groups and the nature of their culture has not been examined in detail and it seems most likely that we are looking

CALDERDALE
COLLEGE LIBRARY
HALIFAX

at élite groups rather than whole classes. In Britain there is a scarcity of sociological material examining either the culture of the middle classes or the culture of the bourgeoisie *as such*. What dimensions of these cultures are resisted or not resisted by other classes; which elements of these cultures control the culture of the subordinate classes? Is the dominant culture a bourgeois culture or a middle-class culture? Or given the weight of the past in relation to British culture, for example, to what extent does the dominant culture still retain elements of its aristocratic heritage (see, for example, Anderson, 1969). We might also remember here, Eliot's point on the importance of regional and local cultures (see Chapter 1) and ask what these are and what relationship they have to class cultures.

Bourgeois or middle-class culture has been more studied in America, at a very general level, where it is equated with a 'national', common or dominant culture, and sometimes even a 'popular' culture, the 'American way of life', but whether or not this has a class basis is rarely articulated (see Chapter 1 and, for example, Bellah *et al.*, 1985; Warner, 1975). Gans attempts to link class and culture through the notion of 'taste publics'. He differentiates within the 'middle class', using the concept of class in the sense of status group, in the tradition of Warner. Partly because of this and partly because he defines culture as being about 'taste' rather than 'lived' he tells us little about the relationship of culture to the rest of society (Gans, 1974). Both in Britain and America culture has been studied at the level of the community, but such studies are not always explicitly studies of culture distinguished from social structure (see Chapter 1). The community-studies approach to culture frequently takes an anthropological approach, seeing the community as a whole, often seeing its rural or urban character as important and class as only one factor among many which determine the overall culture (for example, see Frankenberg, 1969). It is also the case for America that ethnicity and region are often seen as more important defining characteristics than class, or at least that they are inextricably intertwined (for example, see Hartman (ed.), 1974). As well as the conceptual confusion and conflation surrounding the notion of middle class or bourgeois cultures, it is relevant here to remember Gouldner's point that sociologists have largely studied the 'underdog', a practice he compares with 'the anthropologist's (one-time) romantic appreciation of the romantic savage' (Gouldner, 1975).

Popular culture and class culture

There is also considerable conceptual and ideological confusion surrounding the term 'popular culture' and much of this appears on the one hand to relate to the problems of class analysis and culture we have discussed, and on the other to continuing debates on the nature of 'mass' culture. The CCCS tradition in Britain has spilled over to America where there is also a much longer tradition of the critical analysis of mass culture (Dunn, 1986; Gallafent, 1990). As we have seen, 'high culture' is culture as defined by élite or dominant class groups and 'popular culture' is the culture of 'the people', the lower classes. Simon Frith argues that popular culture is not simply lower-class culture and that in Australia and the USA for example, popular culture is 'by self-proclamation, a "classless" mass culture' (Frith, 1984, p. 5), but as MacCabe states, 'Any sustained consideration of popular culture inevitably erodes the distinction between it and "high culture" and fits with the idea of culture as a way of life, as lived' (MacCabe (ed.) 1986, p. ix).

Frith also states that 'Popular culture produces "the people"', but this posits a one-way determinism which we have already criticised (Frith, 1986). Popular culture may well have an active relationship with and contain cultural forms which are part of high or élite cultures, as well as being a commercialised 'mass' culture, but we can argue that essentially what defines it is that much of it derives from working-class culture (Frith, 1984, p.4). A simple but topical example of the dialectical process which creates popular culture is the adoption of the operatic aria '*Nessum Dorma*' (high culture), as the theme tune for TV coverage of the 1990 soccer world cup (popular culture), resulting in the operatic star Pavarotti, gaining a place in the pop-record hit charts (also see the comparison of novelists Jane Austen and Georgette Heyer, 'On Reading Trash' in Robinson, 1986; also see Gans, 1974). Making a similar point, a recent study of popular culture in America states 'The writers in this volume condemn the manipulative qualities of commercial culture. But they just as vehemently reject nearly all of what has passed for Marxist (or liberal or conservative) orthodoxy on popular culture', by which they appear to mean the idea that popular culture is simply 'low' or inferior. Instead, they state 'American culture, at its best, has ever been the genius of the ordinary writ large. We have no other aesthetic sources'; and the essays in this volume cover a range of genres and types of culture, much of it rooted in blue-collar working-class life (Buhle (ed.) 1987, p. xi).

In his discussion of American popular culture Ross argues:

> While it speaks enthusiastically to the feelings, desires, aspirations, and pleasures of ordinary people, popular culture is far from being a straightforward or unified expression of popular interests. It contains elements of disrespect, and even opposition to structures of authority, but it also contains 'explanations' . . . for the maintenance of respect for those structures of authority (Ross, 1989, p. 3).

In the tradition of British cultural studies and using a Gramscian analysis Ross discusses the contradictions contained in popular culture and sees it as mediating 'the hidden injuries of class'. But he warns too of the danger of 'locating *pure* political value in popular culture'.

A separate tradition from outside sociology, and often outside academe, which has been concerned with the culture of 'the people' is folklore, which 'may refer to types of barns, bread molds, or quilts; to orally inherited tales, songs, sayings, and beliefs; or to village festivals, household customs, and peasant rituals' (Dorson, 1959, p. 2). Beginning in nineteenth-century Britain as the home-based equivalent of early anthropologists' concern with 'savage customs', in Britain and America today it is often a valuable source of detail about traditional aspects of culture not studied by other disciplines (Dorson, 1959; Dorson, 1968). While folklore lacks an explicit theoretical base, failing to relate the specifics of culture to other structural aspects of society, it also has an ideological role in the attempt of modern Western societies to create a 'symbolic past'. What is interesting in this context is that it emphasises the culture of the 'folk', rather than high culture.

Recently, some historians too have focused more on 'the people's culture', particularly the French 'Annales' school and the English History Workshop studies. Since present popular culture, like high culture, contains elements from the past, these historical studies (often involving oral or ethnographic history) can be seen as an important element of the sociology of culture and have been acknowledged as such by writers in the British cultural studies tradition and by Marxist historians like E. P. Thompson because they are concerned with the way in which popular culture is 'made' and 'lived' (Ladurie, 1978; Steedman *et al.*, 1985; Bushaway, 1982; Golby and Purdue, 1984; Wright, 1985; also see Chapter 10 for E. P. Thompson). Written in this vein, but also drawing on an older community-studies tradition, *Living the Fishing* (Thompson *et al.*, 1983), for example, shows that fishing as a way of life varies considerably in different parts of Britain. Each fishing community has a complex culture and set of social relations based on the economy of family-owned fishing-boats, but this is also part of the wider social and economic structure. Such a study concentrates on working-class culture, but as a lived set of relationships, not a sociological category. So too, does Bernice Martin's essay 'The Kingdom of Terminus' (Martin, 1981). Although she writes in a more eclectic and specifically non-Marxist vein, using some of the ideas of Mary Douglas on order and control (see Chapter 2), she draws on a wide range of other studies including older British community studies and her own recollections, to write about working-class culture in Lancashire in the 1940s. She is particularly interesting, for example, on the symbolic importance of the unused front parlour with its lace curtains presenting 'the family face to the world'. What is unclear from Martin's richly descriptive work is what general conclusions we can make about class culture.

Cultural studies of class

Despite many criticisms, the work of cultural-studies writers in Britain and America allows us to speak more confidently of 'class culture' and also accept the idea that there exist a variety and a complexity of cultures and subcultures. This variety and complexity appear to settle the controversy surrounding the notion of the declining 'collectivist' culture of the working class which posited a homogeneous working-class culture, rather than a working-class culture fragmented not only by geographical unevenness and parochialism, but also by the social, sexual and racial divisions of labour. In Britain the CCCS revived the importance of the idea of classes in struggle, in opposition, but show that these struggles are often carried out in a resourceful and creative way, through culture. In their working-through of the Althusserian legacy of theoretical problems and formulations, the group paved the way for a consideration of the Gramscian concept of hegemony which, whilst not without its own problems, is a useful tool of analysis in the consideration of class and culture (see Chapter 2). The CCCS has also provided us with some vivid accounts of differing lifestyles and cultural struggles which show a range of human resources and creativity and remind us that both culture and class are not determined in a mechanistic way but are products of the experiences and actions of human agents.

In his article, 'Recreation in Rochdale 1900–1940', Paul Wild attempts to trace the changes in recreational pursuits in Britain which occurred with increased leisure time and improvements in living standards (Wild, 1979, p. 159). He demonstrates the way in which the economic ordering of society changes the leisure and cultural patterns of 'more or less stable working-class communities' and traces the emergence of leisure pursuits which correspond to the structured time of the industrial working week. Critcher examines, again the themes of cultural change and working-class life, by focusing on football (Critcher, 1979a). The centrality of football to the common British working-class experience is noted and discussed in terms of changes to what was once a 'pure traditional working-class activity' (ibid, p. 183). However, this raises the issue of to what extent organised football was ever a 'pure' or 'organic' working-class activity. If we examine the history of football, it is clear that it became incorporated into working-class life from without, rather than developing spontaneously from within. Association football was encouraged by priests working among the working classes in the late nineteenth century, and later, there were works teams, usually founded and encouraged by paternalistic employers (Wagg, 1984, p. 4).

A recent study by Hargreaves makes a similar but more general point concerning the way in which the 'dominant class' aimed to 'reconstruct popular sports and pastimes' and transform them into 'rational recreation' which would facilitate the creation of a healthy, morally upright and compliant workforce. Although there was considerable resistance to this development:

> divisions within the working class placed limits on the extent of
> that resistance and on the capacity of working-class people to
> innovate in this area, and so significant changes in the way
> subordinate groups related to sport and recreation were induced
> along rational recreation lines . . . [but] the reform of popular

sports and pastimes was accorded quite limited legitimacy within the class as a whole (Hargreaves, 1986, p. 205).

Hargreaves also shows that cultural hegemony in this area was strengthened by alliances between radical and religious working-class fractions and middle-class groups.

Hargreaves also attempts to tackle the articulation of race and gender in relation to questions of culture and class (see Chapter 7 on gender and sport). He points out that 'Football culture, both traditionally and its latter-day version, is stridently male chauvinist, sporadically violent and is the focus of fierce local patriotism. Now it has acquired in addition a racist, white-nationalist dimension' (ibid, pp. 106–7). The localism and patriotism of football can be seen as a form of class consciousness and solidarity which excludes those identified as 'outsiders', who are often members of ethnic minorities.

Theoretical problems reconsidered

A recent attempt to grapple with the complexities of the question of class and culture is that of Amariglio, Resnick and Wolff (1988). The discussion on class power and culture by these writers is handled in a very abstract theoretical fashion. This is an attempt to discuss the issues in a non-reductionist fashion and to provide methodological guidelines for further studies. However, for the most part, the result is that the issues are merely reduced to incoherence. So, for example, they write:

> Cultural processes always emerge and are reproduced in certain locations with specific conditions of existence. As the conditions of existence vary from location to location, cultural processes are dispersed and differentiated. The specific forms in which art, music, literature, and history exist are the combined result of forms of economic processes (including the class process) and forms of political processes (including the ordering of social behaviour). Similarly, the concept of culture is equally conditioned, and it emerges as a specific discursive field only by virtue of its overdetermination by concepts of other social processes and by non-discursive processes (Amarigio, Resnick, and Wolff, 1988, pp. 488–9).

Many of the theoretical problems of definition and conceptualisation around the area of class and culture are also general theoretical
problems in the analysis of culture which we have attempted to deal
with throughout this book. More important than a fruitless search
for *the* theory of class is to make clear the implications of different
theories of class for the analysis of culture. It may also be that
stratification studies (see Giddens, 1973; and Crompton and Mann,
(eds), 1986) are more useful than studies of class in identifying
clusters of strata which by virtue of their position in the market-
place, as Weber argued, share similar access to goods, needs, wants
and desires and experiences and therefore culture. If we retain the
concept of class in our attempts to analyse culture, then the issue of
class 'boundaries' in relation to shared cultural experiences needs to
be considered, as also the problem of class as a determining structure
and class as process. An attempt must be made to reconcile the
dimensions of culture as a *structure* that individuals are born into and
culture as a *process* which they create and re-create. We need to
analyse the ways in which culture is an area of resistance, negotiation
and incorporation, some of which may involve class consciousness
and action.

We also need to explore cultural similarities as well as cultural
differences, between classes and between societies. So, for example,
generalising rather rashly, we can argue that peasant food, whether
it be in Ireland or Hungary, India or Poland, shares a similar
composition, a similar form. Historically, similarities of form can be
found in the cultural styles of the aristocracy in different societies –
for example, the status of the French language amongst these
groups. Such similarities seem to point to the conclusion that a
similar location of a group (a class or a strata) in the social and
economic structure of any society produces similarities of culture
across societal boundaries. Rather than examining cultural content
alone, we should perhaps be examining cultural form and this might
produce less contradictory, relativist, accounts of culture and class.
The emphasis on contradiction and 'over-determination' in some of
the work in cultural studies might lead us to pose the question 'is the
cultural world too complex and contradictory to be understood?'
But we must also take on board more recent post-modernist
criticism of totalising theories and concepts, of which 'class' is a
classic example.

7 Gendered Cultures

Gender and cultural differentiation

Details of the 'discovery' of gender in sociological inquiry, do not belong here, but this chapter shows the importance of 'gendered' culture as an aspect of collective life and addresses the question of how culture is involved in the constitution of gender and gender relations. Although the definition of culture remains problematic, the notion that culture is 'gendered' presupposes two characteristics: that culture is about how we live and is not homogeneous or monolithic but cut across by major social divisions. We and others have argued that culture is a reflection and working through of social relations, class in particular. It is unsurprising then, that culture also has a complex relationship to and is part of the structural process of gender-differentiation and the production and reproduction of 'gendered subjectivity'. Post-modern theories (for example, see Fraser and Nicholson, 1988) would emphasise that 'gender' and 'gendered subjectivities' are not homogeneous or monolithic either. Recently, sociologists, feminists and others have explored these processes in Western industrial societies and shown how cultural forms such as popular romance fiction, soap operas, advertisements, illustrations, pop music, adventure films, and cultural activities like sport, are part of gender representation and reproduction, although the way in which this occurs may be complex and contradictory.

Social anthropologists studying non-Western societies were quick to document the differentiation of culture along gender lines, but 'rigid' gender differentiation was interpreted as characteristic of their 'primitive' state. Only with recent interest in studying Western culture (see Chapter 1) has gender differentiation in all societies

119

CALDERDALE
COLLEGE LIBRARY
HALIFAX

become the subject of theoretical debate and empirical study. 'The secondary status of women in society is one of the true universals, a pan-cultural fact' (Ortner, 1974, p. 67). Using culture to include the totality of social structure, beliefs and values, and following Lévi-Strauss, Ortner states that:

> every culture implicitly recognises and asserts a distinction between the operation of nature and the operation of culture (human consciousness and its products); and further, that the distinctiveness of culture rests on the fact that it can . . . transcend natural conditions (ibid, pp. 72–3).

In all societies women are seen as somehow 'closer to nature' and men, by definition closer to 'culture', to 'civilisation'. Evidence to support the 'pan-cultural' existence of this notion appears inconclusive and Ortner falls into the trap of biological determinism, but the idea that women are 'closer to nature' yet also part of culture does seem to underlie many Western cultural notions of the basis for gender differentiation (Moore, 1988; Sydie, 1987; Lowe and Hubbard (eds), 1983, Harding, 1986, pp. 128–31). It is over-simple but useful here, to argue that in all societies we can distinguish relatively separate female and male cultures, and in some, homosexual cultures, but at the same time, gender is a dimension or axis of all culture. That is, in order to study gendered culture we need to examine it at a number of different levels. There are two major problems then, involved in theorising 'gendered culture'. First, what relationship do these female and male cultures have to the overall culture of a society – how do they articulate with each other, with homosexual cultures, and with the dominant culture? Second, how do these 'separate' gendered cultures articulate with the gender dimension of culture at a more general level?

Like class, gender is not simply a social category but relative and relational: women and men as social groups are defined in terms of each other (Hirst and Woolley, 1982; Sydie, 1987). The gender dimension of culture involves this relativity and the notion of heterosexuality is one way in which this is expressed. Similarly, homosexual culture must be understood in relationship to heterosexual culture. That culture is gendered means that it embodies and represents ideas, beliefs and practices about women's and men's roles, work and leisure, and sexuality. Although the basis of gender and sexuality in any society lies in 'real' biological differences between the sexes, the social perception and acting-out of these differences is embedded in cultural and social practices and structures, which vary considerably. All cultures assume heterosexuality as the norm – that the major relationships of gender are about women and men – whatever the precise cultural patterns of this and however flexible these are within a particular culture. Thus emphasis and status given to homosexuality are also variable across cultures.

Since heterosexuality and sexual difference are given priority in gender relations, we can say that gendered culture is always about this duality. 'Separate' male and female cultures help to maintain the heterosexual duality of gender, but at the same time each contains links or bridges to the other. An example would be the ideal of romantic love in Western societies. Discussion and concern with this is very much part of female culture, symbolised by receiving and wearing engagement, eternity and wedding rings, celebration of anniversaries and many other rituals, and reinforced in cultural forms like romance fiction and magazines. Women's concern with romantic love, however, links them indissolubly to men because men are the object or the goal for such emotions (McRobbie, eds, 1982; Cowie and Lees, 1981; Lees, 1986). Although men, like women 'marry for love', men's culture puts less emphasis on discussion and cultivation of romantic love than on their need for sexual and domestic services (Metcalf and Humphries (eds) 1985; Easthope, 1986; Weeks, 1981). Since women are the sexual objects of men in this culture, this is a bridge back to what we have called women's culture. We might argue that in Western societies the idealised nuclear or conjugal family which sociologists, politicians and others tell us is the key to a stable society, is also the major link between women's and men's culture.

The family as the articulation between female and male culture is a view grounded in industrialisation and increasing differentiation of family and workplace. By the nineteenth century in Britain and America, the dominant view was that middle-class women were more 'cultured' than men, culture here meaning both 'high' culture and 'civilisation' (see Chapter 1). This related to the idea that women were morally superior to men and the guardians of society's morality and should therefore not enter the public and morally corrupting world of politics and business, but remain in the 'private' sphere of home and family (for example, see Davidoff and Hall, 1987). 'The focus of the new democratic culture [in America] was on male roles. But the ethic of achievement articulated by men was sustained by a moral ecology shaped by women' (Bellah *et al.*, 1985, p. 40). Women were seen as transmitters of the dominant culture but not as its creators, although creation of the products of 'high' culture was (and is) often seen as somehow effeminate (Tuchman, 1975).

Women and cultural marginality

As sociology and feminism have shown us, the structural relationship between the two sexes is almost always one of inequality, in which women are the subordinate group. Thus we would expect an important aspect of the relationship between 'female' and 'male' cultures to encompass this inequality. Let us look more closely at the relationship between female and male cultures in theoretical terms. As we saw in Chapter 2, in the 1960s and 1970s British sociologists and others explored the phenomenon of youth subcultures. In the seminal study *Resistance Through Rituals*, girls appeared to be marginal to the largely male cultural groups discussed, but this male 'dominance' was countered by the inclusion of a pioneering essay on girls and subcultures and further discussion ((McRobbie and Garber, 1976). Powell and Clarke point out that it is inadequate to conceptualise the dominant or mainstream culture 'as if the social totality, and subcultural activity within it, can be explained in terms of what men do' and simply to see what women do as somehow marginal to this (Powell and Clarke, 1976, p. 223). Nevertheless, this conceptualisation does focus attention on the fact that things which men do are commonly treated as more important than things which women do: a simple example here would be the greater television coverage given to sport, rather than, say, to cookery or needlework programmes. This larger 'cultural space' given to men reflects their greater power as a group. There is a parallel here with the way in which 'high' culture is defined as the culture of the élite and powerful (see Chapter 3).

This example also illustrates another important point: gendered culture is part of the ideological status of women's and men's roles. Although the majority of women are involved in the waged labour force for most of their adult lives it is assumed that they are primarily wives and mothers. What we have called women's culture reflects this as, similarly, men's culture reflects their position in the world of work. One way of conceptualising this relationship is to see women as largely concerned with the 'personal', 'private', less visible world of family and home, and men with the more 'impersonal', instrumental and 'public' world of work (Powell and Clarke, 1976, p. 224; Gamarnikow *et al.*, 1983). Although helpful, this conceptualisation fails to show the precise relationship between these two spheres of culture, including the relationship of each to the wider culture. Until recently, much sociological theory has tended to reflect the 'commonsense' view that it is the 'public' sphere which is most important – either in terms of meeting the goals of society, as structural functionalism argues, ensuring that the competing interests posited by liberal pluralists are served, or in meeting the needs of the capitalist system, as structural Marxism argues.

Regardless of this tendency to make women theoretically 'invisible', structural-functionalism, liberal pluralism and Marxism all indicate that the two spheres cannot be seen in isolation. Although the 'public' and the 'private' may be analytically separate, empirically, in terms of everyday reality, and in terms of most theories about society, they are each part of the other. Powell and Clarke argue that women and men have different trajectories or paths through the complexities of cultural life in Western societies and that the 'space' for girls' cultural activity is not so much marginal to that for boys, as more tightly structured, reflecting and reinforcing the different and unequal structural position of women and men. We would add to this insight that each of these different trajectories always takes into account the other: we cannot understand the 'cultural map' without understanding this relationship. The differentiation of cultural space by gender is indicated by Figure 7.1 which shows the passage from the role of teenager to adult for working-class young people.

In this cultural process (which includes what sociologists often call socialisation) the importance of work for men and family for women is emphasised and this is functional for the structurally different roles which men and women have.

The study of Endo culture in Kenya, shows that social space is divided according to a value system which draws on the divisions between women and men in this society. Other areas of conflict and tension are expressed in terms of the opposition between males and females. Although men are dominant in this society, a position

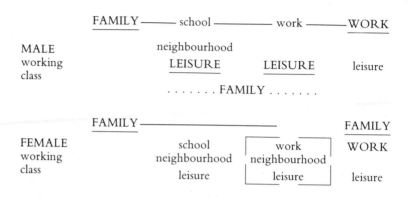

Figure 7.1

Source: Powell and Clarke (1976) p. 225.

achieved by making such dominance appear 'natural', their ownership rights in land and stock are circumscribed by the rights which
women have to use of the land. Also much of Endo women's
culture challenges and constrains men's dominance (Moore, 1986).
While women's culture in any society cannot be adequately
conceptualised as marginal to men's and both can only be understood in relation to the other, we need to look more closely at the
implications of the inequality of gender relations at the level of
culture as a whole.

The concept of the 'private' and 'public' spheres of society seems
to imply a symbiotic relationship, but this ignores that in advanced
capitalist or industrial societies the 'public' and instrumental world
of work and politics dominates the world of family and personal
relationships. Although there are problems with the notion of a
dominant culture (see Chapter 2), it does incorporate the idea that
culture includes beliefs, ideas and practices which reflect and
reproduce the relations of power and domination. In this sense,
the dominant culture incorporates aspects of both male and female
cultures, but at the same time, the dominant culture is much more
male-oriented: that is, it reflects the interests and power of men,
rather than women. The male orientation of culture has meant that
until recently women's culture has often been ignored by
sociologists.

Women are also represented in popular culture as attractive sexual objects for men. Feminists have argued that such sexual attractiveness implies that women should be passive rather than instrumental or powerful. They are powerful only as mothers. This cultural prescription of passivity and non-directiveness for women is contradicted in Britain in the 1990s by the fact that until recently the two most prominent people in our political system have been women – the Queen and the Prime Minister. This contradiction is solved in cultural terms by the Queen being seen as 'above' politics, a symbol of national unity and continuity, given cultural significance by her role as mother (and grandmother) in her own family. She engages in public events and activities which highlight this, allowing the media controlled access to her 'private' sphere so that her family role can be seen to symbolise the 'family' of the United Kingdom. The contradiction of being a powerful public woman has been resolved in Margaret Thatcher's case by calling into play alternative cultural stereotypes: she has been characterised as a bossy headmistress or housekeeper, or a 'nanny' – an extra-powerful surrogate mother. Neither of these women has been allowed to step outside the cultural stereotypes of 'normal' women. Complex symbols come into play to legitimise apparent contradictions and reaffirm the prescription that women and men have different roles and that the public work of politics is for men.

Fictions of all kinds, novels, plays, operas, films, contain alternative representations of gender, but these only make sense to us as readers of these texts because of our knowledge of prescribed or dominant representations. A good example here is the *femme fatale* character, the high-class courtesan, the sexually 'forward' or liberated woman, the Carmen of Bizet's opera, the Bohemian Musette of Puccini's opera and the heroines of modern steamy novels by Judith Krantz and Jackie Collins. (This image is also diffused throughout much of modern clothes and make-up styles suggesting the 'vamp' or the 'tart' – to the middle-ageing writer of this chapter, at least!) Such women are 'the antithesis of demure feminine propriety' but both types 'propagate normative clichés about the typically masculine and feminine, and about the ideal amorous relations between the male and female types as thus characterized' (Pels and Crébas, 1988, pp. 580 and 599–600). The conventional heroine and the 'decadent' femme fatale are both part of the 'bourgeois-romantic' ideal of love in which the woman is unattainable by men, underlining 'the evident truth' that men and women live in two utterly different worlds' (Pels and Crébas, 1988, p. 600; see also Chapter 9).

'Men and boys only'

Sociologists are paying increasing attention to leisure, including sport, another area of Western culture where we can see a clear male-orientation and domination, not simply gender divisions (for class divisions and sport see Chapter 6). Willis draws attention to the idea that performance in sport is based on 'natural' and 'commonsense' differences between the sexes and is central to its ideological operation. On one level, sport appears to have some autonomy and separateness from other areas of society and to be concerned with leisure and enjoyment for both sexes, but at another level it acts as a powerful source of legitimation for the dominant culture. It is not the differences in performance between women and men in themselves, but the way that these are understood as a part of Western culture and the cultural symbols and values which are important: 'to know, more exactly, why it is that women can muster only 90 per cent of a man's strength cannot help us to comprehend, explain or change the massive feeling in our society that a woman has no business flexing her muscles anyway' (Willis, 1985, p. 119)

Historically, as now, sport has been about the formation of male identities, glorifying the qualities of aggression, determination, control, and also the leadership, teamwork and physical fitness required for the public work of government and industry to take place. Recently, 'sports have come to symbolize a national way of life' (Hargreaves, 1986, p. 220) and we saw earlier that symbolically nationalism involves masculinity. At the same time, a major difference in modern sport is that women are both participants and spectators, which has created some interesting cultural changes but left the male-orientation of sport intact. 'There is a very important thread in popular consciousness which sees the very presence of women in sport as bizarre' and this seems to be an expression of the desire to maintain the differentiation between the two sexes. It involves 'reference, all the time to what are taken as the absolute values, the only yardstick, of achievement – *male* achievement' (Willis, 1985, p. 121). Physical achievement is perceived as masculine achievement. Lenskyj's study of Canada and the USA indicates this and shows how once women's physical capacity to engage in sports became accepted, earlier in the twentieth century, a whole range became identified as women's sports which had 'health and beauty functions', while men's sports were still concerned with making boys into 'real' men (Lenskyj, 1986, p. 141).

This concern for reinforcing gender differentiation in sports has remained: 'It is imperative that the masculine concepts of certain sports be retained . . . Male children, both present and future cannot afford to be deprived of yet another factor which influences masculine orientation' (*Physical Educator*, quoted in Lenskyj, 1986, p. 97). 'Locker-room' jokes and rugby-club activities, including bawdy songs, are all part of this cultural process and are separate from and closed to women, to some extent cutting across class divisions (for example, see Lyman, 1987). Although the idea that women and men should play together in sports which involve close body contact is usually expressed in terms of physiological 'mismatching' or sexual impropriety, it functions similarly to retain a clear division between women and men.

Sports culture maintains the reproduction of its masculine orientation by ensuring that the norm of performance and style is masculine (and by definition heterosexual). One aspect of this has been the representation of sportswomen as 'masculine' – not 'real' women. The suggestion, from the 1950s, that some East European female athletes were sexually abnormal – not biologically women – is an extreme example of this. Another aspect of this masculine norm has been to discourage Western sportswomen from adopting 'masculine' styles and mannerisms, to remain 'feminine', laying stress on their achievements as sports*women*. Yet another way of retaining this essentially masculine orientation is the alternative representation of certain kinds of sport as suitable for women, in particular those aesthetically pleasing sports which have developed more in recent years, for example, figure-skating, rhythmic gymnastics and synchronised swimming. Stress on the essential 'feminine' sexuality of sportswomen 'evident in the "cutesy-pie routines" of some gymnasts, figure-skaters and synchronised swimmers' and the clothes worn by ice-skaters and tennis-players, indicates these are sports of a different kind from the truly 'masculine' ones – soccer, rugby, snooker and so on' (Lenskyj, 1986, p. 105). Media presentation enhances the emphasis on appearance in the spectator-oriented 'aesthetic' sports, while reinforcing the dominance of masculine sports by far greater coverage. It was indicated earlier that sport has become a national symbol and the reproduction of gender differentiation within it both reinforces gender divisions in society and the identification of the dominant masculine culture with a national way of life.

Women's work and men's leisure

The wider area of leisure, is also an 'engendered' part of culture (Clarke and Critcher, (eds) 1985; Green, Hebron and Woodward, 1987) illustrating both the separation and connectedness of female and male culture. Most writers agree that leisure is analytically separate from work, although there is an articulation and in some cases an overlap between work and leisure. Given most women's involvement in domestic work – which is separate from wage-labour but has no clear timespan – the notion of leisure as separate from work for women is problematic. '[W]hat is most obvious is the apparent absence of leisure as a significant force in the lives of many women' (Deem, 1987, p. 210), and that whereas men have 'work and 'not work', women have only 'less work' and 'more leisure' (Stanley, 1987). While there are material constraints affecting women's access to leisure facilities – lack of money, transport, child-care and safety in public places – it is the cultural meanings of leisure activities which are important here (Wimbush and Talbot, (eds) 1988).

A reflection and reinforcement of male dominance in Western societies is the way that male 'policing' of women in public places occurs (Stanley, 1987, p. 2; Green, Hebron and Woodward, 1987). Such policing involves marginalisation of women in male preserves like golf and sports clubs, control of space – playgrounds, sports fields, pubs and drinking clubs – and intrusion of men into the 'private' leisure spaces of women. An example of the latter is the sports centre where one of the writers attends a women's 'keep-fit' class. Boys and young men habitually watch this class in a voyeuristic and often amused manner, through a glass partition. This is acknowledged by the teacher's injunctions to 'ignore the fellas because they can't do the exercises anyway', or 'let yourselves go, there are no fellas watching', and sometimes by management who cover the glass with a blind. Similarly, Farran's study of an outdoor water-pursuits centre shows the girls were constantly splashed and joked at by the boys. A special girls' afternoon was organised each week 'cos some girls want time to be on their own without the lads messin' so they can have a laugh and play on the rafts and that' (Farran, 1986, p. 28, quoting a participant).

It might appear that youth clubs are places where young males and females participate in a shared culture but historically they developed to control and contain young working-class males. Recent studies in Britain show that such clubs still largely provide leisure facilities for young males. Nava argues that 'outside the home, girls are observers of boys' activity and boys are observers and *guardians* of girls' passivity . . . thus the policing of girls is assured' (Nava, 1984, p. 12). She shows also that boys 'lay claim to the territory of the club and inhibit attempts by girls to assert their independence from them': through control of space, enforcing a 'double standard' of sexual morality and ridiculing gender inappropriate behaviour as unfeminine (ibid, p. 13).

Men's domination of cultural space in the British pub and the American bar, emphasises male solidarity; the importance of the pub or bar as a centre of leisure activity for many men is underlined by the numerous television beer advertisements depicting pubs as places of hearty masculine activity, often after various sporting heroics. Pubs are also areas where work and leisure overlap – business deals may be transacted, work problems discussed and informal deals agreed there. Although the male camaraderie of pubs is intersected by social class they are essentially cultural spaces where women are tolerated only within clearly defined parameters. British soap operas like *Coronation Street*, *East Enders* and *The Archers*, and the American comedy series *Cheers*, all feature pubs (or bars) as community centres, portraying women in very different roles from men in these places.

Hey (1986) suggests there has been considerable continuity from the Victorian period when drinking was associated with male virility, the only women to be tolerated in pubs were prostitutes and barmaids, and drunken women were associated with sexual immorality. Even today, the stereotype of a barmaid is a woman who is both sexual and maternal and there is a fund of jokes to emphasise this. Upper-class male clubs and lower-class working-men's clubs are able to exclude women completely (because they are private – see, for example, Rogers, 1988). Although pubs are public spaces they are not considered places where respectable women go alone and those who do are likely to be subjected to various forms of sexual harassment as a way of underlining that 'their place' is elsewhere (see Green, Hebron and Woodward, 1987, p. 86.) Groups of women are less likely to be harassed. The mythology of the pub emphasises it as a place where men can escape from women, particularly wives, but masculine culture also emphasises women's sexuality as something to be controlled by 'their' men, a fact underlined by the 'soft porn' calendars often found in bars largely frequented by men – the old-style public bar, rather than the lounge. However, the pub is increasingly a place to which respectable women can be taken by a male escort and this underlines the centrality of men to women's leisure activities, and how male and female cultures intersect.

In Western societies where a high value is placed on such activity for creating stable relationships and socialising children, women's leisure frequently involves the family. In contrast to men, women's leisure activities are often confined to their own homes or those of friends and relatives. Studies show the importance of both friendship networks and what we might call 'emotional work' for the 'less work and more leisure' activities which are part of a specifically female culture (Stanley, 1987; Deem, 1986). Women's culture concerns the reproduction of femininity, and the latter involves much of the emotional work of society.

Private girls and public boys

Earlier, we mentioned work on youth subcultures. Now we will expand on theoretical and empirical links between these and the broader notion of women's and men's cultures. Although the concept of subculture is problematic, subcultural studies of young working-class men in Britain claim to tell us something about the culture of class relationships and its articulation and intersection with

CALDERDALE
COLLEGE LIBRARY
HALIFAX

masculine culture (also see Chapter 6). Working-class male youth subcultures are said to be an aspect of class resistance, their deviant and often bizarre style of dress a way of making sense of their marginal position in society (Hall and Jefferson (eds) 1976; Willis, 1978; Mungham and Pearson (eds) 1976; Hebdige, 1979). Feminist criticism of such studies is first, that gender-blind male researchers have ignored girls; second, that when girls have appeared they have been seen either as marginal to subcultural groups or simply as 'sex objects' for the lads; and third, that subcultural theory has not dealt with sexuality, sexual relations and the relationship of subcultures to this aspect of the wider parent culture (McRobbie and Garber, 1976; Brake, 1985; Frith, 1984). The gender-blindness of subcultural studies is being corrected by research on girls by women sociologists, but to the extent that subcultural research emphasises the 'public' rather than 'private' side of those cultures it omits girls, and girls' and boys' interaction. Research on male subcultures stressing their exclusive masculinity fails to inform us how young men make the transition from these groups to the shared culture of domestic life. On the face of it, the emphasis on masculinity and male bonding is not functional for 'domestic culture'.

McRobbie and Garber state that if girls have not been simply ignored but really are marginal or absent from subcultures then the reasons for this are important. They argue that it is women's different structural position from that of men which makes them problematic in subcultural terms: their absence from or marginality to male subcultures reflects and reinforces their primarily domestic role (also see Brake, 1985, and Frith, 1984). We need to ask therefore, where are girls and what are they doing when young men are involved in subcultural activities?

Before attempting to answer this it is important to mention a further criticism of subcultural studies. In Britain at least, by their focus on the deviant and bizarre, they tell us little about most 'ordinary' working-class youths (Cohen, 1980, pp. iff). It is possible that they are involved in a shared culture with young women rather than the culture of their peers in subcultures. In the popular soap opera *Neighbours*, and other series now screened in Britain at young people's peak viewing-time, conventional romantic girl–boy relationships are shown, but girls and boys are also shown studying and pursuing leisure activities in mixed groups. Earlier we showed that women's leisure activity is constrained and defined in terms of their domestic role and relationship with men. Young women's and men's culture prepares them for the engendered culture of adult women and men. Although they spend leisure and informal parts of their schooling with the same sex peers, both sexes are involved in the culture of romantic love, through dating, courting and 'going steady'. Yet studies of girls' and young women's culture show this to be very different from young male culture and there are tremendous contradictions between the ways that each sex views sexuality and relationships with the opposite sex (Griffin, 1985; McRobbie and Nava, (eds) 1984; McRobbie, 1978; Smith, 1978; Thompson, 1984).

The origins and nature of these contradictions lie in the wider gendered culture. Dominant male culture and subcultures which draw from it emphasise male sexual aggression and control over women. Part of this is the injunction that while sexual activity for young men is a sign of proper masculinity, such activity for girls is prohibited:

> Girls have to be sexually inviting but not sexually experienced; attractive enough to raise the boy's status but not so experienced that there is no kudos in having a relationship with her. They are expected to be a surrogate wife, servicing the boy domestically (Brake, 1985, p. 172).

Some writers have argued that much of masculine culture, including the ritualised aggression and antagonism often expressed against women indicates an underlying deep fear of women's sexuality (for example, see Hey, 1986, and Whitehead, 1976). A more convincing explanation is that control over women's sexuality represents a continuance of male dominance in the domestic sphere (for example, see Green, Hebron and Woodward, 1987). Proprietorial terms used by men 'my woman/girl/bird/piece', 'the wife', 'her indoors', all symbolise such control. Supposed male fear of women's sexuality perhaps indicates that male control of women is always tenuous, conflicting with other cultural prescriptions: romantic love, reverence for motherhood and so on.

Willis has attempted to show the functional relationship between boys' 'anti-school' masculinist culture, the requirements of labour and shopfloor culture (Willis, 1977 and in Clarke *et al.*, 1979). Similarly, there is a functional relationship between girls' culture and the requirements of women's domestic labour. Boys are allowed more free time away from home than girls, who are more likely to be engaged in domestic chores or activities like baby sitting. Girls' domestic obligations enable parents to keep a closer watch on them than boys and this serves to control adult female sexual activity. Studies show that while all young women and men have to negotiate with parents for time and space away from home and with friends, girls are subject to much closer constraints concerning the time they arrive home, where they go and who they go with (Frith, 1984, p. 52ff). Frith points out that these are expectations for girls rather than descriptions of actual behaviour, but we might add that the cultural penalties for not meeting these expectations are high: girls who engage in the same promiscuous sexual behaviour as boys are likely to be labelled as problems (Hudson, 1984, pp. 46–7). Sexual experimentation and activity may also be a form of individualistic cultural resistance for girls, although at the same time it reproduces their sexual subordination (for example, see Griffin, 1985). Even if we reject explanations of young people's subcultural activity as a form of class resistance and see 'youth culture' as an expression of autonomy before taking on adult roles, ways in which girls express their autonomy during this transition period are subject to greater controls.

At the same time that girls are proscribed in their activities, they are immersed in a teenage female culture which is part of the transition to adult female culture. 'Bedroom culture' involves a girl, with her 'special' girl friends, learning the paraphernalia of femininity – clothes, make-up, sexual knowledge and the myths of romantic love. Since these cultural activities take place in the home, mothers and other adult women may be peripherally involved. This culture utilises popular magazines for teenage girls together with adult women's magazines (McRobbie, 1982; Walkerdine, 1984). Teenage magazines prepare girls for womanhood by familiarising them with the world of love and romance. Women's magazines are concerned with women's work – getting and keeping 'a man', children, cooking and other domestic work, and more recently, how to combine this with a career (Winship, 1987; Ferguson, 1983). Although middle-class women have more cultural options than working-class women, all girls and women are immersed in female culture to some extent.

'It's a man's world'

Gendered culture is based upon and helps to resolve a fundamental contradiction in Western societies: the assumption that men live in a man's world of work and women in a women's world of home and family. Men's culture does not appear functional for domestic life as such – only for becoming and remaining the breadwinner. Similarly, women's culture does not appear to incorporate the fact that most women spend much of their lives in paid labour, as well as domestic labour. The partial resolution of this contradiction is in ensuring, through the process of 'separate' male and female cultures, that women continue to carry out the emotional work involved in 'social reproduction' (see Mackintosh, 1981) by giving this work priority, whatever their position in the waged labour force. Men are thus 'free' to concentrate on their role of breadwinner, requiring the male 'bonding' discussed earlier and strategies for successfully making a way through the occupational structure, including ways of dealing with authority and power.

Women in waged work, full- and part-time, continue to define themselves primarily as women – as mothers and wives (for example, see Sharpe, 1984; Hunt, 1980). This definition does not rest simply on the material division of labour and gendered segregation of the labour market, but on the lived culture in which women and men are immersed outside the occupational structure. The working-class culture of the shop-floor is essentially masculine and aggressive 'masculinity' a prerequisite for male survival in the world of work (see also Morgan, 1987; Hearn and Parkin, 1987). Masculine culture then, is the vehicle by which the material world of work penetrates and dominates the rest of culture. In the intersection between female culture and the rest of culture this relationship is reversed. Feminine culture is taken from the home into the (public) workplace by women workers.

Recent ethnographic studies show how female culture of romantic love, marriage and children forms part of workplace culture. These themes are constantly discussed by women workers. Many tobacco-factory workers in Pollert's study, for example, defined themselves as full-time wives and mothers despite working full-time (Pollert, 1981). Westwood's study of hosiery workers (many belonging to ethnic minorities) shows that women's strategies for making alienating work more bearable include 'domestication' of the workplace: bringing in domestic work, decorating machines with family photos and celebrating birthdays, engagements, weddings, and births (Westwood, 1984). Some of the rituals involved in these celebrations show women's awareness and resentment of their subordination. Female workers are often supervised by men and part of shopfloor culture revolves around this. Women (and men) use sexual strategies including banter and outright harassment. Interesting parallels can be drawn here with Endo women's culture in Kenya, where women come together and physically ill-treat a man who has mistreated his wife and also engage in ritual verbal abuse of men during initiation rites (Moore, 1986, pp. 174–7).

Ironically, it is by colluding with the very culture which is part of their subordination that women workers in the West develop a shopfloor culture enabling them to function adequately as both wage-workers and domestic labourers. Studies of women workers in typically female occupations show clearly that female culture is an integral part of such work and a most important way of ensuring that women remain low-paid, low-status workers (Cunnison, 1986; Finch and Groves (eds) 1983; Ramazanoglu, 1987). By 'naturalising' caring and emotional skills female culture operates to validate the existing division of labour in society.

Alternative gendered cultures

We must beware of portraying women and men as passively manipulated, simply because the cultural and ideological content of media representations are more easily accessible to us than knowledge about culture 'as it is lived'. Race and class cut across gender and we need to acknowledge the differences and similarities, between native and ethnic minority groups in Britain, for example (Bryan *et al.*, 1985; CCCS, 1982; also see Chapter 5). We also need to distinguish actual cultural behaviour from that which is prescribed (Welsh, 1989a). For individuals within a marriage or family situation, or indeed in a wider cultural sense, the balance of power between males and females and the way in which their gendered subjectivity is realised may be different from the cultural norms. We also need to note the existence of alternative sexualities and alternative gendered cultures and the way in which these articulate with 'mainstream' gendered culture. As we have indicated earlier, the status and role of homosexuality and lesbianism varies in different societies (Whitehead, 1981).

A study of Swahili Muslims in Mombasa, for example, shows that male homosexuality operates on a patron–client basis, alongside heterosexual marriage. It provides economic opportunities for poor young men. These men are admitted to the secluded company of women, along with close kin and children, but they join in religious rituals with men, and women are excluded from these. In a society where wealthy men hold most power, homosexual men are in competition with women, but they do not have to attract men with their domestic accomplishments, as women do. In this sense, homosexual men in Mombasa remain part of male culture. Lesbian women remain part of women's culture too, and such women compete with each other in conventional feminine terms. Lesbianism is also a way in which wealthy women develop an influence and power not possessed by most women in Swahili culture. It is suggested that rank is more important in Mombasa than gender divisions and crossing sex boundaries appears to be of less note than crossing those of rank (Shepherd, 1987).

In Britain and America many aspects of male homosexual culture echo the dominant male culture in their emphasis on violence and power. It is possible to argue that this 'gay machismo' is less threatening to conventional gender divisions than the cultural style of the 'effeminate' homosexual (Humphries, 1985). Since the 1970s in particular, lesbianism for many women is a consciously chosen way of life and a political rejection of inequalities inherent in Western heterosexual culture. It allows women to be involved in an alternative female culture which nevertheless connects to 'mainstream' female culture. Despite rejecting the aggressiveness of male–female relationships, some lesbians do act out these roles with their partners, as male homosexuals do. It appears that our socially constructed gendered subjectivities and hence culture operate at a psychological level which a conscious change of cultural style does not entirely alter (Cartledge and Ryan (eds) 1983; Snitow *et al.*, 1984; Billington, 1982).

In discussing dominant patterns of gendered culture in the West, there is a danger that we ignore its heterogeneity and also post-modernist criticism of false generalisation and essentialism (for example, Fraser and Nicholson, 1988; Weedon, 1987). Largely as the result of the gay liberation and feminist movements of the 1970s, there have been attempts by women and men to develop alternative or 'counter-hegemonic' femininities and masculinities (Welsh, 1989b). Amongst these, apart from several varieties of lesbianism and male homosexuality, we might mention successful and powerful career women, 'emasculated' men who are heterosexual but reject a dominant masculinity, male heads of single-parent families who carry out nurturing roles, and reversed-role marriages. However, although these are alternative *roles*, hegemonic processes ensure they are incorporated into the dominant gendered cultures and it is difficult to demonstrate that these roles are much more than individual or small group resistances. The hegemonic processes which ensure the reproduction of gendered cultures do not exclude cultural heterogeneity, contradiction and resistance.

8 Education

Selecting from culture

Education is a major transmitter of culture and from Matthew Arnold to F. R. Leavis, debates about English or British culture have been in part, debates about education. In *The Long Revolution* (1961, 1965), Raymond Williams focused on this connection and made it theoretically explicit. He notes that although we often assume that education is 'a settled body of teaching and learning, and . . . [that] the only problem it presents to us is that of distribution', this is misleading:

> It is not only that the way in which education is organised can be seen to express, consciously and unconsciously, the wider organisation of a culture and a society . . . It is also that the content of education, which is subject to great historical variation, . . . expresses . . . certain basic elements in the culture, what is thought of as 'an education' being in fact a particular selection, a particular set of emphases and omissions (Williams, 1965, p. 145).

Williams sees what is defined as education in a particular society as being a selection from its culture. It has three inextricably related but distinguishable purposes – to pass on:

(i)   accepted behaviour and values of society;
(ii) general knowledge and attitudes appropriate to an educated man [sic];
(iii) a particular skill by which he will earn a living.

To the extent that the 'pattern of culture' in a particular society is generally accepted, education towards it will be seen as a natural training which everyone must acquire. However, when society is changing or there are alternative cultures, education can become a contested area and one group's 'education' can be another's 'indoctrination'. Williams traces English male education from the sixth century to show not only the historically varying conceptions of education but also 'the actual and complex relations between the three aims cited'. Changing definitions of education are clearly seen to be related to the changing character of English society and to the outcome of conflicts between different social groups.

The first schools were for training priests and monks. Latin grammar (including comprehension and commentary) was their basis and remained the basis of academic education for a very long time. However, the curriculum gradually broadened as schools proliferated and with the establishment in Oxford (in the thirteenth century) of the first colleges, the beginnings of a university. Although education remained within a firm Christian framework the concept of a 'liberal' education as a general preparation for specialised study of law, medicine, or theology began to form. The development of philosophy, medicine and law was accompanied by the universities struggling for their independence from direct supervision by the Church. Their success was accompanied by the creation of virtually independent schools, such as Winchester and Eton, in close relation to the colleges. This school and college system was paralleled by a chivalry system in which young boys from noble households were sent as pages to great houses and trained to knighthood, and by an apprenticeship system for craftsmen and tradesmen. Education was vocational and organised in relation to 'a firm structure of inherited and destined status and condition' (Williams, 1965, p. 152) from which women and the labouring poor were largely excluded.

The Reformation reduced the power of the Church over the grammar schools, but the schools remained central. Often sponsored as private foundations, the curriculum was narrow and largely untouched by the Renaissance. It was in the Dissenting Academies, set up by religious Non-conformists excluded from traditional institutions, that the curriculum really began to change in the eighteenth century. Mathematics, geography, modern languages and the physical sciences were included and a new, recognisably modern definition of a general education developed. There was some development too, of the university curriculum, to include mathematics and science, but universities (Oxford, Cambridge and later, St Andrews and Edinburgh) still largely served to train the clergy, and adhered to the old curriculum. Legal and medical training were mainly outside them as was training in the new professions in science, engineering and the arts. Women were completely excluded until the late nineteenth century.

Education for the poor was scanty but problems associated with increasing urbanisation gave rise to the Charity School movement, from the end of the seventeenth century. Its intention was the 'moral rescue' of the poor coupled with a more formal notion of an elementary education suitable for that social class. Education of the poor, however, was not universally regarded as a good thing:

> It is doubtless desirable that the poor should be generally instructed in *reading*, if it were only for the best purposes – that they may read the Scriptures. As to *writing* and *arithmetic*, it may be apprehended that such a degree of knowledge would produce in them a disrelish for the laborious occupations of life' (quoted in Williams, 1965, p. 156).

These sentiments of a JP of 1807, echo those of Bernard de Mandeville's 'An Essay on Charity and Charity Schools' of 1723:

> To make the Society Happy and People Easy under the meanest Circumstances, it is requisite that great numbers of them should be Ignorant as well as Poor . . . The Welfare and Felicity there-fore of every State and Kingdom, require that the Knowledge of the Working Poor should be confin'd within the Verge of their Occupations, and never extended beyond what relates to their Calling (Mandeville, 1970, p. 294).

Williams notes that by the end of the eighteenth century the shift from a system of social divisions based on localities, to a national system of social classes was more or less complete and its result a new kind of class-determined education (also see Chapter 6). 'Higher education became a virtual monopoly, excluding the new working class, and the idea of universal education, except within the narrow limits of moral rescue, was widely opposed as a matter of principle' (Williams, 1965, pp. 156–7).

Gradually, schools were provided for the poor but at first they gave training of a very limited kind and the reports of major parlia-mentary commissions in the nineteenth century all emphasised the class- and gender-based nature of education, with the secondary level reserved for middle- and upper-class males. Nevertheless, modern notions of a liberal education for all, including women, were taking shape under the twin pressures of the growth of industry and democracy (see Chapter 1). The growth of an organised working class, demanding education was a significant factor, although it failed to get precisely what it wanted (Johnson, 1979). It was also widely recognised – for example, in the Forster Act of 1870 – that industrial prosperity depended on the speedy provision of education for the workforce. The fundamental nature of education and its role in relation to the economy and the general character of a society was fiercely debated throughout the nineteenth century.

Williams distinguishes three responses amongst those who wished to reform education: a genuine response to the growth of democracy by men such as Mill, Carlyle, Ruskin and Arnold; a protective or moral rescue response to the growth of democracy from those who feared the extension of the franchise and believed 'our future masters . . . should at least learn their letters'; and a practical vocational response from those who linked education with industrial prosperity. The arguments of the nineteenth-century debate were complex, and strange alliances between groups of protagonists with opposed principles were formed. However, three broad groupings, still recognisable today, are identified:

(i)   *Industrial trainers* defined education narrowly, in terms of future adult work and its associated social character – habits of regularity, self-discipline, obedience and trained effort.

(ii) Their definition was contested by *public educators*, a group which believed that governments had a duty to recognise the 'natural right' to be educated in a broader sense, as an essential aspect of democracy. This group nevertheless included individuals with 'widely differing attitudes to the rise of democracy and of working class organisation' (Williams, 1965, p. 162).

(iii) Equally opposed to a narrow vocationally oriented definition of education were the *old humanists* who did much to define a 'liberal education' in the modern sense, but were concerned about its vulgarisation if extended to the masses. They were often fundamentally antipathetic to democracy (a similar position to elitest theorists of culture discussed in Chapter 1).

The public educators tended to support the industrial trainers in their drive to extend education, whilst allying themselves to the old humanists in fighting to retain a wider concept of education. The outcome was a compromise but, unfortunately from Williams's point of view, the reforms more strongly reflected the industrial than the democratic argument (except in the case of women's education, which Williams ignores). A major reorganisation of elementary, secondary and higher education along lines, still broadly followed today, was accomplished.

Williams's discussion of the process of 'selecting from culture' in English education draws our attention to the way in which divisions and conflicts in society are reflected in struggles to define education. He is on the side of the democrats, the public educators, and believes in the need for common schools and a common curriculum, but does not believe that the question of our common culture has been addressed. He sees the curriculum today as reflecting a compromise between inherited and new interests. Particular forms of knowledge have been included or excluded as the outcomes of struggles and they do not represent a genuine common culture.

Writing from a different political perspective, G. H. Bantock shares Williams's view of education as a selection from culture, grappling with the problems which this posed in the mid- to late 1960s. Bantock is not concerned with the democratic argument. His position has some affinity with that of nineteenth-century 'old humanists', identifying a 'high' cultural tradition based on literacy and preserved by a small minority, but also presents a view of education for the masses. He shares T. S. Eliot's denial of a common culture, explaining the failure of mass education by the attempt to force an alien literary culture on the masses (Bantock, 1971).

The culture of the school, Bantock argues, is the 'high culture' of the book and 'it nowhere seriously touches those cultural experiences in terms of which a considerable majority are going to spend the rest of their lives' (ibid, p. 28). It largely excludes teachers, drawn from the upper working or lower middle classes, as well as pupils. Therefore cultural apathy reigns in our colleges and schools and 'no organisational changes will improve our education if the teachers are not able to provide classes with vital cultural experiences' (ibid, p. 42).

Instead of force-feeding children a diluted version of high culture we need a curriculum with roots in the oral and mythic traditions of a folk culture. Bantock defines a folk culture as 'one which arises largely out of the face-to-face interests of the folk, and out of their primary experience' (ibid, p. 48). Whilst reading and writing are important, this culture is identified essentially in terms of intuition, emotion and creativity, rather than abstract rational analysis. It finds expression in motor skills and communal participation. Folk culture predates industrialisation. In some ways it has been replaced by pop culture, which appeals to the mythic, intuitive and emotional, but is oriented to consumption rather than to participation, whereas folk culture is grounded in the organic life of the people, in their work and their communities. Bantock's argument here is similar to 'mass society' theories discussed in Chapter 1. He argues that the ills of our education system can only be remedied by providing cultural life-chances, rooted in the real cultural life of the people, rather than simple equality of opportunity.

Williams's and Bantock's work is relevant to contemporary curriculum debates because it raises issues about what counts as education (what to teach, to whom) and links between education and the wider culture of a society. Bantock is not concerned with social and economic opportunity but raises important questions about the quality of cultural experiences provided by education in a culturally plural society. Williams sees the contested nature of the curriculum as clearly connected with issues of democracy and equality. In arguing that the achievement of a common general secondary education for all, in Britain, would involve much more than wider distribution of opportunities and resources, he anticipates curriculum debates of the 1970s (also see Squires, 1987).

Culture, structure and educational inequality

British and American sociologists of education were, however, preoccupied with problems of educational inequality conceived as a question of distribution. Early research revealed a systematic bias in achievement, against children from lower socioeconomic strata, and the argument of Williams's 'industrial trainers' found expression in 'human capital' theory (see Karabel and Halsey, 1977). In addition, the liberal individualistic ideologies of Britain and America are built on a presupposition of fairness, expressed in terms of equality of opportunity, which demands a manifestly fair education system (in part the 'public educator's' argument). In Britain after the Second World War emphasis was on providing empirical evidence to influence policy-makers to improve access to secondary and higher education. In the 1960s, in addition, selection of children for different types of secondary education (academic or vocational) was criticised and the Labour government began the change to comprehensive education. Following the Robbins Report(1963), higher education was dramatically expanded and the growth of sociology and the sociology of education was a direct result of this.

By the late 1950s and early 1960s the increasing doubts of sociologists about the efficacy of policies aimed at bringing about greater equality coincided with critiques of the dominant paradigms of structural-functionalism and positivism. In common with other areas of sociology, the sociology of education shifted its interest towards culture and in particular the culture of educational 'under-achievers'.

In Britain, several studies drew attention to the connection between working-class culture and educational failure (Mays, 1962; Jackson and Marsden, 1962). Whereas Williams had related the content of education to the problem of inequality, these studies treated culture, in particular the culture of children's homes, as an independent variable. They focused on supposed cultural deficits of working class and, particularly in America – ethnic-minority cultures and how to 'compensate' for them. Bernstein's important early work (for example, Bernstein, 1974) stressing the discontinuity between working-class home and school culture, was partially misunderstood and his notion of restricted and elaborated language codes seen as providing strong support for the notion of cultural deficit. Even David Hargreaves's (1967) and Colin Lacey's studies (1970), unusual in placing emphasis on the interaction between home and school cultures in the process of schooling, did not seriously question the prevailing definition of education. Typical policy outcomes of this period were pre-school 'compensatory education' programmes and 'educational priority areas' in Britain and 'Headstart' in America.

Lack of success of such schemes, theoretical developments within sociology and wider political and intellectual movements, contributed to a further shift in focus. In the 1970s curriculum content claimed the attention of sociologists, whose concern was with greater equality in education and society and who carried the torch of the 'public educators'. The 'new sociology of education' heralded by the volume, *Knowledge and Control: New Directions for the Sociology of Education* (Young (ed.) 1971), was united by the intention of questioning the 'taken for granted' nature of education. Earlier work was seen as simply 'taking' problems predefined by educators rather than 'making' the assumptions of the educators problematic in themselves. Bernstein commented:

> How a society selects, classifies, distributes, transmits and evaluates the educational knowledge it considers to be public, reflects both the distribution of power and the principles of social control . . . Educational knowledge is a major regulator of the structure of experience (quoted in Young, (ed.) 1971, p. 47).

This summarises issues now deemed central and they recall those signalled earlier by Williams.

Focusing on how curriculum knowledge is selected does not, as such, imply a relativist stance on the nature of knowledge, but there was certainly an inclination towards such a position amongst 'new' sociologists of education. This perceived relativism was the focus of attack by liberal philosophers of education such as Paul H. Hirst who were themselves seeking to defend a common curriculum based on distinct 'forms of knowledge', conceived as being free from cultural bias (see, for example, Hirst, 1974, and Pring, 1972).

The new sociology of education reflected the range of 'new' perspectives emerging more generally in sociology (Whitty, 1985). The phenomenological, interpretative tradition had the strongest initial impact and focused attention on the construction and maintenance of social reality, in the everyday culture of schools, through the negotiation of meanings (see, for example, Keddie, in Young, (ed.), 1971; Woods, 1983). The 'structural' tradition incorporated neo-Durkheimian, neo-Marxian and French structuralist influences and gained ascendancy as the general impact of structural critiques of cultural studies was felt (see above, Chapter 2).

Interest thus shifted to the role of education as an aspect of culture and to the way in which it reflects and contributes to the reproduction of class power. Whilst the phenomenological tradition generated an enormous amount of often-under-theorised empirical research, the structural tradition was preoccupied with theoretical questions. Work in a neo-Marxist vein focused on capitalist economic relations. It was influenced by the Americans, Bowles and Gintis (1976) and the more sophisticated analyses of Althusser. Neo-Durkheimian questions concerning the legitimation of patterns of class power were raised by the work of Bourdieu and Bernstein which centred more specifically on issues concerning the curriculum and examinations. Later work, such as Sharp and Green's study of social control in a primary school (1975) and Willis's *Learning to Labour* (1977), has tried to bridge the gulf between structural and interpretative perspectives (which are tensions within sociology more generally) and begin to explore the complexities increasingly perceived in the interrelationships between culture and structure.

Work in both traditions recognised the importance of explicit curriculum content and 'the hidden curriculum'. This refers to values and patterns of behaviour which, although not formally taught, are integral to the process of schooling. Bourdieu, for instance, links his notion of 'cultural capital' to styles of teaching and learning, patterns of thinking and of using language, rather than the content of the curriculum as such (Bourdieu and Passerant, 1977). He argues that the advantage of middle class over working class (and Parisian over provincial) children is maintained through possession of cultural capital, their familiarity with the middle-class cultural forms – literature, art and logic – of the education system, an explanation of working-class failure not unlike Bantock's (also see discussion of Gouldner in Chapter 6). Bourdieu, however, questions the justice of an élite culture. He argues that cultural domination by the middle class is maintained by 'symbolic violence'. This involves creating an illusion of deserved superiority, through success in a system which, although apparently fair, is rigged in its favour from the start.

Whilst class issues predominated in British and European work, in the USA, the cultures of blacks, native Indians and other ethnic minorities were problematised. Until fairly recently, little attention was given to gender and the role of female cultures in education, but this gender-blindness has been challenged by feminists and many of the theoretical concepts developed recently in the area of education and culture can be used to analyse gender in this context (Arnot and Weiner (eds) 1987; Weiner and Arnot (eds) 1987; also see Chapter 7).

Industry, education and the two cultures

By 1969, the 'progressive' developments of the public educators were under attack and a return to 'traditional standards' advocated. In Britain this was marked by the publication of a series of 'Black Papers' initiated by Cox and Dyson (Cox and Dyson, 1969). This right-wing attack was followed up by a speech, in 1976, by James Callaghan, the Labour Prime Minister. He suggested that the education system should become more accountable to popular wishes and more responsive to the needs of industry. Science education, for example, required a more technological bias towards practical applications in industry. This ushered in the Labour Party's 'Great Debate' (see Department of Education and Science, 1977.) Questioning of the 'progressive' reforms of the late 1960s and early 1970s was joined by forces further to the left. The effectiveness of educational reforms in creating social change became an issue for structurally oriented sociologists of education (see Bernstein, 1970 and 1977). The CCCS volume, *Unpopular Education* (1981), noted that the reforms were unpopular with working-class parents who felt their children were being denied the basic skills they required (a point borne out by the much-publicised William Tyndale dispute).

Amidst the strands of this debate a strong vocationalist ('industrial trainers') argument is clear. In the context of the 'Great Debate', the demands of industry are linked with fears about so-called educational standards. Industry is deemed to require an intelligent, highly educated work force and the education system is accused of failing to supply it. Roy Edgely has cogently argued, however, that modern industrial skills generally demand a low level of intelligence and education (Edgely, 1977). Employers seek obedience, a sense of discipline and loyalty and place these above academic attainment. 'The industrial demand for a *more educated* workforce lies in the hope that more education *of the kind suggested* will help to restore the discipline needed in the subordinate ranks of industry's political hierarchy.' In support of this contention he quotes a member of the Harvard Business School:

> I suggest that the excessive educational and skill specification is a serious mistake and potential hazard to our economic and social system. We will hurt individuals, raise labour costs improperly, create disillusion and resentment, and destroy valid job standards

by setting standards that are not truly needed for a given task (Edgely, 1977, p. 29).

It is perhaps not surprising, then, that the demand for education to meet the needs of industry has been linked, in both Britain and America, with an attack on liberal views and a demand to get back to 'basics'. A modern American 'public educator's' point of view strangely mirrors the fears Bernard de Mandeville expressed in 1723 (quoted earlier):

> General education helps to develop attitudes and dispositions which do not dispose students to a later acceptance of the disciplinary requirements of the workplace . . . [But] when the English teacher's job becomes instruction in effective letter writing (to the exclusion of expressive composition and literature), then the English class no longer offers an occasion for unwanted attitudes and dispositions . . . Despite its claims for a restoration of traditional learning, the implementation of the back-to-basics ideal results in the decomposition of more general subject matter into specific technical skills (quoted in Whitty, 1985, p. 112).

Explicit emphasis on skill actually conceals a real process of 'deskilling', in Braverman's sense of separating low-level skills from the more theoretical knowledge connected with greater control (Braverman, 1974). This process can be linked with developments like the introduction of teaching 'packages' in schools, which constrain teachers, making it difficult to organise the social relations of the classroom in such a way as to contest the implicit messages in the material (see Apple, 1982; and Shor, 1986).

Science education figures strongly in modern vocationalist arguments and Williams argues that science and technology have never been fully incorporated as dimensions of English 'culture'. In the nineteenth century it was the industrial trainers who saw the practical vocational significance of science and pressed for its inclusion in the school curriculum. The old humanists, defending the 'old' learning and a liberal education, against vocationalism, tended to adopt 'the absurd defensive reaction that all real learning was undertaken without thought of practical advantage' (Williams, 1965, p. 163). This attitude affected the character of the science eventually admitted within the liberal educational framework and an emphasis on the superiority of 'pure' over 'applied' knowledge is still current. Issues posed by the impact of science on our cultural vision and hence on a culturally relevant conception of a general liberal education were addressed by only a few exceptional thinkers, such as T. H. Huxley, who recognised the social significance of a scientific world view.

Culture is still viewed largely as the property of humanists and defined in the traditional élite university curriculum which reflects their anti-industrial bias. Science, seen as the handmaiden of industry, is neither properly appreciated nor subjected to adequate analytical scrutiny. Now, as in the nineteenth century, science education is linked with technical training, not viewed as an important component in general education. It is associated with lower-status institutions – colleges of technology and polytechnics in Britain, community colleges in America (see Weiner, 1981, pp. 132–7).

Twentieth-century industrial trainers in Britain certainly have not had things all their own way since the inauguration of the Great Debate. Whitty (1985, ch. 6), argues that the old humanist lobby, represented by the universities and GCE examination boards, have been able to exploit the tension between the concept of 'standards' and the concept of 'relevance'. They have reasserted their role as upholders of standards and reimposed a conformity on conceptions of school knowledge which had been increasingly challenged in the preceding period, not only by sociologists and progressive and radical teachers, but also from those concerned to make the curriculum serve the needs of industry. It is an interesting comment on the strength of the old humanists that the industrial trainers have been most influential in the lower-status areas of the curriculum and the Manpower Services Commission, a government body outside the education system and the control of the DES, was important in furthering their cause through initiatives such as the Certificate of Pre-vocational Education (CPVE) and the Technical and Vocational Education Initiative. These became a major site of conflict, with GCE boards taking an interest in the CPVE and the views of industrial trainers being taken more into account in setting up the new Secondary Examinations Council and launching the GCSE examinations.

The place of science and technology in education and culture at large is a crucial issue. However, in giving his famous 'two cultures' lecture in 1959, C. P. Snow was crying in as big a wilderness as T. H. Huxley in the nineteenth century (see Chapter 10). The guardians of literary high culture have left largely unasked, questions about ways in which our culture has been changed by science and technology. They recognise a loss of values in modern society, but rather than exploring the challenges of a modern technological society they hark back to a mythical 'golden age' of 'Victorian values' (also see Chapter 1). Some of the most imaginative literary attempts to deal with some of these issues, by feminist writers of science fiction such as Ursula LeGuin and Marge Piercy, are excluded from consideration on the grounds of being both feminist and science fiction and therefore not 'literature'. The question 'what should count as science education?' has not been asked seriously by the old humanists in relation to these wider issues.

Technological culture and school science

Michael Young has related the present form of the British school science curriculum to its roots in the form of abstract science incorporated within the nineteenth-century humanist liberal education framework. The science offered elevates 'pure' science above, and separates it from, technology. It is divided into traditional disciplines and held aloof from daily life and social concerns (Young, 1976). It is inaccessible to the majority of pupils whom it leaves 'scientifically and technologically ignorant in an increasingly technologically dominated society' and generates 'a community of scientists who see the knowledge they are responsible for producing and validating as *necessarily* not available to the community at large' (Young, 1976, p. 51).

The Nuffield reforms introduced in the 1960s did little to change this. Though emphasising experimentation and 'being a scientist for a day' Nuffield science did not relate science to technology or everyday life and often the practical work seemed disconnected from the discipline itself. Moreover, Layton quotes teachers who classed children expecting physics to have something to do with 'trains' or 'cars' as unintelligent whereas those who wanted to know 'how the work fitted into the whole of physics' were seen as intelligent. He comments that this attitude suggests:

CALDERDALE
COLLEGE LIBRARY
HALIFAX

that 'intelligent people are better at physics' and . . . identifies intelligence not only with ability in physics, but with aptitude in a particular approach to physics. Conversely, . . . pupils who were interested in 'practical' applications and 'real life' must therefore be 'unintelligent' (Layton, 1985, pp. 97–8).

Such a view also seems to assume that education is something split off from, and not relevant to, 'real life', not part of 'lived ' culture.

At a time when the new national curriculum is being introduced in Britain it is interesting to consider a provocative paper, 'A Case Against the Core' (West, 1981, pp. 226–36). Science is to form part of the core because of its perceived link with industry's need for a technically literate workforce. West argues that even if this were true, existing syllabuses, from which the core is to be extracted, are unsuitable. In comments similar to those of Layton, he sees A-level physics as legitimated in terms of university degree-course demands and having nothing to do with the broader culture of society. Such a physics education merely gives a general indication of:

> an ability to solve a particular set of intellectual puzzles that have nothing whatsoever to do with the real world of people, politics and the possibilities that exist in the interaction between them. Such qualifications furthermore do not necessarily equip the holder to apply their physics to the real world of industry and commerce . . . (West, p. 232).

West is very much on the side of the public educators, concerned with democracy and social justice. He advocates a science curriculum linked to 'the problems of *being* in modern industrial and post-industrial societies'. So whilst the industrial trainers have assumed that current syllabuses will furnish the science for the 'core', serious questions are being raised about those syllabuses. Some public educators are concerned with science as fundamental to our culture and profoundly critical of what passes for science education.

Very interesting questions have been raised by those concerned with gender differences in science education. Starting from girls' under-achievement in science and the numerical dominance of boys in classes, research has begun to probe the masculine domination of science education. A gendered culture of science education is being revealed. Representation of girls and women in science textbooks, gender differences in 'cultural capital' (science lessons relate more to the interests and experiences that boys bring to them) and the effect of 'masculine' and 'feminine' behaviour in science classes have all been found significant (see, for example, Kelly, 1985). The problem 'is not simply to give equal access to the excluded, but to transform what we mean by science and technology' (Baran, 1987 p. 102). Baran describes an innovative course in a London girls' school which explores technology in 'real-life' contexts, integrating work-place and domestic technology with science and raising social issues about, for example, gender divisions and labour processes.

Education and cultural struggle

It is, nevertheless, the old humanists and the industrial trainers who are in the forefront of current struggles to define the place and form of science education in Britain and these struggles are directly over what Richard Johnson terms the ideological conditions for the mode of production (in Clarke *et al.*, 1979). However, as Johnson also points out, there are cultural elements to which capitalism is *relatively* indifferent, although struggles in those areas may be significant. In the sphere of education it is not surprising then, that some of the most radical curriculum developments have been in the field of art education which, in terms of the new 'core', is one of the frills. It is being starved of resources but, unlike history and social science, its content is not widely perceived as ideologically significant and dangerous to the established social order.

Work of the Department of Cultural Studies of the ILEA's Cockpit Arts Workshop, has centred on photography projects with young people in and out of school. Photography is a powerful medium for a range of reasons: it has popular currency as a leisure pursuit and technological glamour; it is a major means whereby dominant cultural myths are represented – images of glamour, wealth, power, sexuality and so on; and skills to achieve reasonable and powerful results can be quickly acquired. Emphasis is placed on 'establishing a dialogue with young people where they can bring their experience forward in ways they can value and control'. Having developed a practice based on this experience, wider institutional questions can be engaged. In three terms' work on 'territory' what was evident was 'the high degree of serious engagement in questions of their lives; their prospects and likely future, as well as where they had come from. What we realised was how powerfully territory articulated significant meaning' (Dewdney and Lister, 1986. p. 46).

This kind of work has some affinity with that of the Brazilian educator Paulo Freire (see Freire, 1972). His work has inspired radical western educators and his ideas recall those of '*praxis*' Marxists such as Marcuse and Gramsci. In America, the important writings of Michael Apple, Henry Giroux and Ira Shor show Freire's influence, and in Britain it can be felt directly in Chris Searle's work with London schoolchildren (see, for example, Searle, 1973). Freire has worked in Brazil, Chile and America. While his work is concerned largely with the legacy of colonialism it has general application to conditions of oppression. As we saw in Chapter 4, domination involves the imposition of an alien culture which silences the culture of the oppressed. Freire argues that education is never neutral. It is always either for 'domestication' or freedom. Education for freedom is a critical challenging process, committed to, and engaged with, the oppressed in finding a voice for their silenced culture. This culture necessarily contains a critique of the dominant culture and finding a voice initiates a struggle which is likely to be violent and in which the educator participates.

Freire contrasts his concept of 'conscientisation' with a 'banking' concept, where teachers make information deposits into the empty accounts of their students' brains. Conscientisation involves critical awareness of the forces making society and ourselves and of the powers we have to remake ourselves and our conditions. Such a process of education involves teachers in an egalitarian learning relationship with their students. They learn from the students about their conditions, bring skills that the students can utilise on their own behalf, and act with them in collective authorship. The process is one of 'empowerment' and this implies challenging existing power relationships. It contrasts markedly with Bantock's vision of working-class education in a folk culture which can coexist with a literary high culture of the dominant élite. Close connections are made by Freire between self-knowledge (including an understanding of the context of social institutions within which the self develops), personal growth and political action. The consciousness-raising activity of feminists, where women work in groups and struggle to find a voice, a culture, illustrates this well. In expressing their experience, women find themselves necessarily engaged in critique which leads to action. The radical implications of connections between the personal and political, and cultural change seem to have been lost in the development of a very rapidly growing area of the British curriculum 'personal and social development', which claims inspiration from Freire. The depoliticisation of the term 'empowerment' in this context illustrates how radical cultural struggles can be defused as key terms are appropriated by more conservative cultural forces (Hitchin, 1985).

In this chapter we have shown the intimate relationship between a society's culture and what is defined as education; struggles over education are struggles for cultural hegemony. Indeed, the traditional separation between the sociologies of education and culture must itself be seen, in part, in relation to issues of power in the development of knowledge disciplines in the context of the academic and education professions. The work of Foucault discussed in Chapter 2 is relevant to this question.

9 Media: Creating Popular Culture

'Mass' media

As we have seen in previous chapters, the study of culture has provided a subject area for various disciplines and in recent years new areas of film and television studies have emerged. We have also seen that the cultural-studies approach has combined many of the disciplines mentioned (see Chapters 1 and 2). It has also brought to the fore the study of the mass media and its relationship to other aspects of popular culture. The study of 'popular culture' was seen until quite recently, as the study of 'mass culture', with the mass media as part of this: in the USA this still tends to be the case (for example, see Caughie, 1986; Gallafent, 1990; and Chapter 6). The whole area is surrounded by theoretical controversy, some of which has been discussed in earlier chapters. The starting-point for the analysis of culture and the media was from the perspective of the study of mass communications and this has been and continues to be dominated by two disciplines – sociology and literary criticism. Although writers in the United States tended to apply a sociological approach and in Europe, especially England, used the tools provided by literary criticism, both these traditions have been dominated by the theory of 'mass society' discussed in Chapter 1. To a remarkable extent, there was broad consensus during the inter-war years and beyond, for the view that the mass media exercised a powerful and persuasive influence. Underlying this consensus was the creation of mass audiences on an unprecedented scale and the feeling that urbanisation and industrialisation had created a society that was volatile, unstable, rootless, alienated and inherently susceptible to manipulation. Linked to these ideas was the view that modern society did not have the stable value-systems of earlier ones and had already been subject to the manipulation of mass media propaganda during the Second World War.

This view encouraged a model of the media as an all-powerful propaganda agency, 'brainwashing' a susceptible and defenceless public. The media were seen as simply sending out messages which easily penetrated deep into the passive waiting public. The work then, of the sociologist and social psychologist was to measure the content of the messages and the extent to which they were received. This approach accounts for much of the work which attempted to analyse the effects of the mass media in the United States. In the 1940s and early 1950s this theory was seen as unproblematic, requiring only the empirical evidence to substantiate it. In England at this time consideration of the mass media was rooted in the debate on culture conducted by the Leavisites against the same background of fears of a nightmare 'mass society – mass culture'. It was taken for granted that mass culture was inevitably shoddy and lacking aesthetic discrimination and the task of the cultural critics was to rescue the people from this levelling-down of cultural and material life (see Chapter 3).

These concerns became sharper with the introduction of commercial television in the consumer boom of the 1950s when more and more people acquired television sets and tuned them to immensely popular quiz shows, soap operas and comedies. These fears have continued to be expressed by critics of popular mass media:

> there are large and accruing profits to be made from a vast populace rendered intellectually gullible and emotionally indolent. Cliché, sentiment, glossy patter, stereotyped images, instant jingles round the clock, are easy to manufacture, easy to slot to each other, and providing that within the populace there are no sensitive feelings for aesthetic shape and personal truth, easy to distribute not only across 'the provinces', but around the world . . . We need to know whether the casual stance adopted by the intelligent young today derives from a profound sense of cultural relativity fostered by the arbitrary flow of the serious and the trivial, the real and the unreal, which marks television entertainment, magazines, newspapers and radio alike (Peter Abbs: 'Mass Culture and Mimesis', *Tract No. 22*, quoted in Masterman, *Teaching the Media* (Comedia, 1985, p. 42).

It is ironic that the Leavisite mission of using literary criticism to engender a particular 'English' cultural sensitivity and critical intelligence created a legacy which ultimately provided a space in which 'popular culture' as opposed to mass culture could be examined and understood (see Chapter 3). It was from these élitist critical debates that the discussion of media texts eventually became an acceptable and intellectually respectable activity, in Britain and America.

Impetus for the study of popular culture, including mass media, also benefited from the reassessment of mass-society theory which began to take place in the late 1950s and early 1960s. We can point to two reasons for this reassessment. In the aftermath of the plethora of research on media effects a new orthodoxy had emerged which held that the mass media have only a limited influence on people's beliefs and behaviour. This view was succcinctly stated by Klapper in his classic summary of media effects research. 'Mass communications', he concluded 'ordinarily do not serve as a necessary and sufficient cause of audience effects' (Klapper, 1961, p. 8). People, it was argued, manipulated, rather than were manipulated by, the mass media. This view was further reinforced by a number of 'uses and gratifications' studies showing that audiences are active rather than passive and bring to the media a variety of different needs that influence their uses of and responses to the media. It was now argued by people like the sociologist, Daniel Bell, that America was not a 'mass' society made up of isolated, rootless, alienated human beings. Rather, it was a society organised through various groups and organisations whose strong ties and interdependencies created stable group-pressures that shielded the individual from direct media influence (see Bell, 1960, especially ch. 1). Underpinning this new orthodoxy claiming the lack of media influence was a critique of older mass-society theory, but also a positivistic and behaviourist approach stemming in part, it has been argued, from the association of American sociologists with research programmes generated by media instititutions themselves, concerned with audience research (Gitlin, 1978).

Media 'pluralism'?

This liberal-pluralist approach to media sociology views the media as the benign upholders of democracy. The various media allow different views, opinions and issues to be aired and this, it is claimed, contributes to the free and open circulation of ideas,beliefs and values. So, on a political level, the media are no longer viewed as the harbingers of social unrest or totalitarianism. Rather, within this perspective they are viewed as essential to the democratic process. Furthermore, on the issue of mass culture, this new approach pointed out that the media were also responsible for making the established classics of 'high' culture available to a wider audience, whose cultural standards had been lifted with rising educational standards. However, as Andrew Tudor explains: 'A new understanding of the relation between media and society was not immediately forthcoming' (Tudor, 1979, p. 8). He argues that the main emphasis throughout the various approaches to the media from this point on is a shift away from examining media effects as specific to the cultural life of an individual, to an emphasis on the role of the media in providing a framework which directly and indirectly influences the cultural construction and cultural maintenance of a particular world view.

The first area – 'construction' – refers to the role of the media in the area of socialisation. So, for example, a study by Dohrmann (1975) researched the effects of children's educational programmes like *Sesame Street*, *Electric Company* and *Captain Kangaroo* on gender attributes. She analysed the extent to which males were portrayed in these programmes as active, masterful and displaying leadership and suchlike qualities, as opposed to the stereotype of females as passive, as victims, incompetent, and needing advice and protection. In these programmes males/boys were much more likely to demonstrate active masterful roles than passive ones. The male child was shown as having ingenuity, being heroic, whereas the female child tended to be led, and to be helpless. Dohrmann argues that these programmes provide symbolic messages of comparative gender worth, the implication being that such messages affect behaviour.

A further study found that by reversing the stereotype and showing programmes in which girls are shown to be at least as competent as the boys, significant differences in children's behaviour could be produced. This was a study of children in the 5–10 age range, carried out by O'Bryant and Corder-Bolz (1978). The researchers showed four specially made commercials for a fruit drink which varied the role of women. Some of them showed women in their usual traditional work-roles, while others portrayed women in reverse-role situations – as welders, butchers, and so on. The research findings revealed that boys and girls shown traditional-role advertisements displayed more traditional notions of the kinds of work women can do whereas the sample which were shown non-traditional advertisements were less stereotyped in their views about the types of jobs women could do (for further discussion, see Howitt, 1982). These examples may give the impression that the socialisation role of the media is simple and unambiguous, but this is not the case. Rather, the process is complex and mediated by other agencies of socialisation in society, the family and the education system. The complexities of the relationship between media and other aspects of culture may become clearer when we explore the second dimension of the media as creators of our social and cultural framework.

The concept of 'world-maintenance' emphasises the role of the media as providers of 'experience' and 'knowledge' (Tudor, 1979, p. 10). They provide us with much indirect experience of events and processes which happen beyond our own personal social experience. We increasingly 'know' more and in providing this information the media structure the information for us. The media do not simply provide or increase our knowledge of the world but help us to make sense of it. One way in which this is done is by agenda-setting. This term describes a phenomenon that has long been noticed and studied, particularly in the context of election campaigns. An example would be a situation in which politicians seek to convince voters on the issues of a particular campaign. In determining the agenda, what the issues are and their context, the media structure our definition of the situation, what can or cannot be taken to be important.

'Good and bad news'

One area of the media central to this process is 'news'. Although it is common for people to say things like 'don't believe everything you read in newspapers or see on television', most people reading the newspaper or watching a TV news broadcast expect that they will get an idea of what are the most important events happening in the world. Studies which have examined the making of print and television news demonstrate the ways in which news is socially constructed and the variety of factors – such as the source of news, the context in which it is produced, media personnel's notion of what is newsworthy – determining which events make up the news (see Cohen and Young (eds) 1981).

A good illustration of agenda-setting and how the media define the issues in a debate can be seen in the reporting of race relations. Studies suggest that while the media do not necessarily encourage racial prejudice, their style of reporting defines the presence of ethnic minorities in society as a 'problem'. Hartmann and Husband (1972) found that in Britain, in areas without large immigrant populations, children obtained their ideas and opinions about black people predominantly from the media. Moreover, as a result of media coverage, black people were viewed as causing trouble and conflict, as being 'social problems' in themselves. This occurs because the media tend to focus on the immediate social and political tensions of the presence of immigrants, with little real analysis of their position. For instance, in the early 1970s, 'black mugging' received considerable media coverage, but the economic, social and educational deprivations of black people in this country did not. Perhaps even more pertinent, analysis of the context in which post-war immigration from the Commonwealth into Britain occurred is largely neglected in the media. A similar process and effect can be seen in media handling of crime.

Cohen and Young (eds, 1981) and also Cohen (1980) stress the role of media in the creation of 'folk-devils', in which 'moral panics' take root, exaggerating the incidence of a phenomenon and whipping up concern over its supposed epidemic proportions. For example, Teddy Boys, Mods and Rockers, Hippies, Skinheads, 'drug-takers' and football hooligans have all been prime targets for media identification as 'folk-devils' and the subsequently created 'moral panic' has served to reinforce and legitimise various 'law and order' political campaigns in Britain.

Media ideology and consensus

One of the most important elements of this process is the reliance of the media on the idea that society operates on the basis of a shared common culture: that the majority, if not all of its members, are in agreement on a wide range of norms, values and ideas and there is

CALDERDALE
COLLEGE LIBRARY
HALIFAX

agreement on what are reasonable and acceptable patterns of behaviour. As Stuart Hall writes:

> it is assumed that we share a common stock of cultural knowledge with our fellow men [*sic*] . . . This 'consensual' viewpoint has important political consequences, when used as the taken-for-granted basis of communication. It carries the assumption that we also all have roughly the same interests in the society, and that we all roughly have an equal share of power in the society . . . the media are among the institutions whose practices are most widely and consistently predicated upon the assumption of a national consensus (Hall *et al.*, 1978, p. 55).

This idea of national consensus and the media's role in upholding this view is well illustrated by the work of the Glasgow Media Group which examined the role of the media in relation to industrial relations in Britain. The general conclusion to be drawn from such research is that trade unions, workers and strikers tend to be portrayed unfavourably as the root cause of national economic problems and under-performance in terms of industrial output; of industrial trouble and disruption and of harm and inconvenience to the lives and interests of other citizens. Specifically, industrial relations tend to be discussed in the context of notions of a unifying 'national interest', so that the range of images and interpretations employed by the media are contained within a set of assumptions about the relations between capital and labour. Thus strikes are located within the context of their impact on the national economy. The idea contained in this is that we all benefit equally from the smooth running of the national economy and when it is disrupted we all suffer equally.

So, for the media, 'strikes' are invariably 'bad news' and to be deplored, regardless of any inherent justice in the strikers' grievances or demands, or in the principle on which the strike is based. The idea of the 'national interest' is the ultimate barometer against which action is to be measured, so that trade-union action is reported and analysed primarily within the context of national economic performance and only incidentally, if at all, within a framework which assesses the inherent validity or justice of their actions. In fact, union leaders are invariably asked to provide justification for industrial actions *vis-à-vis* society with little regard for the internal merits of the case. The Glasgow Media Group also showed how the TV news had a tendency to seek 'facts' and information from official management sources and to rely on workers to provide the filmable 'newsworthy' events. They showed how official spokespeople and management are far more likely to be interviewed in comfortable offices while questions to workers are presented 'on the run', presenting a stereotyped version of industrial culture.

The language in which disputes are presented is also part of the framework of interpretation provided by the media: use of such terms as 'moderates', 'militants', 'extremists', 'violence on the picket lines'. These expressions constitute symbolic codes, through which the media help to structure interpretations of social reality, presenting a partial account of that social reality by drawing on particular sets of values to interpret action and events. The Glasgow Media Group stress that this news presentation is not simply a question of a deliberate, conspiratorial process of manipulation nor a question of the expression of bias in particular news items or on the part of particular media personnel. More fundamental are the kinds of assumptions regularly invoked in interpreting certain events – so the content of the media is organised around particular explanations and solutions. This in turn shapes the ideas and beliefs and hence the consciousness of people in society and as such constitutes an important dimension of the interrelationship of media and culture (Glasgow University Media Group, 1976, 1980, 1982). Various pertinent criticisms have been levelled at the the Glasgow Media Group (for example, see Harrison, 1985) but our concern in this section has been to identify the process to which they draw attention rather than to present a complete analysis of the studies. Like education (see Chapter 8) the media in all societies are an aspect of culture which help to shape and interpret what is defined as knowledge (also see Chapter 4).

The dominant theme in this new approach to the study of an important area of popular culture then, is to understand in what ways popular cultural products represent and reproduce a particular version of reality. This approach asks how these representations are understood and analysed by those who receive them. It also asks what the process is, by which cultural products represent particular class or group interests and if, indeed, specific cultural products can be said to represent specific class interests at all. Theoretical refinement of these types of questions was aided by the resurgence of both the 'new' Marxism of the early 1960s and the contribution of semiology to the study of meaning systems.

Historically, as discussed in more detail in Chapter 2, Marxist approaches to culture rested on a particular understanding of the concept of ideology as a false or mistaken notion concealing the real interests and needs of a social group or class. As we have seen, reformulations of the concept of ideology, particularly those of Althusser, countered accusations that the earlier Marxist concept of ideology was based in a rigid economic determinism. More recent reformulations have provided the space and basis for an analysis of media and popular culture in terms of the relative autonomy of both, but also as part of the processes involved in the nature of the reproduction of the material conditions of capitalism.

An important article by Stuart Hall, 'Culture, the Media and the "Ideological Effect"' (Hall, 1977), provides an interesting example of the new approach. He points to three functions performed by ideological cultural processes:

(i)   masking;
(ii) fragmenting;
(iii) reuniting.

Masking is the process whereby the real nature of the social and economic system is hidden. Fragmenting refers to the division of the totality of the social world into isolated and unconnected parts which are then reunited in an imaginary or misleading way, so that, for example, basic class antagonisms are submerged in references to the 'nation', 'nationhood' and a 'common consensus'. When this process is translated to the ideological role played by the media, Hall argues, the media carry out cultural functions and these cultural functions are vital to the reproducing of the capitalist system. The first of these functions we have already mentioned, that is, the media provide us with a particular perspective on the social world: Hall calls this 'selective construction'. Second, the media reflect on the diversity of life styles which they present and catalogue. They assign them a place or a particular status and show either their acceptability or carry out the work of exclusion, of downgrading certain aspects of social reality. The media's function here is:

> The provision of social realities where they did not exist before or the giving of new directions to tendencies already present, in such

a way that the adoption of the new attitude or form of behaviour is made a socially acceptable mode of conduct, whilst failure to adopt is represented as socially disapproved deviances (Halloran, 1970, quoted in Hall, 1977, p. 341).

This brings us to the third function of the media which is the way in which they provide an overall view or definition of a cultural consensus. In so doing they give us a special kind of self-image for society. This is not to say that we are simply manipulated by the media: rather, Hall stresses the fact that the ideological effects of the media are much more subtle, much more complex and contradictory. But in terms of the overall effect, the media does not question the *status quo* and a particular way of understanding the world in terms of what passes for a 'commonsense' view of events.

Economic organisation and media production

Such an analysis of the relationship of media and culture is not without either its critics or its problems. Not only from those who doubt the validity of Marxist arguments, but inside the Marxist paradigm there are different views on ideology and the media and different interpretations of the way that the relationship with culture should be understood. Within the Marxist camp there remains a tension still between those writers who would continue to stress the importance of economic determinants in the production of popular culture and those who see cultural processes as determinants in themselves (also see Chapter 3). Peter Golding and Graham Murdock, for example, point specifically to the concentration of ownership and control of the media. They write:

> The central argument . . . is that sociologists interested in contemporary mass communications need to pay careful and detailed attention to the ways in which the economic organisation and dynamics of mass media production determine the range and nature of the resulting output

and that

> the dominant British currents of Marxist work on the sociology of culture, Hall's included, have persistently failed to explore this

question of economic determinations with any degree of thoroughness' (Golding and Murdock, 1979, pp. 198–200).

They are at pains to stress they are not proposing in any simple way that economic factors are the most significant in shaping the media. Nor are they saying that there is a perfect fit between market forces and decisions on the one hand and the kind of ideological message we receive from the media on the other. That is, they begin by stating that they are not crude Marxists with a simple, reductionist approach to the economy and the media. They also stress that they accept the Althusserian idea of 'relative autonomy' of the broadcasters, production personnel, journalists and all those involved in the production of media culture. However, for them the crucial term is 'relative'. They argue that Stuart Hall makes the same error as certain versions of liberal pluralist analysis. That is, by failing to analyse economic trends influencing the media, Hall dissolves the links between the cultural and the economic, despite the fact that he sees this link as basic to a Marxist interpretation:

> the process of ideological reproduction cannot be fully understood without an analysis of the economic context within which it takes place and of the pressures and determinations which this context exerts. Far from being 'incidental', questions of resources and of loss and profit play a central role in structuring both the processes and products of television production (Murdock and Golding, 1977, p. 19).

On the basis of Hall's emphasis on the significance of counter-vailing sources of power, Murdock and Golding are basically arguing that Hall's view of ideology is similar to the pluralist notion of competing interests. In other words, in attempting to move away from a crude reductionist model of the role of the media Stuart Hall has lost his way. These writers also condemn the over-concentration on textual analysis in much of the 'new' Marxian studies of culture and pose a serious question mark over the value of 'ideological' readings. They argue that simply to focus on the texts as ideology is to remain blind to the forces which lie behind the production of texts. They argue that whilst 'textual analysis will remain important and necessary . . . it cannot stand for the sociological analysis of cultural production' (Golding and Murdoch, 1979, p. 207).

Reading cultural products

Another area of disagreement within Marxism relevant to the discussion of media and culture is the debate between 'culturalists' and 'structuralists'. This debate is not simply about how we conceptualise culture and therefore the media as part of culture, but also how we go about studying culture in general or media in particular. Tony Bennett (1981) provides a good summary of the two positions when he says that culturalism and structuralism are principally distinguishable in terms of their contrasting approaches to the question of meaning. He gives an example of the different approaches by referring to a structuralist account of the rules of a dietary system. This approach concentrates then, on the rules and rituals rather than, for example, examining the ways the people involved give meaning to their eating habits. Bennett compares this approach with a 'culturalist' approach to the festival of Christmas, which would be concerned with attempting to understand the meaning people give to the various customs and rituals associated with Christmas and thus attempt to interpret the meaning of this event for those involved. The distinction between the two approaches is quite difficult to grasp, but basically the difference is that, for culturalism, the interpretation of meaning is a process to be engaged in, while for structuralism, the production of meaning is a process to be analysed.

Debates about meaning and many of the theoretical approaches which we examined in Chapter 2, for example, semiotics and discourse theory, have been incorporated into relatively eclectic 'post-modern' approaches and studies of the media, which there is insufficient space to discuss in this volume. However, most of these debates and approaches to the study of media and culture can be illustrated by examining soap opera as a popular cultural product. Soap opera could be characterised as the epitome of mass culture. Traditionally the genre has been viewed as an inferior trashy product in a simplistic synthesis of the mass-culture, mass-society theory and therefore either not worthy of investigation, or investigated in terms of its assumed pejorative effects (also see Chapter 3 for the values and processes involved in defining 'high' art). Recently Ien Ang has explained the way in which this theory still continues to act as a touchstone for discourses on *Dallas*. Her book is based on viewers' reactions which take the form of letters to the author. In her analysis she points to the way in which

> the rules and judgements of the ideology of mass culture are not unknown to *Dallas* fans. What is more, they too seem to respond to this ideology. But they tend to do so in a completely different way from those who hate *Dallas* or who love it ironically. 'Really' loving *Dallas* (without irony) would seem to involve a strained attitude toward the norms of the ideology of mass culture. And it is this strained relationship which the fans have to try to resolve (Ang, 1985, p. 104).

In earlier studies, for example in the 1930s in America, as explained above, the search was for the effects of soap opera on the female audience. The work of Herzog, Lazarsfeld and Kendall on radio soaps are good examples which look for the behavioural changes brought about by the content of soap operas. In these studies much attention was given to the plots, themes and characters which structured the narrative. Herzog, for example, discussed the appeal of soap opera in functional terms. Soaps were said to act as time-fillers and served as a base for social intercourse. They also compensated for the lack of social intercourse and provided a source of information on the world, from clothing styles, to medicine, through to interpersonal relations and social problems (Herzog, 1944). A more recent study by Downing followed this 'content analysis' and 'uses and gratifications' approach and argued that the appeal of soap opera lay in the fact that the content is both personal and domestic. As she states, 'a study of this much-maligned genre shows that despite her handicaps, the daytime heroine may still be the most adequate human on television' (Downing, 1974, p. 130).

In her book on *Crossroads* (1982), Dorothy Hobson also attempts to understand the appeal of soap opera by interviewing audiences, so her work adopts both the audience-gratification approach and a culturalist approach. In order to establish the importance of studying both the genre and the audience, Hobson approaches the latter as creative, thinking subjects, rather than as passive, unthinking automatons. Though the analysis of popular culture is never addressed directly Hobson seems to indicate that the medium of television cannot be assessed or theorised in the same way or with the same analytical tools as other cultural products:

Broadcasters should recognize that when they do attract a large audience they should not despise that audience nor the programmes which most appeal. A soap opera which appeals to and connects with the experiences of fifteen million people is as valid and valuable as a work of art as a single play or documentary which may attract four million viewers. Neither is better nor worse than the other. They are simply different programmes and each dependent on the understanding which the audience brings to it for its ultimate worth (Hobson, 1982, p. 171).

Peter Buckman's study of soap opera contains similar themes; indeed one of the stated aims of his book is to enable viewers to take pride in their addiction to the genre. The criteria of high culture cannot be applied in this instance, argues Buckman, as he explains that 'The discerning critic is an élitist – which needn't be an insult – who can see merit in what vulgar prejudice condemns. Television is by its nature anti-élitist' (Buckman, 1984, p. 161; also see Chapter 3 above).

A more definitive semiological/structuralist analysis of soap opera is given by the British Film Institute's study of *Coronation Street* (Dyer *et al.*, 1981). The series of articles contained in this monograph develops different aspects of the genre, from textual to ideological analysis, but the audiences are not as individuated as in the studies previously discussed, though they are viewed as active rather than passive. For example, it is suggested that the fascination for viewers of *Coronation Street* may lie in the fact that it provides the space for people to be onlookers, *voyeurs* on human problems, eavesdroppers on intimate conversations. If we think of the limited space there is in our society for open discussions on emotional desires, needs and frustrations to take place, this argument does have a certain force. The emphasis throughout the study is on the narrative and ideological structuring of the genre, that is, the continuous serial form with the subsequent lack of narrative closure and the multiplicity of plots. Thus the pleasure and appeal of soap opera is explained to some degree by the form.

However, in her essay, Lovell points to the ideological and cultural contradictions of the genre. Not only do women occupy quite powerful places in soap opera but they are also portrayed as strong, vital, and some have careers and independence (Lovell, 1981). Soap opera also deals with women as human beings, not simply as sex objects nor solely in terms of male activities and interests. Women are portrayed as responsible members of society, whose opinions are sought and acted upon. They are also shown as enjoying the friendship of other women. So this genre could be said to offer women a validation and celebration of those interests and concerns with which they engage, activities which are not highly valued within the dominant culture. It is also argued that the complexity and contradictions of human nature placed in 'domestic situations' portrayed by this genre constitute part of its popularity, especially for women, as this form expresses 'the hopes and aspirations of the dominated which are thwarted under capitalism and patriarchy' (Lovell, 1981. p. 49). In other words, soap operas and popular culture on a wider level embody dreams and desires which are lacking in the 'real' world. The texts contain a subversive promise that life could be different, there are alternatives. Thus the cultural impact of *Coronation Street* has been investigated on a number of levels, but emphasising essentially an ideological reading of the text and the role of similar cultural products in maintaining or questioning a particular 'hegemonic' totality,

Similar approaches and themes are discussed by Robert C. Allen (1983) and Tania Modleski (1984). Modleski argues that it is important to recognise that 'soap opera allays real anxieties, satisfies real needs and desires, even while it may distort them' (Modleski, 1982, p. 108). The contradictory nature of the role of the media within culture is well-illustrated by a study of the particular cultural form of soap opera and the debates on its message and effect in relation to different 'readings' of popular culture. On the one hand a case can be made for the 'progressive' reading of the text, especially in relation to women: it can be seen as an aspect of women's cultural space which provides meaning for them. On the other hand the extent to which the primacy of the dominant social order, including its ideological components, is fundamentally challenged is questionable. A similar conclusion was reached in a recent study of popular romance fiction where it was argued that it is not surprising if 'the reader remains unsure as to whether the romance should be considered fundamentally conservative on the one hand or incipiently oppositional on the other', but that

> If we can learn to look at the ways in which various groups appropriate and use the mass-produced art of our culture, I

suspect we may well begin to understand that although the ideological power of contemporary cultural forms is enormous, indeed sometimes even frightening, that power is not yet all-pervasive, totally vigilant, or complete (Radway, 1984, pp. 209–22).

10 Disintegrations and Reintegrations: Future Directions in the Sociology of Culture

Conceptual boundaries in studying culture

We have seen that historians, sociologists, anthropologists, literature specialists and others have made significant contributions to our understanding of culture and in turn the study of culture has led to the breaking-down of disciplinary boundaries. The history of the study of culture is therefore complex and it is difficult to indicate directions without seeming to suggest an oversimplified unilinearity. Bearing this in mind, nevertheless, it might be said that as the study of culture has developed, conceptual distinctions have been made and refined. For example, high culture has been distinguished from low culture and concepts of mass and popular culture developed. In order to distinguish the specifically cultural aspects of a society and refine the theoretical usefulness of the concept of culture the distinction between social structure and culture has generally been drawn. Marxist researchers have located culture within the super-structures and some have distinguished more general aspects of culture from those with the specifically ideological function of reproducing the social relations of production. In all this it has mostly been taken for granted that knowledge, particularly scientific knowledge, could be distinguished from the general pattern of beliefs in society which could be seen as culturally defined.

Some, perhaps all, of these conceptual distinctions are still useful in helping us to grapple with the complexities of culture. However, just as theoretical concepts clarify issues and problems, they also

172

simplify, by abstracting and allowing us to focus on some aspect of the social world. It is perhaps inevitable then, that as research progresses and analyses are pursued the limitations of conceptual boundaries themselves become theoretical issues. This has certainly been true in the study of culture. Just as disciplinary boundaries have been challenged so have conceptual distinctions. Looking towards the future of the sociology of culture the breaking-down of barriers and separations seem to be an increasing preoccupation. Integration of disciplines and areas within disciplines, *rapprochements*, reintegrations and perhaps disintegrations occur as the search for conceptual order and clarity capitulates in the face of a seemingly disordered and immensely complex reality and the challenge of post-modernism.

In this final chapter we shall examine what seem to us to be some of the more significant aspects of this process of disintegration and reintegration for the future of the sociology of culture. We shall explore the breakdown of structural differentiations and the structure/culture, base/superstructure distinctions, in the light of post-structuralist and other challenges. We shall also consider the erosion of boundaries between the sociology of culture and the sociology of knowledge – in particular the sociology of science – and the challenge which this poses to conceptions of truth and reason. Finally, we shall consider the general assault on rationality and all forms of progress launched by post-modernism.

Culture and structure

Within sociology the distinction between structure and culture has proved useful. For example, it has made it possible to talk about structural inequalities along the lines of race, class and gender, to identify material disadvantage such as lack of employment opportunities and to examine these in themselves, distinct from cultural dimensions. The latter can then be identified as dependent variables or causal factors in the reproduction of structural inequalities. So the 'working class' could be economically defined and 'working-class culture' seen as a production of class position and perhaps as a causal factor in the reproduction of the class system (see Chapter 6 for criticism of this position). Similarly, poverty could be distinguished from 'the culture of poverty', and 'blacks' and 'women' as categories of economic deprivation could be treated as analytically separate from ethnic minority cultures and cultures of femininity. This kind of separation is analytically useful and, particularly within the Marxist base/superstructure model, allows us to think in terms of a direction of causal effectiveness. Within sociology and philosophy differing but related theoretical distinctions have also been made between action and structure, individual and society, subjective and objective, mental and material. There is an interrelationship between these distinctions: culture is often associated with subjective experience, whereas structure or the 'material base' is understood in terms of the objective conditions of existence. Different theorists see the issues differently and we would not wish to under-emphasise the importance of differing conceptualisations, but for our purposes, to give some indication of the issues, we will concentrate on the base/superstructure distinction.

Base/superstructure, structure/culture models have been gradually undermined as the complexity of society and culture has been acknowledged. As we saw in Chapter 2, Althusser's sophisticated view of a 'structure in dominance' has been particularly influential in British and European work. It allows for some complexity in causal relations, yet identifies the economic base as determinant in the last instance and thus crucial in defining the general character of a given social formation at a specific conjuncture, by determining the overall pattern of its causal relations. This makes for conceptual clarity and generates causal explanations in a way not possible, for example, with a Weberian model which suggests causal complexity without attempting to identify any priority or overall direction to those causal forces.

However, with a historian's eye for detail and taste for the particular and complex relations of specific situations, E. P. Thompson expressed his outrage at the attempts of Althusser and his followers to build philosophical and sociological models of social totalities at the expense of complex reality. *The Poverty of Theory* (1978) was his most sustained attack and it is not possible here to do justice to its richness. His scorn for the oversimplification of base/ superstructure distinctions is clearly and more coolly conveyed in *Whigs and Hunters* (1977). Here Thompson argues that historically, in agrarian England, it was difficult to distinguish between 'law' and 'production':

the distinction between law, on the one hand, conceived as an element of 'superstructure', and the actualities of productive forces and relations on the other hand, becomes more and more untenable. For the law was often a definition of actual agrarian *practice* . . . How can we distinguish between the activity of farming or quarrying and the rights to this strip of land or to that quarry? The farmer or forester in his daily occupation was moving within visible or invisible structures of law (Thompson, 1977, p. 261).

Thompson's identification of the political implications of Althusserian theory – which builds a model of the social totality and the process of historical change and attempts to grasp the whole in a unified and unifying vision – with Stalinism (for example, Thompson, 1978 p. 323) is echoed in later post-structuralist attacks on the political terror they see inherent in all totalising theory (see Lyotard, 1984, pp. 37 and 81).

Althusser's conceptual gymnastics can be seen as something of a last-ditch attempt to grasp in an orderly theoretical model the impossibly complex causal interactions of the social world. Stuart Hall, nevertheless, is keen to defend it. Althusser, he argues, takes full account of 'difference'. However, unlike post-structuralists, such as Foucault (see Chapter 2), he avoids the shift from practice to discourse and the 'perpetual slippage of meaning', 'the endless sliding of the signifier' which in Foucault 'is pushed *beyond* the point where it is capable of theorising the necessary unevenness of a complex unity . . .' (Hall, 1985, p. 92). Foucault assures us that 'nothing ever fits with anything else'. He substitutes difference for unity whereas Althusser stresses 'the necessity of thinking unity and difference; difference in complex unity'. 'Articulation' becomes a key theoretical term, the key to understanding how different levels of practice or different discourses relate together in a complex whole. Without this understanding there can be no real grasp of the way that State power functions, for example:

> The function of the State is, in part, precisely to bring together or articulate into a complexly structured instance, a range of political discourses and social practices which are concerned at different sites with the transmission and transformation of power . . . for example, familial life, civil society, gender and economic relations (Hall, 1985, p. 93).

Hall argues there is some virtue in holding on to a way of theorising unity while allowing for complexity. The insistence on the economic being determinant 'in the last instance' recognises a mode of articulation and a structured pattern of causality. Hall also considers Althusser's model valuable in the way it conceptualises the subject as central to the process of social reproduction.

Coming from the direction of anthropology, Maurice Godelier is as critical as E. P. Thompson of the Althusserian model which

> represented society as a kind of cake composed of superimposed and unequal layers, the hardest of which (the infrastructure) supported the others (the superstructures). The latter became less and less firm as one approached the uppermost level, which comprised all those ideas and ideologies human beings have in their heads that reflect, in a partial and distorted manner, both the inner and the outer realities of their society (Godelier, 1986, p. 9).

Similarly, he argues that the Parsonian structural-functionalist model of sociologists and economists, that sees society as a 'global system articulating economic, political, religious, etc. subsystems with specialised functions' is fundamentally ethnocentric (ibid, p. 28, also see Chapter 1 above).

The crucial distinction is not a structural one, between levels or institutions nor is it a distinction between the mental and the material, because at the heart of all human relations with material reality is 'a complex ensemble of representations, ideas, schemas, etc.'. The crucial distinction, argues Godelier, is one between functions. Relations of production are the fundamental relations in any society, as human beings transform nature and produce society in order to live. However, in certain types of society kinship relations can function 'from the inside' as social relations of production, as can politics and religion. It is only in certain societies, particularly capitalist ones, that the distinction between functions coincides with a distinction between institutions. Godelier, then, seeks to maintain the useful conceptual distinction between base and superstructure but draws it in a different way because the usual notion of structure is at odds with his anthropological experience of non-capitalist societies.

We can see that the struggle for conceptual and theoretical clarity is often difficult to reconcile with the complexity of issues generated by empirical studies. We strive for theoretical order and are constantly confronted by disorderly experience. At best, this can be seen as a fruitful tension through which we refine and develop our knowledge. In all this we hold on to the distinction between 'knowledge' and its object – in this case, 'culture'. This is yet another problematic distinction which we shall now explore, taking science, as it often is and is understood, as the paradigm for knowledge.

Culture and science

In Chapter 8 we saw that in nineteenth-century England, in struggles between 'old humanists' and 'industrial trainers', a view of culture was defended by the former which excluded science. T.H. Huxley complained, 'How often have we not been told that the study of physical science is incompetent to confer culture; that it touches none of the higher problems of life'. He agreed with Arnold, that the 'criticism of life' is the essence of culture, but disagreed that literature contains the materials which suffice for the construction of such a criticism:

> [Culture] implies the possession of an ideal, and the habit of critically estimating the value of things by comparison with a theoretic standard. Perfect culture should supply a complete theory of life, based upon a clear knowledge alike of its possibilities and of its limitations . . . [The] distinctive character of our own times lies in the vast and constantly increasing part which is played by natural knowledge. Not only is our daily life shaped by it, not only does the prosperity of millions of men depend upon it, but our whole theory of life has long been influenced, consciously or unconsciously, by . . . physical science . . . (Huxley, 1967, pp. 200–2).

Science, then, was denigrated by the traditional cultural élites and effectively excluded from consideration as a 'humanising' or civilising cultural force in the nineteenth century. At the same time 'high culture' was set to develop along the lines of an established literary tradition ignoring the challenge to values posed by science and technology (see Chapter 3 for how these values were established). C. P. Snow gave his lecture, 'The Two Cultures' at Cambridge University in 1959 (Snow, 1969.) In many ways, his complaint echoes that of Huxley and testifies to the success of the old humanists in maintaining their position, which Huxley had described as the 'Levites in charge of the ark of culture' (Huxley, 1967, p. 200). Nearly a century later, Snow observed a 'total incomprehension' between two polar groups: 'at one pole we have the literary intellectuals, who incidentally while no one was looking took to referring to themselves as "intellectuals" as though there were no others' and at the other, the physical scientists who for the most part are ignorant of literature and find even Dickens hard to read. Snow warned of the dangers of this separation for both our cultural and practical future and he was concerned with the cultural attitudes that lead us to disregard the political urgency of putting scientific knowledge to work in tackling the problems of world poverty. He referred to 'intellectuals' as 'natural Luddites', but also warned of the general attitude of superiority towards applied knowledge of which 'pure' scientists are also guilty. He noted that, rather after the fashion of Chinese Mandarins, as young research workers at Cambridge he and his colleagues prided themselves 'that the science we were doing could not, in any conceivable circumstances, have any practical use' (Snow, 1969, p. 32).

The 'two cultures' lecture provoked a venomous debate in which an attack on Snow by Leavis is noteworthy, both for the quality of its invective and for its fierce defence (in Arnold's footsteps) of literary high culture and its critical function. This modern debate was as much about power as was its nineteenth century precursor.

Science as the model of reason

Despite the attitudes and power of 'old' and more recent humanists, since the nineteenth century there has been a widespread veneration of science:

> In many minds indeed, the possibilities of science replaced the slowly waning certainties of religion . . . Natural science became increasingly one of the dominant spiritual forces of the time, the key to solve, as well, all the practical problems of life: it was, as Chesterton wrote, 'in the air of all that Victorian world' (Greenleaf, 1983, p. 238).

Science rapidly became a standard in relation to which policies and practices were judged and justified. Although excluded from the realms of culture 'at home', traditional cultures abroad were judged in relation to their levels of scientific and technological development (see Chapters 1 and 4). So successful has been the rise of scientific thinking, that today it is widely accepted throughout the developed Western capitalist world as the model for all rational thought. Greenleaf refers to this as 'Scientism':

> the many and varied forms of belief resting on the notion that the only effective method of thinking and analysis is that deriving from, or deemed characteristic of, the inquiries of modern natural science and technology . . . The implication . . . is that scientific method . . . is the only means to ensure effective understanding of any aspect of human or natural experience and that genuine knowledge of man and society can only be acquired in the same way that mastery of nature is achieved (Greenleaf, 1983, p. 239).

Science then, gained power, outside and in opposition to the sphere of high culture where questions of social and cultural value, 'the criticism of life', are at issue. Indeed, the success of scientific reason is partly associated with its so-called value freedom, its drive to describe and explain the natural world, and by extension the social world, impartially, without making moral, political or aesthetic judgements. Under the umbrella of science, a model of reason and truth developed, incorporating canons of 'discovery' and 'proof', uncontaminated by messy questions of value. Nevertheless, the notion of a disinterested pursuit of truth itself sets a high moral tone, justifing the superiority of pure science over applied science and technology. As we shall see, this conceals a thrust to dominate and control nature (and society) rooted in the scientific world view (also see Chapter 8 and discussion of Gouldner in Chapter 6).

It can be said that our age is dominated by forms of thinking and expression shaped by science and technology and science has attained a dangerously privileged position as the yardstick of all human reason. 'Scientism' contends for the status of the metaphysics of the modern age and operates as a powerful ideology. Whatever the naiveties of C. P. Snow's argument and his misplaced faith in the virtues of science, he correctly discerned dangers in the separation of cultures. Science may and does throw up moral problems but has not refined the tools required to engage with them. Moral reasoning has been defined as outside its scope although the very existence of science and scientific reason depends on the prior acceptance of an ethic, including such principles as truth-telling, abstaining from fraud, attending to evidence and respecting the discoveries of others, which cannot be justified scientifically.

The danger is, that in a climate of 'scientism', it is easy to believe that because moral principles and social ends are not amenable to scientific reason they cannot be reasoned about at all. Humanists concerned to preserve the critical function of culture have failed to extend its scope to include the challenges posed by a technocratic civilisation and, as Peter Scott has argued, 'the intellectual system that has produced the bomb has failed to produce the moral categories which permit such knowledge to be civilised in the service of man'.

> Our culture élites are often in bondage to technocratic and scientific knowledge. We can best describe technocratic thought by the discrepancy between its claims and its consequences. It claims to be a full description of reality but its consequences frequently entail a systematic inhibition of the moral imagination (Scott, 1983).

Modernisation, rationality and technological change

It is illustrative of this separation of cultures that despite the growth of cultural studies in general and the sociology of culture in particular, little attention has been paid by mainstream work to the technological character of modern culture, since the earlier mass-society critics (see Chapter 2). However, Jacques Ellul's examination of technological society was first published in 1954 and Herbert Marcuse's *One-Dimensional Man*, in 1964. Marcuse, and following him, Habermas, have sought to develop Weber's analysis of Western capitalism (see also Chapter 6) finding in his concept of rationalisation, a key to understanding technological society. According to Weber, the process of rationalisation involves the extension of the criteria of rational decision-making into increasing areas of social life. This instrumental rationality (*zweckrationalitat*) involves calculating the most efficient means to achieve our purposes or goals. It is a formal 'value-free' conception of reason, linked to the rational procedures of science. It requires quantification, rational experiments and proofs and generates organisations of technically trained officials. Ends and purposes are outside the scope of this reason (see also Chapter 8).

Employed in the pursuit of calculable economic efficiency, through the use of capital accounting methods and measured in terms of profit, it was an effective tool of capitalist development in the West. Combined with ascetic Protestantism, requiring diligence in a worldly calling, coupled with a frugal life style, its effectiveness increased because profit was used in the pursuit of yet more profit. As the religious beliefs that provided its rationale declined, the profit motive remained and became the driving force of capitalist enterprise. Weber argued that this economic order would become an 'iron cage', a self-perpetuating system, with the United States an example of 'the last stage of cultural development', consisting of 'Specialists without spirit, sensualists without heart; this nullity imagines that it has attained a level of civilisation never before achieved' (Weber, 1974, p. 182; also see Eldridge (ed.) 1971).

Marcuse characterises Weber's rationality as 'technical' reason concerned with 'the production and transformation of material (things and men) through the methodical-scientific apparatus . . . Its rationality organises and controls things and men, factory and bureaucracy, work and leisure' (Marcuse, 1972, p. 205). But, he asks, to what purpose does it control them? Marcuse, unlike Weber, argues that technical reason is not value-free because calculable efficiency is linked to productivity. To produce more and to produce more efficiently, are values internal to the system, entailing the domination and control of nature and human beings. As this rationality unfolds, its inherent irrationality becomes apparent, for example, as planned obsolescence becomes a social necessity and

> higher productivity, domination of nature, and social wealth become destructive forces. This destruction is not only figurative, as in the betrayal of so-called higher cultural values, but literal: the struggle for existence intensifies both within national states and internationally, and pent-up aggression is discharged . . . in the scientifically organised destruction of men (Marcuse, 1972, p. 207).

Noting how Weber recognised that 'Capital accounting in its *formally* most rational mode . . . presupposes *the struggle of man with man*' (ibid, p. 211), Marcuse argues that the system tends towards a new form of domination, not by the bourgeois class, but by 'total bureaucracy'. The system has a logic of its own to which all are subject. Domination has become rational but without losing its political character. It is rational in that a system can be maintained which makes the growth of the 'forces of production', coupled with scientific and technical progress, the basis of its legitimation. Because increasing productivity and domination of nature increases the comfort in which individuals live, the oppressive nature of the system tends to disappear from consciousness. Moreover, the existing 'relations of production', rather than being thrown into question by the developing 'forces of production', are seen as the technically necessary organisational form of a rationalised society:

> today domination perpetuates and extends itself not only through science and technology but *as* science and technology, and the latter provides the great legitimation of the expanding political power, which absorbs all spheres of culture.
>
> In this universe, technology also provides the great rationalisation of the unfreedom of man and demonstrates the 'technical' impossibility of being autonomous, of determining one's own life (Marcuse, 1970, p. 130).

Marcuse's vision of dehumanisation and oppression by the same 'rational' technology that offers to humanise nature and bring comfort and prosperity is one which has powerful fictional parallels in films and novels, from Chaplin's *Modern Times* and Fritz Lang's *Metropolis* to Huxley's *Brave New World*. It develops Weber's theme of the power of the unintended consequences of human action to create a culture which enslaves, and echoes the concern of mass-society theorists.

Habermas, a later Frankfurt School theorist (see Chapter 1), acknowledges Marcuse as the first to make the political content of technical reason the point of departure in his analysis of advanced capitalist society (Habermas, 1971). However, Habermas draws back from Marcuse's position which takes domination as internal to the logic of scientific reason. Marcuse's analysis leads him to conclude that social emancipation would require a revolutionary transformation of the character of science, away from a logic of control, towards one governed by the intention of preserving, fostering and releasing the potentialities of nature. Habermas argues that Marcuse is ambivalent in his attitude towards technological reason and unclear about the possibility of a alternative. Drawing on Arnold Gehlen, Habermas argues that technological rationality is intimately connected with purposive-rational action (*zweckrationalitat*) and rooted in the nature of the human organism. It is action regulated by its own results and is in fact the structure of work. So long as we have to achieve self-preservation through social labour and with the aid of means that substitute for work we cannot renounce technological reason for a qualitatively different form of reason. Habermas agrees with Marcuse's formulation that 'when technics becomes the universal form of material production, it circumscribes an entire culture' (Marcuse, 1970, p. 127), but sees the problem not in terms of the nature of scientific reason, but of its extension beyond its proper sphere.

Habermas uses Weber's concept of rationalisation, following his attempt to grasp the impact of scientific and technical progress on the institutional framework of societies undergoing the process of modernisation and developing Weber's analysis by distinguishing between 'work' and 'interaction'. He argues that the purposive-rational action associated with work is governed by technical rules and strategies which are tested empirically and modified according to their effectiveness. Interaction, on the other hand, is grounded in social norms which depend on inter-subjectivity and mutual understanding. This is the sphere of 'communicative action' and the basis of the institutional framework of society. In traditional societies interaction predominates and purposive-rational action is subject to consensual norms. However, as the productive forces develop, the institutional framework is challenged to adapt ever more rapidly. In Marx's words:

All fixed frozen relations, with their train of ancient and venerable prejudices and opinions, are swept away, all new formed ones become antiquated before they can ossify. All that is solid melts into air, all that is holy is profaned . . . (*Communist Manifesto*, p. 36: Marx and Engels, 1950).

The institutional frameworks of modern societies are subordinated to the self-legitimating demands of technological progress implemented by a new 'technological intelligentsia' (see Chapter 6 and Gouldner, 1979, pp. 37–9).

Habermas comments that it was with regard to the passive adaptation of the institutional framework compared with the active subjection of nature that Marx asserted that 'men make their own history, but not with will and consciousness'. Like Marx, Habermas is concerned to facilitate the transformation of the secondary adaptation of the institutional framework into an active one, and to bring the structural change of society under human control. For history to be made with will and consciousness, purposive-rational action would have to be resubordinated to the systems of communicative action which themselves must undergo a process of rationalisation. Habermas argues that rationalisation at the level of the institutional framework can only occur in the sphere of interaction itself and it would involve the removal of restrictions on communication such that it would be undistorted by relations of domination. So, the problem for Habermas is not scientific and technical reason itself, which brings the benefits of the technical control of nature, it is rather the lack of a strong rationalised institutional framework capable of providing a value critique adequate to the challenges posed by technological progress. We can see here still, the Frankfurt School (and earlier theorists') concern with a standard of absolute 'rational' values. Habermas exonerates technological reason from Marcuse's charge that its character is fundamentally repressive, because he separates purposive-rational action from the sphere of interaction. Purposive-rational action operates on nature, guided by technical rules and strategies which are analytically true or empirically testable. If constrained by a framework of rational values, it remains an indispensable tool. Habermas's concern in this early work is similar to Snow's concern with the separation of cultures. However, his more sophisticated analysis seeks to explain the separation and present a view of their proper relation and its development. The domination of nature is not itself a problem for Habermas in the way it is for Marcuse.

Scientific culture

This position is open to challenge in the light of post-Kuhnian developments in the sociology of scientific knowledge which would tend to support a more Marcusian position (Kuhn, 1962). Early sociological studies of science made a distinction between the technical and social aspects of scientific knowledge, concentrating on the social conditions under which scientific knowledge is produced. Newer approaches include the technical content of scientific knowledge within their enquiries. The detailed practices of scientists, their technical activities and ways of making judgements and theoretical interpretations have been studied. Sociologists engaged in this work are in a similar position to those who study religious cultures. In order to understand the meaning of much that is going on they have to understand something of the shared knowledge and beliefs of the group. This, of course, means understanding the science that is going on. Like Kuhn, many researchers are trained scientists with an interest in the social processes involved in the construction of scientific knowledge and they have often been concerned with philosophical questions.

Sociological studies of science then, have different theoretical antecedents from those in the mainstream of the sociology of culture. This, combined with the peculiarly technical content of the former, has perhaps inhibited cross-fertilisation. Nevertheless, recent work in this tradition suggests that the construction of scientific 'truth' is a social and cultural process more akin to communicative action and the inter-subjective definition of consensual norms than the model presented as purposive-rational action. Amongst the most accessible and suggestive work in this area is that of H. M. Collins, (1985). For example, he looks at debates about the development of apparatus designed to detect the gravitational waves predicted by Einstein's theory of relativity, concluding that the apparatus is assessed on the basis of its ability to produce the proper experimental outcome, which is consensually defined by the community of scientists. Similarly, experimentation is an acquired skill and debates about competence are linked to debates about the proper outcome of experiments. In the absence of any agreed normal criterion (when there is not yet an established consensus – a working tradition of research) scientists disagree about which experiments are competently done.

Particularly interesting, because of the way they link with Marcuse's view of scientific rationality as a rationality of domination, are studies combining a post-Kuhnian with a feminist perspective and raising the issue of the domination of nature as well as of humanity as a problem. This logic of domination is linked to a masculine conception of rationality, extending our notion of culture as gendered (see Chapter 7). It is impossible here to do justice to the complexity of the issues raised but see, for example, *Feminist Approaches to Science* (Bleier (ed.) 1986). Sandra Harding's *The Science Question in Feminism* (1986), explores the various issues and perspectives in some depth and Brian Easlea's *Fathering the Unthinkable* (1983), examines the relationship between the masculinity of science and the nuclear arms race.

Such work notes that rationality is frequently contrasted with emotionality. Mind, objectivity and activity are identified as masculine qualities and elevated above bodily concerns, subjectivity and passivity, which are associated with the feminine. Western science, at least since the sixteenth century, has abounded in sexual metaphors. Nature is depicted as female and knowledge created as an act of aggression – passive nature has to be interrogated 'unclothed', 'unveiled', 'penetrated', forced to reveal her most intimate secrets. It is argued that all this reveals something wrong, with Western rationality in general and science in particular, that is rooted in the way men relate to nature, to each other and to women. It has as its logical outcome the 'exterminism' of today's science. Jane Caputi's detailed study, *The Age of Sex Crime* (1987), provides an interesting broader analysis of the aggressive sexuality of modern Western patriarchal culture which keys into much that is being said about science:

> While the pornography of the Age of Sex Crime pictures women as plastic, displayed, dead, dismembered victims/objects, its Nuclear Age counterpart depicts the Earth as a threatened, abused, halved, shrunken, malleable, replaceable, and ultimately artificial object (Caputi, 1987, p. 194).

It can be argued that it is impossible to imagine just what non-sexist science/rationality would entail as we are bound within our own profoundly sexist structures of rationality. Nevertheless, some inkling may be gained in the process of critique of existing science. It would be one

> in which no rigid boundary separates the subject of knowledge (the knower) and the natural object of knowledge; where nature itself is conceptualised as active rather than passive, a dynamic and complex totality requiring human cooperation and understanding

rather than a dead mechanism, requiring only manipulation and control (Fee, 1986, p. 46).

Conceptions of nature and natural knowledge embodying similar ideas can be found if we look outside European, colonial, white and bourgeois cultures. Joseph Needham's studies of Chinese science, writings on African philosophy and American Indian views of nature are cited as examples and parallels drawn between feminist critiques of Western science and those of ecological movements. Feminist science fiction such as Marge Piercy's *Woman on the Edge of Time* (1978) also provides alternative visions, performing what Kingsley Amis calls its most important task of dramatising social enquiry and providing a fictional mode in which cultural tendencies can be isolated and judged (Lefanu, 1988).

Such ideas have become possible as science and rationality have increasingly been seen as cultural constructions, in the wake of the work of Kuhn and others. These ideas are controversial and dangerous however, because in subverting the traditional view of scientific knowledge as 'uncontaminated' by social factors they threaten to undermine any faith in rationality at all. We have seen that Habermas is prepared to defend scientific rationality and argues the need for the additional rationalisation of communicative interaction.

Modernisation and the legitimation crisis

We have noted that the process of modernisation subjects the institutional framework of a society to continual challenges to adapt in the face of the rapidly developing productive forces. Marshall Berman borrows Marx's phrase 'All that is solid melts into air', for the title of his book sketching the relations between modernisation, modernity or the character of life, particularly nineteenth- and twentieth-century city life, under capitalism and modernism in the arts (Berman, 1983). Modernisation and modernity are associated with ideals of progress and rationality which sweep away traditional beliefs, ways of life and patterns of authority. Modernist movements in the arts such as cubism, surrealism 'stream-of-consciousness' writing and Bauhaus architecture were always critical of modern life, rejecting bourgeois values and mass culture (see also Chapter 3)

CALDERDALE
COLLEGE LIBRARY
HALIFAX

but did so in the name of social progress and in order to build a better, more rationally ordered world. However, as Berman notes:

> The innate dynamism of the modern economy, and the culture that grows from this economy annihilates everything that it creates – physical environments, social institutions, metaphysical ideas, artistic visions, moral values – in order to create more, and to go on endlessly creating the world anew (Berman, 1983, p. 288).

This constant upheaval and undermining of values, truths and authority produces the 'legitimation crisis' of modern times and one of the imperatives of modernity has been to resist the tendency towards the relativisation of all authority, truths and values by establishing their rational basis. We are all forced to grapple 'with the question of what is essential, what is meaningful, what is real in the maelstrom in which we move and live' (Berman, 1983, p. 288). Habermas identifies this imperative with the project of the eighteenth-century Enlightenment. The Enlightenment outlook was radically new, concerned to liberate intellectual endeavour from authority, myth and tradition. Responsibility for determining truth and value was placed on individuals. The notion of rational subjects pursuing an intelligent ordering of life was fundamental to Enlightenment thinking. Since political authority must be acceptable to their judgement, political liberalism and the idea of progress followed naturally. Also central to the project was the effort to develop objective science, universal morality and law, and autonomous art, according to the inner logic of the belief that these specialised cultures would enrich everyday life by promoting the control of natural forces, an understanding of the world and the self, moral progress, the justice of institutions and the general happiness of human beings (see Chapter 1).

Habermas is critical of the way that these expert cultures have impoverished rather than enriched the everyday public world by their distance and impenetrability. He is also critical of the location of reason within the minds of individual subjects and of the belief in timeless truths and values. Nevertheless, he strongly defends rationality against relativism. He allows that the pursuit of knowledge is rooted in human interests but insists that those interests include the development of rational understanding which has a liberating potential. His later theory of 'communicative action' places reason within the context of acts of communication rather than in the heads of individual subjects. He argues that a commitment to standards of validity is presupposed in the act of communication. Genuine argument – communication – would have no basis if we could not suppose the possibility of genuine agreement about the truth of a statement. However, communication is systematically distorted, for example, by social relations which are unjust or unfree. Seeking rational decisions involves striving after a grounded consensus which moves beyond current practice towards an 'ideal speech situation' where communication is free from systematic distortions. Hence the struggle towards an ideal speech situation involves a struggle towards free and just social relations (for example, see, Habermas, 1976; and McCarthy, 1976). For Habermas, however, modernity is an unfinished project.

Apocalypse now: Post-modern culture and the death of value

The post-modern label first gained currency in the field of art history, chiefly in connection with architecture. However, the term now has a much wider significance and is associated with those who have declared the project of modernity 'dead'. Debate has centred around the meaning of the concepts of modernisation, modernism and modernity on the one hand and post-modernism and post-modernity on the other. The issues are complex and there is considerable conceptual confusion. Merquior notes, for example, that the 'post-modern' label has been attached to at least three things:

(a) a style or mood born of the exhaustion of, and dissatisfaction with, modernism in art and literature;
(b) a trend in French philosophy, or, more specifically, in post-structuralist theory;
(c) the latest cultural age in the West (Merquior, 1986).

It is impossible here to do justice to the complexity of issues involved in the modernity/post-modernity debates, but by focusing on the confrontation between Habermas and Lyotard it will be possible to give some indication of what is at stake. Lyotard distrusts all totalising theories as inherently 'terrorist', whereas Habermas considers Lyotard, Foucault and Deleuze as neo-conservatives because they offer us no theoretical reason to move in one political direction rather than another.

During approximately the same period as Habermas has been working to refine the Enlightenment viewpoint, a number of French thinkers, including Foucault (see Chapter 2) and Gilles Deleuze became critical of Marxist belief in the rationality of the historical process. They turned to Nietzsche for inspiration and rejected all forms of dialectical thought. Their work eventually produced a generalised 'post-structuralist' assault on all philosophical conceptions of reason and truth, which were declared to be repressive. Following Nietzsche they sought to reassert 'the infinity of the world' against totalising philosophies and the 'immodesty and naivety of science'. Like Weber, they argued that the world can never be grasped within a single unified theoretical system. Life is inherently multifarious and contradictory and all thinking and evaluation limited within perspectives. Jean-François Lyotard, previously active in left politics and involved in the development of post-structuralism, became concerned with the tendency of this 'left Nietzscheanism' to equate truth with power. He drew back in his later works, as did Foucault, from Nietzsche's acceptance of the fact that

> if claims to universality can never be more than the mask of particular forces and interests, then 'life' cannot take the form of a harmonious plurality of standpoints, but is essentially appropriation, injury, over-powering of the strange and weaker, suppression, severity, imposition of one's own forms, incorporation and at the least and mildest, exploitation (Dews, 1987, p. 218).

Totalising visions of truth may be inherently repressive but the denial of universal principles does not guarantee toleration and a right to difference. In 1979 Lyotard published two books in French, *Au Juste*, (later translated as *Just Gaming* with Thébaud) and *The Post-Modern Condition*. In the first he tries to develop a political account of the concept of justice on an anti-universalistic and anti-rationalist basis. In the second he attempts to connect this conception of justice to a broad characterisation of the present age and its political possibilities. In this work he maintains the post-structuralist stance against comprehensive and unifying perspectives which he calls the great 'meta-narratives' of the modern period. These are the overarching belief systems originating from the Enlightenment –

beliefs in rationality, science, progress and human emancipation (see Chapter 1) – which have served to solve the legitimation crisis over the past two centuries.

Lyotard maintains the Nietzschean attack on the possibility of consensus in learning or any universally valid knowledge for humanity. The demand for consensus indeed contains the seeds of terror and totalitarianism:

> The nineteenth and twentieth centuries have given us as much terror as we can take. We have paid a high enough price for the nostalgia of the whole and the one . . . Under the general demand for slackening and for appeasement, we can hear the mutterings of the desire for a return of terror, for the realization of the fantasy to seize reality. The answer is: Let us wage a war on totality . . . (Lyotard, 1984, pp. 81–2).

When we think of Auschwitz, Stalinism and Khomeini, it is easy to see Lyotard's point. It is certainly difficult to retain the idea of human progress, particularly moral progress and rationality in a world facing such momentous consequences of human folly as ecological disaster and nuclear annihilation.

Nevertheless, we can also sympathise with Habermas in his struggle to hold on to reason and the struggle for human betterment. If we give up this struggle, must we accept that anything goes and might substitutes for right, the tendency in French post-structuralist thinking that Lyotard came to distrust? In a slightly different vein, Frederic Jameson, the Marxist literary critic, sees the collapse of reason and authority making way for the universal logic of the market where no values prove timeless or authentic and the measure of everything is its market price. Jean Baudrillard, sometimes dubbed the high priest of post-modernism presents a nightmare vision of a media-and-consumer society (modernised 'mass society') where reality disintegrates altogether into images – where TV is the world:

> theorists of the post-modern often talk of an ideal-type channel-hopping MTV (music television) viewer who flips through different images at such speed that she/he is unable to chain the signifiers together into a meaningful narrative, she/he merely enjoys the multiphrenic intensities and sensations of the surface of the images (Featherstone, 1988, p. 200).

People are caught up in the play of images that have less and less relationship to an external 'reality'. Concepts of the social, political, or even 'reality', no longer seem to have any meaning and the 'gooey, sticky, blurry omnipresent and ubiquitous media-saturated consciousness' (Baudrillard's metaphors) destroys the concept of meaning itself, which depends on stable boundaries, fixed structures, shared consensus (see Kellner, 1987, p. 127).

Lyotard shares Habermas's concern for justice. In *Just Gaming* and *The Post-Modern Condition* he distances himself from the reduction of reason and truth to power and, far from associating post-modernism with rampant consumerism and the annihilation of meaning, he seeks to identify its liberating potential. In rejecting Habermas's search for consensus he turns to the view of science found in the writings of Kuhn and Feyerabend, draws on Wittgenstein's notion of language games (see Chapter 2) and indicates the democratic potential of a computerised data-bank society.

We no longer have recourse to the grand narratives, argues Lyotard, but 'the little narrative remains the quintessential form of imaginative invention, most particularly in science' (Lyotard, 1984, p. 60). Following Kuhn, he says that research that takes place under the aegis of a paradigm tends to stabilise. This is what Kuhn calls normal science. It is the result of the puzzle-solving activity generated by questions suggested within the current consensual paradigm of the scientific community. However, what is striking is that someone always comes along to disturb the order of 'reason'. The rules of the game on which consensus is based are challenged. Such challenges are often ignored or repressed bescause they tend to destabilise the system. Lyotard says that such repressive behaviour is terrorist and akin to that of any ordinary power-centre whose behaviour is governed by a principle of homeostasis. The terrorism involves 'eliminating or threatening to eliminate, a player from a language game'. The player is silenced or consents, not because he/she has been refuted, but because her/his ability to participate has been threatened. Nevertheless, destabilisation is inherent in scientific activity. Science provides us with a model of an open system in which a statement is relevant if it generates ideas, that is 'if it generates other statements and other game rules' (Lyotard, 1984, pp. 63–4). It is the function of imaginative or 'paralogical' activity in science to point out the current rules of the game and to petition the players to accept different ones. The only legitimation for this is that the new rules will generate ideas.

Lyotard asks whether this 'open system' model of science presents a possible model of an open community or whether it is limited to the game of learning. There is nothing comparable to the temporary consensus represented by the scientific paradigm identifiable for a 'social collectivity' as a whole. Social pragmatics are immensely more complex than scientific pragmatics and it would be impossible to identify the prescriptive rules of all the language games in circulation within a social collectivity. Language games take a variety of forms and are subject to a variety of sets of pragmatic rules. Nevertheless, this model of science is one which suggests that consensus is not the goal of dialogue but only a particular state of discussion. It suggests that the end, on the contrary, is 'paralogy' (discursive novelty). Lyotard argues:

> This double observation (the heterogeneity of the rules and the search for dissent) destroys a belief that still underlies Habermas's research, namely, that humanity as a collective (universal) subject seeks its common emancipation through the regularisation of the 'moves' permitted in all language games . . . Consensus has become an outmoded and suspect value (Lyotard, 1984, p. 66).

However, Lyotard argues, justice as a value is neither outmoded nor suspect. Therefore we must arrive at an idea and practice of justice that is not linked to that of consensus. He says that the recognition of the heteromorphous (varied forms) nature of language games is the first step in that direction because it implies a renunciation of terror. The second step is the principle limiting any consensus on the rules defining a game and the legitimate moves within it. It must be local – agreed by present players and subject to eventual cancellation. In other words, social life is seen to be governed by a multiplicity of little narratives which are inherently open to challenge and cancellation. Post-modernism has the potential of liberating us from the terror consequent upon the search for a totalising grand narrative:

> This orientation corresponds to the course that the evolution of social interaction is currently taking; the temporary contract is in practice supplanting permanent institutions in the professional,

emotional, sexual, cultural, family, and international domains, as well as in political affairs (Lyotard, 1984, p. 66).

Lyotard recognises that the system tends to favour temporary contracts which are flexible and low cost but insists that the relationship is ambiguous, the temporary contract is not totally biased towards the system. A similar ambiguity exists in relation to the computerisation of society which could become 'the dream instrument for controlling and regulating the market system' and in that case it would inevitably involve the use of terror. However, with a computer-literate populace and free public access to the memory and data banks, groups would be aided in formulating challenges to the prescriptive rules governing language games and in promulgating alternatives.

In the end, it is in the claim to reason rather than power that the openness of systems resides. Reason invites challenge and in its very nature is open to argument. Interestingly, Dews (1987, p. 220 ff.) suggests that Lyotard's position is not so different from that which Habermas has adopted in his later work. He says that for the post-structuralists it is the universality implicit in the conception of truth that appears as a threat but they overlook that it is the very universality of truth claims which makes for their vulnerability.

The post-modern attack on unifying perspectives has contributed to the growing suspicion, within cultural studies of all universalistic categories. Feminists in particular have argued that concepts such as 'women', 'male/female gender identity', 'reproduction' and 'mothering' can obscure difference and, far from being unproblematically liberating, such categorisations can be oppressive (see, for example, Fraser and Nicholson, 1988). The loss of any notion of a unified 'subject' as a whole, separate, rational, autonomous being, 'an essential self', agonised over by some has been welcomed by others as the overthrow of the dominant 'masculine', 'bourgeois' conception of the subject and this informs a fresh look at portrayals of subjectivity in feminist fictions (see, for example, Waugh, 1989). In summary, the notion of post-modernity captures the sense of flux and uncertainty which is a source of both anxiety and excitement in our culture and which continues to be reflected in the study of culture.

Bibliography

Many of the books cited have been through several editions, including paperback. Where possible later editions cited in the text are those most easily accessible to the reader.

Abbott, P. and Sapsford, R. (1987) *Women and Social Class* (London: Tavistock).

Abercrombie, N., Hill, S. and Turner, B. (1980) *The Dominant Ideology Thesis* (London: Allen & Unwin).

Abrams, M. H. (1957) *A Glossary of Literary Terms* (New York: Holt Rinhart Winston).

Abramson, H. J. (1980) 'Assimilation and Pluralism', in S. Thermstrom (ed.) *Harvard Encyclopedia of American Ethnic Groups* (Cambridge, Massachusetts: Harvard University Press).

Allen, R. C. (1983) 'On Reading Soaps: A Semiotic Primer', in E. A. Kaplan (ed.) *Regarding Television* (Frederick, Maryland: American Film Institute Monograph, University Publications of America).

Althusser, L. (1977) *For Marx* (London: New Left Books).

Althusser, L. and Balibar, E. (1977) *Reading Capital* (New Left Books, 2nd edn.

Altick, R. D. (1957, 1963) *The English Common Reader* (University of Chicago Press).

Amariglio, J. L., Resnick, S. A. and Wolff, D. R. (1988) 'Class, Power and Culture', in C. Nelson and L. Grossberg (eds) *Marxism and the Interpretation of Culture* (London: Macmillan).

American Academy Conference on the Negro American (Transcript) *Daedelus*, 95, (1966) vols 94 & 95 Special issue on 'The Negro American'.

Amos, V. and Parmar, P. (1984) 'Challenging Imperial Feminism', *Feminist Review*, no. 17.

Anderson, P. (1969) 'Components of the National Culture', in R. Blackburn and A. Cockburn (eds) *Student Power* (Harmondsworth: Penguin).

Ang, I. (1985) *Watching Dallas* (London: Methuen).

Apple, M.W. (1982) 'Curricular Form and the Logic of Technical Control' in M.W. Apple (ed.) *Cultural and Economic Reproduction in Education* (London: Routledge & Kegan Paul).

Appignanesi, L. (ed.) (1986) *Postmodernism*, ICA Documents 4 & 5, (London: Institute of Contemporary Arts).

Arnot, M. and Weiner, G. (eds) (1987) *Gender and the Politics of Schooling* (London: Hutchinson).

Asad, T. (ed.) (1973) *Anthropology and the Colonial Encounter* (New Jersey: Ithaca Press).

Ashcroft, B., Griffiths, G. and Tiffin, H. (1989) *The Empire Strikes Back* (London: Routledge & Kegan Paul).

Austin-Broos, D.J. (1987) 'Clifford Geertz: Culture, Sociology and Historicism', in Austin-Broos (ed.) *Creating Culture*.

Austin-Broos, D.J. (ed.) (1987) *Creating Culture: Profiles in the Study of Culture* (London: Allen & Unwin).

Ballard, R. and Ballard, C. (1977) 'The Sikhs: The Development of South Asian Settlements in Britain' in J. Watson, *Between Two Cultures*.

Bantock, G.H. (1971) 'Towards a Theory of Popular Education', in R. Hooper (ed.) *The Curriculum, Context, Design and Development* (Oliver & Boyd).

Banton, M. (1970) *Race Relations* (London: Tavistock).

Baran, G. 'Teaching Girls Science', in M. McNeil (ed.) *Gender and Expertise* (Free Association Books).

Barrett, M., Corrigan, P., Kuhn, A. and Wolff, J. (eds) (1979) *Ideology and Cultural Production* (Beckenham: Croom Helm).

Barthes, R. (1973) *Mythologies* (London: Paladin).

Batsleer, J., Davies, T., O'Rourke, R. and Weedon, C. (eds) (1985) *Rewriting English: Cultural Politics of Gender and Class* (London: Methuen).

Beattie, J. (1964) *Other Cultures* (London: Cohen & West).

Becker, H. (1963) *Outsiders: Studies in the Sociology of Deviance* (Illinois: Free Press).

Bell, D. (1960) *The End of Ideology: On the Exhaustion of Political Ideas in the Fifties* (Illinois: Free Press).

Bell, D. (1979) *The Cultural Contradictions of Capitalism* (London: Heinemann) 2nd edn.

Bell, D. (1980) *Sociological Journeys: Essays, 1960–1980* (London: Heinemann).

Bellah, R.N., Madsen, R., Sullivan, W.M., Swidler, A. and Tipton, S., (1985) *Habits of the Heart: Individualism and Commitment in American Life* (Berkeley: University of California Press).

Benjamin, W. (1970) *Illuminations* (London: Cape).

Bennett, T. (1981) 'Popular Culture: History and Theory', in Open University *Popular Culture Themes and Issues 2* (Milton Keynes: Open University Press).

Bennett, T., Boyd-Bowman, S., Mercer, C. and Woollacott, J. (1981) *Popular Television and Film* (London: British Film Institute).

Bennett, T., Martin, G., Mercer, C. and Woollacott, J. (eds) (1981) *Culture, Ideology and Social Process: A Reader* (London: Batsford).

Bensman, J. and Lilienfeld, R. (1973) *Craft and Consciousness* (New York: John Wiley).

Berger, J. (1972) *Ways of Seeing* (London: BBC and Pelican).

Berger, P. (1977) *Facing Up To Modernity* (Harmondsworth: Penguin).

Berman, M. (1983) *All That Is Solid Melts Into Air* (London: Verso).

Bernstein, B. (1970) 'Education Cannot Compensate For Society', *New Society* (February).

Bernstein, B. (1971) 'On the Classification and Framing of Educational Knowledge', in Young (ed.) *Knowledge and Control*.

Bernstein, B. (1974, 1977) *Class Codes and Control* (London: Routledge & Kegan Paul).

Beynon, H. (1984) *Working For Ford* (Harmondsworth: Penguin).

Billington, R. (1982) 'Ideology and Feminism: Why the Suffragettes Were "Wild Women"', *Women's Studies International Forum*, no. 5.

Blackburn, R. (ed.) (1972) *Ideology in Social Science: Readings in Critical Social Theory* (London: Fontana).

Blauner, R. (1976) 'Colonized and Immigrant Minorities', in G. Bowker and J. Carrier, *Race and Ethnic Relations: Sociological Readings* (London: Hutchinson).

Bleier, R. (ed.) (1986) *Feminist Approaches to Science* (Oxford: Pergamon).

Bocock, R. (1986) *Hegemony* (London: Tavistock).

Bourdieu, P. (1986) *Distinction: A Social Critique of the Judgement of Taste* (London: Routledge & Kegan Paul).

Bourdieu, P. and Passerant, J.C. (1977) *Reproduction in Education, Society and Culture* (London: Sage).

Bowles, S. and Gintis, H. (1976) *Schooling in Capitalist America* (London: Routledge & Kegan Paul).

Boyd-Barrett, O. (1977) 'Mass Communication in Cross-Cultural Contexts: The Case of the Third World', in Open University, *Mass Communication and Society*, (Milton Keynes: Open University Press).

Brake, M. (1985) *Comparative Youth Culture: The Sociology of Youth Cultures and Youth Subcultures in America, Britain and Canada* (London: Routledge & Kegan Paul).

Bramson, L. (1961) *The Political Context of Sociology* (Princeton, New Jersey: Princeton University Press).

Braverman, H. (1974) *Labour and Monopoly Capital: The Degradation of Work in the Twentieth Century* (New York: Monthly Review Press).

Brecht, B. (1977) 'Against Georg Lukacs, in Bloch, E. et al (eds) *Aesthetics and Politics*, (London: New Left Books).

Brunt, R. and Rowan, R. (eds) (1982) *Feminism, Culture and Politics* (London: Lawrence & Wishart).

Bryan, B., Dadzie, S. and Scafe, S. (eds) (1985) *The Heart of the Race: Black Women's Lives in Britain* (London: Virago).

Buckman, P. (1984) *All For Love: A Study in Soap Opera* (London: Secker & Warburg).

Buhle, P. (ed.) (1987) *Popular Culture in America* (Minneapolis: University of Minnesota Press).

Bulmer, M. (ed.) (1975) *Working Class Images of Society* (London: Macmillan).

Burrow, J.W. (1970) *Evolution and Society: A Study in Victorian Social Theory* (Cambridge: Cambridge University Press).

Bushaway, B. (1982) *By Rite: Custom, Ceremony and Community in England, 1700–1800* (London: Junction Books).

Butters, S. (1976) 'The Logic of Enquiry of Participant Observation: A Critical Review', in Hall and Jefferson (eds) *Resistance Through Rituals.*

Caplan, P. (ed.) (1987) *The Cultural Construction of Sexuality* (London: Tavistock).

Caputi, J. (1987) *The Age of Sex Crime* (London: Women's Press).

Cartledge, S. and Ryan, J. (eds) (1983) *Sex and Love: New Thoughts on Old Contradictions* (London: The Women's Press).

Cashmore, E. (1979) *Rastaman* (London: Allen & Unwin).

Castles, S. and Kosack, G. (1973) *Immigrant Workers and Class Structure in Western Europe* (Oxford: Oxford University Press).

Cassirer, E. (1955–7) *The Philosophy of Symbolic Forms,* (New Haven, Connecticut: Yale University Press) 3 vols.

Caughie, J. (1986) 'Popular culture: Notes and Revisions', in MacCabe (ed.) *High Theory/Low Culture.*

Cayton, H. and Drake, St C. (1946) *The Black Metropolis* (London: Jonathan Cape).

Centre for Contemporary Cultural Studies (1981) *Unpopular Education: Schooling and Social Democracy in England Since 1944* (London: Hutchinson).

Centre for Contemporary Cultural Studies (1982) *The Empire Strikes Back: Race and Racism in 70s Britain* (London: Hutchinson).

Chesneau, E. (1887) *The English School of Painting* (London: Cassell) 3rd edn.

Child, I. L. and Siroto, L. (1971) 'Bakweley and American Aesthetic Evaluations Compared', in C. Jopling (ed.) *Art and Aesthetics in Primitive Societies.*

Clarke, J. and Critcher, C. (1985) *The Devil Makes Work: Leisure in Capitalist Britain* (London: Macmillan).

Clarke, J., Critcher, C. and Johnson, R. (eds) (1979) *Working Class Culture: Studies in History and Theory* (London: Hutchinson).

Clarke, J., Hall, S., Jefferson, T. and Roberts, B. (1976) 'Subcultures, Cultures and Class', in Hall and Jefferson (eds) *Resistance Through Rituals.*

Clecak, P. (1983) *America's Quest for the Ideal Self: Dissent and Fulfilment in the 60s and 70s* (Oxford: Oxford University Press).

Cohen, P. (1988) 'The Perversions of Inheritance: Studies in the Making of Multi-Racist Britain' in P. Cohen and S. W. Bains (eds), *Multi-Racist Britain.*

Cohen, P. and Bains, S. W. (eds), (1988) *Multi-Racist Britain* (London: Macmillan).

Cohen, S. (1980) *Folk Devils and Moral Panics* (Oxford: Martin Robertson) 2nd edn.

Cohen, S. and Young, J. (1981) *The Manufacture of News: Deviance, Social Problems and the Mass Media* (London: Constable) revised edn.

Collins, H. M. (1985) *Changing Order* (London: Sage).

Collins, R. *et al.* (eds) (1986) *Media Culture and Society: A Critical Reader* (London: Sage).

Connell, R. W. (1983) *Which Way is Up?* (London: Allen & Unwin).

Connell, R. W. (1987) *Gender and Power* (Cambridge: Polity Press).

Connerton, P. (ed) (1976) *Critical Sociology* (Harmondsworth: Penguin).

Coser, L.A. (1965) *Men of Ideas: A Sociologist's View* (New York: Free Press).

Coser, L. A. and Rosenberg, B. (eds) (1964) *Sociological Theory: A Book of Readings* (West Drayton, Collier-Macmillan).

Cowie, C. and Lees, S.(1981) 'Slags or Drags', *Feminist Review*, vol. IX, pp. 17-31.

Cox, C.B. and Dyson, A. E. (1969) *Fight for Education: A Black Paper* (London: Critical Quarterly Society).

Cox, O. C. (1959) *Caste, Class and Race* (New York: Monthly Review Press).

Critcher, C. (1979a) 'Football Since the War', in Clarke *et al.*, *Working Class Culture*.

Critcher, C. (1979b) 'Sociology, Cultural Studies and the Post-War Working Class', in Clarke *et al*, *Working Class Culture*.

Crompton, R. and Mann, M. (eds) (1986) *Gender and Stratification* (Cambridge: Polity Press).

Crowley, D. J. (1971) 'An African Aesthetic', in C. Jopling (ed.) *Art and Aesthetics in Primitive Societies*.

Culler, J. (1981) 'Semiology: The Saussurian Legacy', in Bennett, *et al.*, *Culture, Ideology and Social Process*.

Culler, J. 1983 *Barthes* (London: Fontana).

Cunnison, S. (1986) 'Care on the Cheap: Gender, Consent and Exploitation Among Sheltered Housing Wardens', in Purcell, K., Allan S. and Wood, S. (eds) *The Changing Experience of Employment: Restructuring and Recession* (London: Macmillan).

Curran, J., Gurevitch, M. and Woollacott, J. (eds) (1977) *Mass Communication and Society* (London: Edwin Arnold).

Curran, J. and Seaton, J. (1981) *Power Without Responsibility: The Press and Broadcasting in Britain* (London: Fontana).

Davidoff, L. and Hall, K. (1987) *Family Fortunes: Men and Women of the English Middle Class, 1780–1850* (London: Hutchinson).

Davis, H. H. (1979) *Beyond Class Images: Explorations in the Structure of Social Consciousness* (Beckenham: Croom Helm).

Davis, H. and Walton, P. (eds) (1983) *Language, Image, Media* (Oxford: Blackwell).

Deem, R. (1986) *All Work and No Play: The Sociology of Women and Leisure* (Milton Keynes: Open University Press).

Deem, R. (1987) 'The Politics of Women's Leisure', in J. Horne *et al.*, *Sport, Leisure and Social Relations*.

Dennis, N., Henriques, F., and Slaughter, C. (1956) *Coal is Our Life* (Andover: Eyre & Spottiswood).

Department of Education and Science (1977) *Education in Schools* (London: HMSO).

Dewdney, A. and Lister, M. (1986) 'Photography, School and Youth Culture: The Cockpit Arts Project', in S. Bezencenet and P. Corrigan (eds) *Photographic Practices; Towards a Different Image* (London: Comedia).

Dews, P. (1987) *Logics of Disintegration* (London: Verso).

Dohrmann, R. (1975) 'A Gender Profile of Children's Educational TV', *Journal of Communication*, no. 25, pp. 56-65.

Dorfman, A. (1983) *The Empire's Old Clothes* (London: Pluto Press).

Dorfman, A. and Mattelart, A. (1973) *How To Read Donald Duck* (New York: International General).

Dorson, R. (1959) *American Folklore* (Chicago: University of Chicago Press).

Dorson, R. (1968) *The British Folklorists: A History* (London: Routledge & Kegan Paul).

Douglas, M. (1966, 1978c) *Purity and Danger: An Analysis of Concepts of Pollution and Taboo* (Harmondsworth: Pelican).

Douglas, M. (1978a) *Implicit Meanings* (London: Routledge and Kegan Paul).

Douglas, M. (1978b) *Natural Symbols* (Harmondsworth: Penguin) 2nd edn.

Douglas, M. (1980) *Evans-Pritchard: His Life, Work, Writings and Ideas* (Brighton: Harvester Press).

Douglas, M. (1982) *In the Active Voice* (London: Routledge and Kegan Paul).

Downing, M. (1974) 'Heroine of the Daytime Serial', *Journal of Communication*, no. 24, pp. 130–7.

Dunn, T. (1986) 'The Evolution of Cultural Studies', in D. Punter (ed.) *Introduction to Contemporary Cultural Studies* (London: Longman).

Durkheim, E. (1971) *The Elementary Forms of the Religious Life* (London: Allen & Unwin).

Dyer, R., *et al.* (1981) *Coronation Street* (London: BFI Publishing).

Easlea, B. (1983) *Fathering the Unthinkable* (London: Pluto Press).

Easthope, A. (1986) *What a Man's Gotta Do: The Masculine Myth in Popular Culture* (London: Paladin).

Eco, U. (1979) *A Theory of Semiotics* (Indiana: Indiana University Press).

Eco, U. (1986) *Travels in Hyperreality* (London: Picador) first published as *Faith in Fakes* (London: Secker & Warburg).

Edgely, R. (1977) 'Education For Industry', *Educational Research* 20, pp. 26–32.

Eldridge, J. E. T. (ed.) (1971) *Max Weber: The Interpretation of Social Reality* (Walton-on-Thames: Nelson).

Eliot, T. S. (1948, 1983) *Notes Towards the Definition of Culture* (London: Faber & Faber).

Elliott, B. (1986) *Victorian Gardens* (London: Batsford).

Ellul, J. (1964) *The Technological Society* (New York: Vintage Books).

Erikson, E. H. (1966) 'The Concept of Identity in Race Relations: Notes and Queries', *Daedelus*, no. 95, pp. 145–71.

Fanon, F. (1967) *The Wretched of the Earth* (Harmondsworth: Penguin).

Fanon, F. (1969) *Toward the African Revolution* (New York: Grove Press).

Farran, D. (1986) *'Leisure': Some Practical Considerations*, Studies in Sexual Politics (Sociology Dept., Manchester University).

Featherstone, M. (1990) 'Global Culture: An Introduction', *Theory, Culture and Society*, no. 7, special issue on global culture.

Featherstone, M. (1988) 'In Pursuit of the Postmodern', *Theory, Culture and Society*, no. 5.

Fee, E. (1986) 'Critiques of Modern Science: The Relationship of Feminism to Other Radical Epistemologies', in R. Bleier (ed.) *Feminist Approaches to Science*

Ferguson, M. (1983) *Forever Feminine: Women's Magazines and the Cult of Femininity* (London: Heinemann).

Fernandez, J. W. (1971) 'Principles of Opposition and Vitality in Fang Aesthetics', in C. Jopling (ed.) *Art and Aesthetics in Primitive Societies*.

Finch, J. (1983) *Married To the Job: Wives' Incorporation in Men's Work* (London: Allen & Unwin).

Finch, J. and Groves, D. (eds) (1983) *A Labour of Love: Women, Work and Caring* (London: Routledge & Kegan Paul).

Forster, E. M. (1961) *Aspects of the Novel* (Harmondsworth: Penguin).

Foucault, M. (1977) *Discipline and Punish: The Birth of the Prison* (London: Allen Lane).

Foucault, M. (1979) *The History of Sexuality: Volume I, An Introduction* (London: Allen Lane).

Frankenberg, R. (1969) *Communities in Britain: Social Life in Town and Country* (Harmondsworth: Penguin).

Franklin, J. H. (1965) 'The Two Worlds of Race: A Historical View', *Daedelus*, no. 94, pp. 899–920.

Fraser, N. and Nicholson, L. (1988) 'Social Criticism Without Philosophy: An Encounter Between Feminism and Post-Modernism', *Theory, Culture and Society*, no. 5.

Frazier, E. F (1932) *The Negro Family in Chicago* (Chicago: University of Chicago Press).

Freire, P. (1972) *The Pedagogy of the Oppressed* (Harmondsworth: Penguin).

Frith, S. (1984) 'Introduction' to C. McGregor, *Pop Goes the Culture* (London: Pluto Press).

Frith, S. (1985) *The Sociology of Youth* (Causeway Press, 1984), reprinted in M. Haralambos (ed.) *Sociology: New Directions* (Causeway Books, 1985).

Frith, S. (1986) 'Hearing Secret Harmonies', in C. MacCabe (ed.) *High Theory/Low Culture*.

Fry, R. (1937) *Vision and Design* (London: Chatto and Winduss, 1920; Harmondsworth: Pelican edn, 1937).

Frye, N. (1976) *The Secular Scripture: A Study of the Structure of Romance* (Cambridge, Massachesetts: Harvard University Press).

Fryer, P. (1984) *Staying Power: The History of Black People in Britain* (London: Pluto Press).

Gabriel, T. H. (1982) *Third Cinema in the Third World*, (London: UMI Research Press).

Gallafent, E. (1990) 'Trouble is Their Business', *Over Here: Reviews in American Studies*, no. 10.

Gans, H. (1974) *Popular Culture and High Culture: An Analysis and Evaluation of Taste* (Basic Books, New York).

CALDERDALE
COLLEGE LIBRARY
HALIFAX

Garfinkel, H. (1967) *Studies in Ethnomethodology* (Englewood Cliffs, New Jersey: Prentice-Hall).

Garmarnikow, E. *et al.* (eds) (1983) *The Public and the Private* (London: Heinemann).

Gasset, J. O. Y (1961) *The Revolt of the Masses* (London: Allen & Unwin, 1932; London: Allen & Unwin, 1961).

Geertz, C. (1973) *The Interpretation of Cultures* (New York: Basic Books).

Gerth, H. and Mills, C. W. (eds) (1948) *From Max Weber: Essays in Sociology* (London: Routledge & Kegan Paul).

Giddens, A. (1973) *The Class Structure of Advanced Societies* (London: Hutchinson).

Giddens, A. (1984) *The Constitution of Society* (Cambridge: Polity Press).

Giddens, A. (1989) *Sociology* (Cambridge: Polity Press).

Gilroy, P. (1987) *There Ain't no Black in the Union Jack* (London: Hutchinson).

Gitlin, T. (1978) 'Media Sociology: The Dominant Paradigm', *Theory and Society*, no. 6.

Glasgow University Media Group (1976) *Bad News* (London: Routledge & Kegan Paul).

Glasgow University Media Group (1980) *More Bad News* (London: Routledge & Kegan Paul).

Glasgow University Media Group (1982) *Really Bad News* (London: Writers & Readers).

Gluckman, M. (1960) 'Tribalism in Modern British Central Africa', *Cahiers d'Etudes Africaines*, no. 1.

Goddard, D. (1972) 'Anthropology: The Limits of Functionalism', in R. Blackburn (ed.) *Ideology in Social Science: Readings in Critical Social Theory* (London: Fontana).

Godelier, M. (1986) *The Mental and the Material* (London: Verso).

Golby, J. M. and Purdue, A. W. (1984) *The Civilisation of the Crowd: Popular Culture in England 1750–1900* (London: Batsford).

Golding, P. and Murdock, G. (1979) 'Ideology and the Mass Media', in Barrett *et al.*, *Ideology and Cultural Production*.

Goldmann, L. (1980) 'The Concept of the Significant Structure in the History of Culture', in L. Goldmann, *Essays on Method in the Sociology of Literature* edited by W. Q. Boelhower (Telos Press, St Louis).

Goldsmith, O. (1962; 1966) *Citizen of the World*, in *Collected Works of Oliver Goldsmith*, vol. 2, edited by A. Friedman (Oxford: Oxford University Press, 1966).

Goldthorpe, J. H, Lockwood, D., Bechhofer, F., and Platt, J. (1968–71) *The Affluent Worker in the Class Structure* (Cambridge: Cambridge University Press) 3 vols.

Gott, B. and Cameron, A. C. (1932) *The Film in National Life* (London: Allen and Unwin).

Gouldner, A. (1971) *The Coming Crisis of Western Sociology* (London: Heinemann).

Gouldner, A. (1975) *For Sociology: Renewal and Critique in Sociology Today* (Harmondsworth: Penguin).

Gouldner, A. (1979) *The Future of Intellectuals and the Rise of the New Class* (London: Macmillan).

Gramsci, A. (1971) *Selections From Political Writings, 1921–26*, edited and translated by Q. Hoare (London: Lawrence & Wishart).

Gramsci, A. (1971) *Selections From the Prison Notebooks*, edited and translated by Q. Hoare and G. Nowell-Smith (London: Lawrence & Wishart).

Green, E., Hebron, S. and Woodward, D. (1987) 'Women, Leisure and Social Control', in Hanmer and Maynard (eds) *Women, Violence and Social Control*.

Greenleaf, W. H. (1983) *The British Political Tradition* (London: Methuen) 2 vols.

Griffin, C. (1985) *Typical Girls: Young Women From School To the Job Market* (London: Routledge & Kegan Paul).

Gurevitch, M. *et al* (1982) *Culture, Society and the Media* (London: Methuen).

Habermas, J. (1976) 'Systematically Distorted Communication', in P. Connerton (ed.) *Critical Sociology*.

Habermas, J. (1971) *Toward a Rational Society* (London: Heinemann).

Hall, S. (1977) 'Culture, the Media and the "Ideological Effect"', in Curran *et al.*, *Mass Communication and Society*.

Hall, S. (1980a) 'Cultural Studies and the Centre: Some Problematics and Problems', in Hall *et al.*, *Culture, Media Language*.

Hall, S. (1980b) 'Race, Articulation and Societies Structured in Dominance' in UNESCO, *Sociological Theories: Race and Colonialism* (Paris: UNESCO.

Hall, S. (1981) 'Cultural Studies: Two Paradigms', in Bennett *et al.*, *Culture, Ideology and Social Process*.

Hall, S. (1982) 'Culture and the State', in Open University, *The State and Popular Culture 1* (Milton Keynes: Open University Press).

Hall, S. (1985) 'Signification, Representation, Ideology: Althusser and the Post-Structuralist Debates', *Critical Studies in Mass Communication*, no. 2.

Hall, S., Critcher, C., Jefferson, T., Clarke, J. and Roberts, B. (1978) *Policing the Crisis* (London: Macmillan).

Hall, S., Hobson, D., Lowe, A. and Willis, P. (1980) *Culture, Media, Language: Working Papers in Cultural Studies, 1972–79* (London: Hutchinson).

Hall, S. and Jefferson, T. (eds) (1976) *Resistance Through Rituals: Youth Subcultures in Post-War Britain* (London: Hutchinson).

Hanmer, J. and Maynard, M. (eds) (1987) *Women, Violence and Social Control* (London: Macmillan).

Harding, S. (1986) *The Science Question in Feminism* (Milton Keynes: Open University Press).

Hargreaves, D. (1967) *Social Relations in a Secondary School* (London: Routledge & Kegan Paul).

Hargreaves, J. (ed) (1982) *Sport, Culture and Ideology* (London: Routledge & Kegan Paul).

Hargreaves, J. (1986) *Sport, Power and Culture: A Social and Historical Analysis of Popular Sports in Britain* (Cambridge: Polity Press).

Harland, R. (1987) *Superstructuralism: The Philosophy of Structuralism and Post-Structuralism* (London: Methuen).

Harrison, M. (1985) *TV News: Whose Bias?* (Newbury: Policy Journals).

Hartman, D. W. (1974) *Immigrants and Migrants: The Detroit Ethnic Experience* (Detroit: Wayne State University).

Hartmann, P. and Husband, C. (1972) 'The Mass Media and Racial Conflict', in D. McQuail (ed.) *Sociology of Mass Communications* (Harmondsworth: Penguin).

Haug, W. F. (1986) *Critique of Commodity Aesthetics* (Cambridge: Polity Press).

Hay, M. and Stichter, S. (eds) (1984) *African Women South of the Sahara* (London: Longman).

Hearn, J. and Parkin, W. (1987) *'Sex' at 'Work': The Power and Paradox of Organisation Sexuality* (Brighton: Wheatsheaf Books).

Hebdige, D. (1979) *Subculture: The Meaning of Style* (London: Methuen).

Heller, J. (1988) *Picture This* (London: Macmillan).

Henn, J. K. (1984) 'Women in the Rural Economy: Past Present and Future', in Hay and Stichter (eds) *African Women South of the Sahara*.

Herberg, W. (1960) *Protestant – Catholic – Jew: An Essay in American Religious Sociology* (New York: Doubleday Anchor)

Herzog, H. (1944) 'On Borrowed Experience', in P. Lazarsfeld (ed.) *Radio Research 1942–43* (New York: Essential Books).

Hewison, R. (1987) *The Heritage Industry* (London: Methuen).

Hey, V. (1986) *Patriarchy and Pub Culture* (London: Tavistock).

Hill, J. (1986) *Sex, Class and Realism* (London: BFI Publishing).

Hirst, P. H. (1974) *Knowledge and the Curriculum* (London: Routledge & Kegan Paul).

Hirst, P. and Woolley, P. (1982) *Social Relations and Human Attributes* (London: Tavistock).

Hitchin, L. (1985) A *Critical Evaluation of the Emergence and Role of Personal and Social Development in the Secondary Education Curriculum* (unpublished dissertation, Humberside College of Higher Education).

Hobson, D. (1982) *Crossroads: The Drama of a Soap Opera* (London: Methuen).

Hodson, P. (1984) *Men: An Investigation Into the Emotional Male* (London: BBC).

Hoggart, R. (1958) *The Uses of Literacy* (Harmondsworth: Penguin).

Hoogvelt, A. (1978) *The Sociology of Developing Societies* (London: Macmillan).

Horne, D. (1986) *The Public Culture: The Triumph of Industrialism* (London: Pluto Press).

Horne, J., Jary, D. and Tomlinson, A. (eds) (1987) *Sport, Leisure and Social Relations* (London: Routledge & Kegan Paul).

Howitt, D. (1982) *Mass Media and Social Problems* (Pergamon Press).

Hudson, B. (1984) 'Femininity and Adolescence', in McRobbie and Nava (eds) *Gender and Generation*.

Humphries, M. (1985) 'Gay Machismo', in Metcalf and Humphries (eds) *The Sexuality of Men*.

Hunt, P. (1980) *Gender and Class Consciousness*, (London: Macmillan).

Husband, C. (ed.) (1982) *'Race' in Britain: Continuity and Change* (London: Hutchinson).

Huxley, T. H. (1967) Extract from 'Science and Culture' (1880) in C. Bibby (ed.) *The Essence of T.H. Huxley* (London: Macmillan).

Jackson, B. and Marsden, D. (1962) *Education and the Working Class* (London: Routledge & Kegan Paul).

Johnson, R. (1979) 'Three Problematics: Elements of a Theory of Working Class Culture', in Clarke *et al.*, *Working Class Culture*.

Jones, G. (1980) *Social Darwinism and English Thought: The Interaction Between Biological and Social Theory* (Brighton: Harvester Press).

Jones, S. (1988) *Black Culture, White Youth: The Reggae Tradition from JA to UK* (London: Macmillan).

Jopling, C. (ed.) (1971) *Art and Aesthetics in Primitive Societies* (New York: Dutton).

Jordin, M. (1984) 'Contemporary Futures: The Analysis of Science Fiction', in C. Pawling (ed.) *Popular Fiction and Social Change* (London: Macmillan).

Karabel, J. and Halsey, A. H. (eds) (1977) *Power and Ideology in Education* (Oxford: Oxford University Press).

Kavolis, V. (1971) 'The Value-Orientations Theory of Artistic Style', in C. Jopling (ed.) *Art and Aesthetics in Primitive Societies*.

Keddie, N. (1971) 'Classroom Knowledge' in M. Young (ed.) *Knowledge and Control*.

Kellner, D. (1987) 'Baudrillard, Semiurgy and Death', *Theory, Culture and Society*, no. 4.

Kelly, A. (1985) 'Changing Schools and Changing Society: Some Reflections on the Girls Into Science and Technology Project' in M. Arnot (ed.) *Race and Gender: Equal Opportunities Policies in Education* (Oxford: Pergamon).

Kelly, A. (1987) 'The Construction of Masculine Science', in Arnot and Weiner (eds) *Gender and the Politics of Schooling*.

Kimmel, M. S. (ed) (1987) *Changing Men: New Directions in Research on Men and Masculinity* (London: Sage).

Kirp, D. L. (1985) 'Racial Inexplicitness and Education Policy', in M. Arnot (ed.) *Race and Gender. Equal Opportunities Policies in Education* (Oxford: Pergamon Press).

Klapper, J. T. (1961) *The Effects of Mass Communication* (Illinois: Free Press).

Kluckhohn, C. (1951; 1964) 'The Study of Culture', in Coser and Rosenberg, (eds) *Sociological Theory* (1964).

Kristeva, J. (1973) article in *Times Literary Supplement*, 12 October 1973, p. 1249.

Kroeber, A. L. (1952; 1964) 'The Superorganic', in Coser and Rosenberg (eds) *Sociological Theory* (1964).

Kuhn, T. S. (1962) *The Structure of Scientific Revolutions* (Chicago: University of Chicago Press).

Kumar, K. (1978) *Prophecy and Progress: The Sociology of Industrial and Post-Industrial Society* (Harmondsworth: Penguin).

Lacey, C. (1970) *Hightown Grammar* (Manchester: Manchester University Press).

Ladurie, E. L. R. (1978) *Montaillou: The Promised Land of Error* (George Braziller, New York).

Laing, S. (1986) *Representations of Working Class Life, 1957–1964* (London: Macmillan).

Lal, B. B. (1986; 1988) 'The 'Chicago School' of American Sociology, Symbolic Interactionism and Race Relations Theory', in Rex and Mason (eds) *Theories of Race and Ethnic Relations*.

Lanternari, V. (1963) *The Religions of the Oppressed: A Study of Modern Messianic Cults* (New York: Mentor).

Lasch, C. (1978) *The Culture of Narcissism: American Life in an Age of Diminishing Expectations* (W. W. Norton, New York).

Lawrence, E. (1982) 'In the Abundance of Water the Fool is Thirsty: Sociology and Black "Pathology"' in Centre for Contemporary Cultural Studies, *The Empire Strikes Back*.

Lawrence, P. (1976) *Georg Simmel: Sociologist and European* (Walton-on-Thames: Nelson).

Layton, D. (1985) *Technological Revolution?: The Politics of School Science in England and Wales Since 1945* (Lewes: Falmer Press).

Leach, E. (1970, 1974) *Levi-Strauss* (London: Fontana).

Leavis, F. R. (1937) 'Literary Criticism and Philosophy: A Reply', *Scrutiny*, no. 6.

Leavis, F. R. (1962) *Two Cultures? The Significance of C. P. Snow*, with an essay by M. Yudkin (London: Chatto & Windus).

Leavis, F. R. and Thompson, D. (1933) *Culture and Environment: The Training of Critical Awareness* (London: Chatto & Windus).

Leavis, Q. D. (1932) *Fiction and the Reading Public* (London: Chatto & Windus).

Lees, S. (1986) *Losing Out: Sexuality and Adolescent Girls* (London: Hutchinson).

Lefanu, S. (1988) *In the Chinks of the World Machine: Feminism and Science Fiction* (London: Women's Press).

Lenskyj, H. (1986) *Out Of Bounds: Women, Sport and Sexuality* (Toronto: Women's Press).

Levine, L. W. (1988) *Highbrow/Lowbrow: The Emergence of Cultural Hierarchy in America* (Cambridge, Massachusetts: Harvard University Press).

Lévi-Strauss, C. (1970) *The Raw and the Cooked: Introduction to a Science of Mythology* (London: Jonathan Cape) vol. 1.

Little, K. L. (1948) *Negroes in Britain* (London: Kegan Paul, Trench, Trubner).

Little, K. (1974) *Urbanisation as a Social Process* (London: Routledge & Kegan Paul).

Little, K. L. (1965) *West African Urbanization: A Study of Voluntary Organisations in Social Change* (Cambridge: Cambridge University Press).

Lockwood, D. (1966) *The Blackcoated Worker: A Study in Class Consciousness* (London: Allen & Unwin).

Lovell, T. (1980) *Pictures of Reality: Aesthetics, Politics and Pleasure* (London: British Film Institute).

Lovell, T. (1981) 'Ideology and Coronation Street', in Dyer *et al. Coronation Street.*

Lowe, M. and Hubbard, R. (eds) (1983) *Woman's Nature: Rationalizations of Inequality* (Oxford: Pergamon).

Lowenthal, L. (1957) *Literature, Popular Culture and Society* (Englewood Cliffs, New Jersey: Prentice-Hall).

Lumley, R. (ed.) (1988) *The Museum Time Machine* (London: Routledge & Kegan Paul).

Lyman, P. (1987) 'The Fraternal Bond as a Joking Relationship: A Case Study of the Role of Sexist Jokes in Male Group Bonding', in Kimmel (ed.) *Changing Men.*

Lyotard, J.-F. (1984) *The Post-Modern Condition: A Report on Knowledge* (Manchester: Manchester University Press).

Lyotard, J.-F. and J. L. Thébaud (1985) *Just Gaming* (Manchester: Manchester University Press).

Mac an Ghaill, M. (1988) *Young, Gifted and Black* (Milton Keynes: Open University Press).

MacCabe, C. (ed.) (1986) *High Theory/Low Culture: Analysing Popular Television and Film* (Manchester: Manchester University Press).

McCarthy, T. A. (1976) 'A Theory of Communicative Competence', in P. Connerton (ed.) *Critical Sociology.*

MacDonald, D. (1957) 'A Theory of Mass Culture', in B. Rosenberg and D. M. White, *Mass Culture* (Illinois: Free Press).

Macdonell, D. (1986) *Theories of Discourse: An Introduction* (Oxford: Blackwell).

Mackenzie, G. (1973) *The Aristocracy of Labour: The Position of Skilled Craftsmen in the American Class Structure* (Cambridge: Cambridge University Press).

Mackintosh, M. (1981) 'The Sexual Division of Labour and the Subordination of Women', in K. Young, C. Wolkowitz and R. McCullagh (eds) *Of Marriage and the Market: Women's Subordination in International Perspective* (London: CSE Books).

McLuhan, M. and Fiore, Q. (1967) *The Medium is the Massage* (Harmondsworth: Penguin).

McQuail, D. (1969) *Towards a Sociology of Mass Communications* (West Drayton: Collier-Macmillan).

McRobbie, A. (1978) 'Working Class Girls and the Culture of Femininity', in Women's Studies Group, *Women Take Issue.*

McRobbie, A. (1982) 'Jackie: An Ideology of Adolescent Femininity', in B. Waites *et al. Popular Culture: Past and Present.*

McRobbie, A. and Garber, J. (1976) 'Girls and Subcultures: An Exploration', in Hall and Jefferson, (eds) *Resistance Through Rituals.*

McRobbie, A. and Nava, M. (eds) (1984) *Gender and Generation* (London: Macmillan).

Madge, J. (1963) *The Origins of Scientific Sociology* (London: Tavistock).

Malinowski, B. (1961) *The Dynamics of Culture Change* (New Haven, Connecticut: Yale University Press).

Mandeville, B. de (1970) *The Fable of the Bees* (Harmondsworth: Penguin).

Mann, M. (1973) *Consciousness and Action Among the Western Working Class* (London: Macmillan).

Mannheim K. (1956) *Essays on the Sociology of Culture* (Oxford: Oxford University Press).

Marcuse, H. (1978) *The Aesthetic Dimension* (London: Macmillan).

Marcuse, H. (1970) *One-Dimensional Man* (Boston: Beacon Press, 1964; London: Sphere Books, 1970).

Marcuse, H. (1972) *Negations* (Harmondsworth: Penguin).

Martin, B. (1981) *A Sociology of Contemporary Cultural Change* (Oxford: Blackwell).

Martin, A. (ed.) (1982) *African Films: The Context of Production* (London: British Film Institute).

Marx, K. (1950) 'Preface to a Contribution to the Critique of Political Economy', in *Marx and Engels: Selected Works* (London: Lawrence & Wishart) vol. 1.

Marx, K. (1973) *Grundrisse* edited by M. Nicolaus (Harmondsworth: Penguin).

Marx, K. and Engels, F. (1938) *The German Ideology* (London: Lawrence & Wishart).

Marx, K. and Engels, F. (1950) 'Manifesto of the Communist Party', in *Marx and Engels: Selected Works* (London: Lawrence & Wishart) vol. I.

Mason, P. (1970) *Patterns of Dominance* (Oxford: Oxford University Press).

Masterman, L. (1985) *Teaching the Media* (London: Comedia).

Matthews, F. H. (1977) *Quest for an American Sociology: Robert E. Park and the Chicago School* (Canada: McGill-Queen's University Press).

Mattelart, A., Mattelart, M. and Delcourt, X. (1984) *International Image Markets* (London: Comedia).

Mays, J. B. (1962) *Education and the Urban Child* (Liverpool University Press).

Merquior, J. G. (1986) 'Spider and Bee: Towards a Critique of the Postmodern Ideology' in Appignanesi (ed.) *Postmodernism*.

Merrill, F. E. (1961) *Society and Culture: An Introduction to Sociology* (Englewood Cliffs, New Jersey: Prentice-Hall) 2nd ed..

Metcalf, A. and Humphries, M. (eds) (1985) *The Sexuality of Men* (London: Pluto Press).

Miles, R. (1982) *Racism and Migrant Labour* (London: Routledge & Kegan Paul).

Miles, R. and Phizacklea, A. (1984) *White Man's Country* (London: Pluto Press).

Miles, R. (1989) *Racism* (London: Routledge).

Mitchell, J. (1971) *Woman's Estate* (Harmondsworth: Penguin).

Modleski, T. (1982) *Loving With A Vengeance: Mass Produced Fantasies For Women* (London: Methuen).

Moore, H. (1988) *Feminism and Anthropology* (Cambridge: Polity Press).

Moore, H. (1986) *Space, Text and Gender: An Anthropological Study of the Marakwet of Kenya* (Cambridge: Cambridge University Press).

Morgan, D. (1987) *"It Will Make A Man Of You"*: *Notes on National Service, Masculinity and Autobiography* (Studies in Sexual Politics, Sociology Department, Manchester University).

Mouffe, C. (1981) 'Hegemony and Ideology in Gramsci', in Bennett *et al. Culture, Ideology and Social Process*.

Mullard, C. (1985) 'Multiracial Education in Britain: From Assimilation to Cultural Pluralism', in M. Arnot (ed.) *Race and Gender: Equal Opportunities Policies in Education* (Oxford: Pergamon Press).

Mulvey, L. (1975) 'Visual Pleasure and Narrative Cinema', *Screen* , no. 16, pp. 6–18.

Mungham, G. and Pearson, G. (eds) (1976) *Working Class Youth Culture* (London: Routledge & Kegan Paul).

Murdock, G. and Golding, P. (1977) 'Capitalism, Communication and Class Relations', in Curran *et al. Mass Communication and Society*.

Murdock, G. and McCron, R. (1976) 'Consciousness of Class and Consciousness of Generation', in Hall and Jefferson (eds) *Resistance Through Rituals*.

Naipaul, V. S. (1977) 'Jasmine', in R. Hamner (ed.) *Critical Perspectives on V. S. Naipaul* (London: Heinemann).

Nava, M. (1984) 'Youth Service Provision, Social Order and the Question of Girls', in McRobbie and Nava (eds) *Gender and Generation*.

Nelson, C. and Grossberg, L. (eds) (1984) *Marxism and the Interpretation of Culture* (London: Macmillan).

Ngugi, T. (1989) 'From the Corridors of Silence', *Weekend Guardian*, 21–22 October.

Notcutt, L. A. and Latham, G. C. (1937) *The African and the Cinema* (Guildford: Edinburgh House Press).

Oakley, A. (1981) 'Normal Motherhood: An Exercise in Self-Control?', in B. Hutter and G. Williams (eds) *Controlling Women: The Normal and the Deviant* (Beckenham: Croom Helm).

O'Bryant, S. L. and Corder-Bolz, C. R. (1978) 'The Effects of Television on Children's Stereotyping of Women's Work Roles', *Journal of Vocational Behaviour*, no. 12, pp. 233–44.

Open University (1982) *Minority Experience* (Milton Keynes: Open University Press).

Oppong, C. (ed.) (1983) *Female and Male in West Africa* ((London: Allen & Unwin).

Ortner, S. (1974) 'Is Female to Male as Nature is to Culture?', in M. Rosaldo and L. Lamphere (eds) *Woman, Culture and Society* (Stanford, California: Stanford University Press).

Ortner, S. B. and Whitehead, H. (eds) (1981) *Sexual Meanings: The Cultural Construction of Gender and Sexuality* (Cambridge: Cambridge University Press).

Parekh, B. (1974) *Colour, Culture and Consciousness* (London: Allen & Unwin).

Park, R. E. (1950) *Race and Culture: Essays in the Sociology of Modern Man* (Illinois: Free Press).

Parmar, P. (1989) 'In Our Own Image', in M. Fuirer (ed.) *Whose Image* (Birmingham: Building Sights).

Parsons, T. (1954) *Essays in Sociological Theory* (Illinois: Free Press).

Parsons, T. (1930, 1968) *The Structure of Social Action* (New York: McGraw Hill, 1937; Illinois: Free Press).

Parsons, T. (1951, 1964) *The Social System* (Illinois: Free Press).

Parsons, T. (1965) 'Full Citizenship for the Negro American? A Sociological Problem', *Daedelus*, no. 94, pp. 1009–54.

Patterson, S. (1965) *Dark Strangers* (London: Tavistock, 1963, Harmondsworth: Penguin, abridged edn).

Pearson, G. and Twohig, J. (1976) 'Ethnography Through the Looking-Glass: The Case of Howard Becker', in Hall and Jefferson (eds) *Resistance Through Rituals.*

Pels, D. and Crébas, A. (1988) 'Carmen – or The Invention of a New Feminine Myth', *Theory, Culture and Society*, no. 5.

Perkin, H. (1969) *The Origins of Modern English Society, 1780–1880* (London: Routledge & Kegan Paul).

Piercy, M. (1978) *Woman On the Edge of Time* (London: Women's Press).

Pollert, A. (1981) *Girls, Wives, Factory Lives* (London: Macmillan).

Porter, M. (1982) 'Standing on the Edge: Working Class Housewives and the World of Work', in J. West (ed.) *Women, Work and the Labour Market* (London: Routledge & Kegan Paul).

Poulantzas, N. (1973) 'On Social Classes', *New Left Review*, no. 78.

Powell, R. and Clarke, J. (1976) 'A Note On Marginality', in Hall and Jefferson (eds) *Resistance Through Rituals.*

Pring, R. (1972) 'Knowledge Out of Control', *Education For Teaching*, no. 89.

Pryce, K. (1979) *Endless Pressure* (Harmondsworth: Penguin).

Purcell, K. (1988) *More in Hope Than Anticipation: Fatalism and Fortune Telling Amongst Women Factory Workers* (Studies in Sexual Politics, Sociology Dept., Manchester University).

Rabinow, P. (ed.) (1986) *The Foucault Reader* (Harmondsworth: Penguin).

Radway, J. (1984) *Reading the Romance: Women, Patriarchy and Popular Literature* (London: Verso).

Ramazanoglu, C. (1987) 'Sex and Violence in Academic Life or You Can Keep a Good Woman Down', in Hanmer and Maynard (eds) *Women, Violence and Social Control.*

Ramazanoglu, C. (1989) *Feminism and the Contradictions of Oppression* (London: Routledge).

Rex, J. (1970; 1983) *Race Relations in Sociological Theory* (London: Routledge & Kegan Paul).

Rex, J. (1986) *Race and Ethnicity* (Milton Keynes: Open University Press).

Rex, J. (1988) 'The Role of Class Analysis in the Study of Race Relations – a Weberian Perspective', in Rex and Mason (eds) *Theories of Race and Ethnic Relations.*

Rex, J. and Mason, D. (1988) *Theories of Race and Ethnic Relations* (Cambridge: Cambridge University Press).

Richardson, J. and Lambert, J. (1985) *The Sociology of Race* (Ormskirk: Causeway Press).

Richmond, A. H. (1955) *The Colour Problem* (Harmondsworth: Penguin).

Riesman, D. (1953) *The Lonely Crowd: A Study of the Changing American Character* (New York: Doubleday).

Riesman, D. (1964) *Abundance For What? And Other Essays* (New York: Doubleday).

Roberts, B. (1976) 'Naturalistic Research into Subcultures and Deviance: An Account of a Sociological Tendency', in Hall and Jefferson (eds) *Resistance Through Rituals*.

Robinson, L. (1986) *Sex, Class and Culture* (London: Methuen).

Rock, P. (1979) *The Making of Symbolic Interactionism* (London: Macmillan).

Rogers, B. (1980) *The Domestication of Women: Discrimination in Developing Societies* (London: Tavistock).

Rogers, B. (1988) *Men Only: An Investigation into Men's Organisations* (London: Pandora).

Rosaldo, M. (1980) 'The Use and Abuse of Anthropology: Reflections on Feminism and Cross-Cultural Understanding', *Signs*, no. 5.

Rose, A. M. (1962) *Human Behaviour and Social Processes: An Interactionist Approach* (London: Routledge & Kegan Paul).

Rose, S., Kamin, L. J. and Lewontin, R. C. (1984) *Not in Our Genes: Biology, Ideology and Human Nature* (Harmondsworth: Penguin).

Rosenberg, B. and White, D. (1971) *Mass Culture Revisited* (Van Nostrand Reinhold, New York).

Ross, A. (1989) *No Respect: Intellectuals and Popular Culture* (London: Routledge).

Runciman, W. G. (ed.) (1978) *Weber: Selections in Translation* (Cambridge: Cambridge University Press).

Rushdie, Salman (1982) 'The New Empire within Britain' *New Society*, 9 December 1982, pp. 417–21.

Ruskin, J. (1877) *The Political of Economy of Art* (London: Routledge).

Said, E. (1978) *Orientalism* (New York: Pantheon).

Samuel, R. (ed.) (1989) *Patriotism: The Making and Unmaking of British National Identity* (London: Routledge) vol. 2.

Saussure, F. (1959) *Course in General Linguistics* edited by C. Bally and A. Sechehaye, trans. W. Baskin (London: The Philosophical Library).

Scott, D. (1989) *The Singing Bourgeois: Songs of the Victorian Drawing Room and Parlour* (Milton Keynes: Open University Press).

Scott, P. (1983) 'The Year of the Bomb', *Times Higher Education Supplement*, editorial, January, 1983.

Scruton, R. (1974) *Art and Imagination: A Study in the Philosophy of Mind* (London: Methuen).

Scruton, R. (1981) *The Politics of Culture and Other Essays* (Manchester: Carcanet Press).

Scruton, R, (1983) *The Aesthetic Understanding* (Manchester: Carcanet Press).

Searle, C. (1973) *This New Season* (London: Calder & Boyars).

Sennett, R. (1977) *The Fall of Public Man* (Cambridge: Cambridge University Press).

Sharp, R. and Green, A. (1975) *Education and Social Control* (London: Routledge & Kegan Paul).

Sharpe, S. (1984) *Double Identity: The Lives of Working Mothers* (Harmondsworth: Penguin).

Shepherd, G. (1987) 'Rank, Gender and Homosexuality: Mombasa as a Key to Understanding Sexual Options', in Caplan (ed.) *The Cultural Construction of Sexuality*.

Sheppard, A., (1987) *Aesthetics: An Introduction to the Philosophy of Art* (Oxford: Oxford University Press).

Shils, E. (1959) 'Mass Society and Its Culture', in N. Jacobs (ed.) *Culture For the Millions? Mass Media in Modern Society* (Wokingham: van Nostrand).

Shor, I. (1986) *Culture Wars: School and Society in the Conservative Restoration 1969–1984* (London: Routledge & Kegan Paul).

Sivanandan, A. (1976) 'Race, Class and the State: The Black Experience in Britain', *Race and Class*, no. 17.

Smart, C. and Smart, B. (eds) (1978) *Women, Sexuality and Social Control* (London: Routledge & Kegan Paul).

Smith, A. D. (1981) *The Ethnic Revival in the Modern World* (Cambridge: Cambridge University Press).

Smith, L. S. (1978) 'Sexist Assumptions and Female Delinquency: An Empirical Investigation', in Smart and Smart (eds) *Women, Sexuality and Social Control*.

Snitow, A., Stansell, C., and Thompson, S. (eds) (1984) *Desire: The Politics of Sexuality* (London: Virago).

Snow, C. P. (1969) *The Two Cultures and A Second Look* (Cambridge: Cambridge University Press).

Solomos, J. (1986; 1988) 'Varieties of Marxist Conceptions of 'Race', Class and the State: A Critical Analysis', in Rex and Mason (eds) *Theories of Race and Ethnic Relations*.

Sperber, D. (1979) 'Claude Levi-Strauss', in Sturrock (ed.) *Structuralism and Since*.

Spykman, N. (1966) *The Social Theory of Georg Simmel* (Atherton Press, New York).

Squires, G. (1987) *The Curriculum Beyond School* (Sevenoaks: Hodder & Stoughton).

Stanley, L. (1987) *Essays on Women's Work and Leisure and 'Hidden' Work*, Studies in Sexual Politics (Sociology Department, Manchester University).

Steedman, C., Urwin, C. and Walkerdine, V. (eds) (1985) *Language, Gender and Childhood* (London: Routledge & Kegan Paul).

Strawbridge, S. (1982) 'Althusser's Theory of Ideology and Durkheim's Account of Religion: An Examination of Some Striking Parallels', *Sociological Review*, no. 30, pp. 125–40.

Strawbridge, S. (1988) 'Darwin and Victorian Social Values', in E. Sigsworth (ed.) *In Search of Victorian Values* (Manchester: Manchester University Press).

Sturrock, J. (ed.) (1979) *Structuralism and Since: From Levi Strauss to Derrida* (Oxford: Oxford University Press).

Sutcliffe, D. and Wong, A. (1986) *The Language of Black Experience* (Oxford: Blackwell).

Swingewood, A. (1977) *The Myth of Mass Culture* (London: Macmillan).

Sydie, R. A. (1987) *Natural Women, Cultured Men: A Feminist Perspective on Sociological Theory* (Milton Keynes: Open University Press).

Thompson, E. P. (1968) *The Making of the English Working Class* (Harmondsworth: Penguin).

Thompson, E. P. (1977) *Whigs and Hunters* (Harmondsworth: Penguin).

Thompson, E. P. (1978) *The Poverty of Theory* (London: Merlin).

Thompson, K. (1986) *Beliefs and Ideology* (London: Tavistock).

Thompson, P., Wailey, T. and Lummis, T. (1983) *Living the Fishing* (London: Routledge & Kegan Paul).

Thompson, S. (1984) 'Search For Tomorrow: On Feminism and the Reconstruction of Teen Romance', in Vance (ed.) *Pleasure and Danger*.

Tuchman, G. (1975) 'Women and the Creation of Culture', in M. Millman and R. M. Kanter (eds) *Another Voice: Feminist Perspectives on Social Life and Social Science* (New York: Doubleday Anchor).

Tudor, A. (1976) 'Theories of Film', in B. Nichols (ed.) *Movies and Methods* (Berkeley: University of California Press).

Tudor, A. (1979) 'On Alcohol and the Mystique of Media Effects', in J. Cook and M. Lewington (eds) *Images of Alcoholism* (London: British Film Insitute).

Tunstall, J. (1969) *The Fishermen* (London: Routledge & Kegan Paul).

Tylor, E. (1891: 1964) 'Culture Defined', in L. A. Coser and B. Rosenberg (eds) *Sociological Theory* (1964).

Vance, C. S. (ed.) (1984) *Pleasure and Danger: Exploring Female Sexuality* (London: Routledge & Kegan Paul).

van den Berghe, P. L. (1986; 1988) 'Ethnicity and the Sociobiology Debate', in Rex and Mason (eds) *Theories of Race and Ethnic Relations* (1986; 1988).

Verma, G. K. (1986) *Ethnicity and Educational Achievement in British Schools* (London: Macmillan).

Wagg, S. (1984) *The Football World: A Contemporary Social History* (Brighton: Harvester).

Waites, B., Bennett, T. and Martin, G. (eds) (1982) *Popular Culture: Past and Present* (Beckenham: Croom Helm).

Walkerdine, V. (1984) 'Some Day My Prince Will Come', in McRobbie and Nava (eds) *Gender and Generation*.

Wallman, S. (1986) 'Ethnicity and the Boundary Process in Context', in Rex and Mason (eds) *Theories of Race and Ethnic Relations*.

Walvin, J. (1971) *The Black Presence* (London: Orback & Chambers).

Walvin, J. (1973) *Black and White* (London: Allen Lane).

Walvin, J. (ed.) (1982) *Slavery and British Society 1776–1846* (London: Macmillan).

Warner, W. L. (1975) *The Living and the Dead: A Study of the Symbolic Life of Americans* (New Haven, Connecticut: Yale University Press, 1959; Greenwood Press, 1975).

Watson, J. L. (1977) *Between Two Cultures: Migrants and Minorities in Britain* (Oxford: Basil Blackwell).

Waugh, P. (1989) *Feminist Fictions: Revisiting the Postmodern* (London: Routledge & Kegan Paul).

Weber, M. (1949) *The Methodology of the Social Sciences* (Illinois: Free Press).

Weber, M. (1974) *The Protestant Ethic and the Spirit of Capitalism* (London: Unwin University Books).

Weedon, C. (1987) *Feminist Practice and Poststructuralist Theory* (Oxford: Blackwell).

Weeks, J. (1977) *Coming Out: Homosexual Politics in Britain, from the Nineteenth Century to the Present* (London: Quartet Books).

Weeks, J. (1981) *Sex, Politics and Society* (London: Longman).

Weiner, G. and Arnot, M. (eds) (1987) *Gender Under Scrutiny: New Inquiries in Education* (London: Hutchinson).

Weiner, M. J. (1981) *English Culture and the Decline of the Industrial Spirit: 1850–1980* (Cambridge: Cambridge University Press).

Welsh, I. (1989a) 'Marketing Masculinity', paper presented to Centre For Gender Studies, Humberside College of Higher Education, 20 November 1989 (unpublished MS made available to Ros Billington by the author).

Welsh, I. (1989b) 'Men, Masculinity and the Social Construction of Peace', forthcoming in *Women's International Forum*.

West, R. W. (1981) 'A Case Against the Core', *School Science Review* (December 1981) pp. 222–36.

Westergaard, J. H. (1972) 'Sociology, the Myth of Classlessness', in Blackburn (ed.) *Ideology in Social Science*.

Westergaard, J. H. (1979) 'Power, Class and the Media', in Curran *et al. Mass Communication and Society*.

Westwood, S. (1984) *All Day Every Day: Factory and Family in the Making of Women's Lives* (London: Pluto Press).

White, H. (1979) 'Foucault', in Sturrock (ed.) *Structuralism and Since*.

Whitehead, A. (1976) 'Sexual Antagonism in Herefordshire', in D. L. Barker and S. Allen (eds) *Dependence and Exploitation in Work and Marriage* (London: Longman).

Whitehead, H. (1981) 'The Bow and the Burden Strap: A New Look at Institutionalized Homosexuality in Native North America', in Ortner and Whitehead (eds) *Sexual Meanings*.

Whitty, G. (1985) *Sociology and School Knowledge* (London: Methuen).

Wild, P. (1979) 'Recreation in Rochdale, 1900–40', in Clarke *et al.*, *Working Class Culture*.

Williams, R. (1958; 1963) *Culture and Society, 1780–1950* (London: Chatto & Windus, 1958; Harmondsworth: Penguin, 1963).

Williams, R. (1961; 1965) *The Long Revolution* (London: Chatto & Windus, 1961; Harmondsworth: Penguin, 1965).

Williams, R. (1980) *Problems in Materialism and Culture: Selected Essays* (London: Verso and New Left Books).

Williams, R. (1983) *Keywords* (London: Flamingo).

Willis, P. (1977; 1978) *Learning To Labour: How Working Class Kids Get Working Class Jobs* (Aldershot: Saxon House, 1977; Aldershot: Gower, 1978).

Willis, P. (1978) *Profane Culture* (London: Routledge & Kegan Paul).

Willis, P. (1979) 'Shop-floor Culture, Masculinity and the Wage Form', in Clarke *et al. Working Class Culture.* (1979)

Willis, P. (1982) 'Women in Sport in Ideology', in Hargreaves (ed.) *Sport, Culture and Ideology.*

Wilson, B. R. (1973) *Magic and the Millennium: A Sociological Study of Religious Movements of Protest Among Tribal and Third-World Peoples* (London: Heinemann).

Wilson, G. (1941) 'An Essay on the Economics of Detribalisation', *Rhodes–Livingstone Institute Papers*, vols V, VI.

Wimbush, E. and Talbot. M. (eds) (1988) *Relative Freedoms: Women and Leisure* (Milton Keynes: Open University Press).

Winship. J. (1987) *Inside Women's Magazines* (London: Pandora).

Wittkower, R. (1949, 1973) *Architectural Principles in the Age of Humanism* (London: Academy Editions) originally published as Vol 19, Studies of the Warburg Institute, London.

Wolff, R. P., Moore, B., Jnr and Marcuse, H. (1969) *A Critique of Pure Tolerance* (London: Jonathan Cape).

Wolpe, H. (1986; 1988) 'Class Concepts, Class Struggle and Racism', in Rex and Mason (eds) *Theories of Race and Ethnic Relations* (1986; 1988).

Women's Studies Group Centre for Contemporary Cultural Studies (1978) *Women Take Issue: Aspects of Women's Subordination* (London: Hutchinson).

Woods, P. (1983) *Sociology of the School: An Interactionist Viewpoint* (London: Routledge & Kegan Paul).

Woolff, J. (1981) *The Social Production of Art* (London: Macmillan).

Wright, E. O. (1980) 'Varieties of Marxist Conceptions of class Structure', in *Politics and Society*, no. 9.

Wright, P. (1985) *On Living in an Old Country: The National Past in Contemporary Britain* (London: Verso).

Wuthnow, R., Hunter, J. D., Bergeson, A. and Kurzweil, E. (eds) (1984) *Cultural Analysis: The Work of Peter L. Berger, Mary Douglas, Michel Foucault, and Jurgen Habermas* (London: Routledge & Kegan Paul).

Yeo, S. (ed.) (1981) *Popular Culture and Class Conflict, 1590–1914* (Brighton: Harvester).

Young, M. (1976) 'The Schooling of Science', in G. Whitty and M. Young (eds) *Explorations in the Politics of School Knowledge* (Nafferton Books).

Young, M. (ed.) (1971) *Knowledge and Control: New Directions for the Sociology of Education* (West Drayton: Collier-Macmillan).

Zeraffa, M. (1976) *Fictions* (London: Peregrine).

CALDERDALE
COLLEGE LIBRARY
HALIFAX

Index

CALDERDALE
COLLEGE LIBRARY
HALIFAX